Community-Based Collaboration

Community-Based Collaboration

BRIDGING SOCIO-ECOLOGICAL RESEARCH AND PRACTICE

Edited by E. Franklin Dukes,
Karen E. Firehock, and Juliana E. Birkhoff

University of Virginia Press

CHARLOTTESVILLE AND LONDON

University of Virginia Press
© 2011 by the Rector and Visitors of the University of Virginia
Printed in the United States of America on acid-free paper

First published 2011
9 8 7 6 5 4 3 2 1

Library of Congress Cataloging-in-Publication Data
Community-based collaboration : bridging socio-ecological research and practice /
edited by E. Franklin Dukes, Karen E. Firehock, and Juliana E. Birkhoff.
    p.   cm.
  Includes bibliographical references and index.
  ISBN 978-0-8139-3153-1 (cloth : alk. paper) — ISBN 978-0-8139-3159-3 (e-book)
 1. Natural resources—United States—Management—Citizen participation.
2. Community development—United States. I. Dukes, E. Franklin. II. Firehock, Karen.
III. Birkhoff, Juliana.
  HC103.7.C555 2011
  333.70973—dc22

                                                          2011006941

Contents

Preface

What is community-based collaboration, and why do so many people care about its impact on environmental issues? Is community-based collaboration transforming how people relate to the land and to each other? Do place-based collaborative efforts to integrate environmental enhancement and economic resilience promote social equity, broaden participation, and increase social capital? Do such efforts improve local economic conditions? Do they really improve the environment?

In short, does community-based collaboration as a socio-ecological movement have value?

This book, a product of the Community-Based Collaboratives Research Consortium (CBCRC), addresses that question.

The CBCRC was begun in October 1999, when a group of about forty people representing critics, funders, researchers, facilitators, and community participants in collaborative efforts came together in Tucson, Arizona, to discuss emerging controversies in community collaboration around environmental issues. The gathering was prompted by growing alarm over the impact of community-based collaboration. The executive director of the Sierra Club, Mike McCloskey, to take one instance, had issued a memo cautioning members against collaboration. (This memo was reprinted as "The Skeptic: Collaboration Has Its Limits," *High Country News,* May 13, 1996.) Articles had also appeared in academic publications alerting readers to the perils of this movement (Coggins 1998). These articles expressed concern that local groups were exerting undue influence over management decisions and policies affecting environmental resources that encompassed public goods, such as public lands, endangered species, and rivers. At the same time, others were claiming unparalleled success in environmental, ecological, and social improvements by bringing together formerly conflicting parties to focus on common values and concerns. And grassroots groups were not waiting for approval by outsiders.

Despite the positioning for or against collaboration by various groups, little empirical evidence existed at the time to support or refute their concerns. Much of what passed for knowledge was found in the "gray" literature rather than in peer-reviewed publications and represented one of two extremes, either unabashed boosterism for any collaboration effort or a fierce "no!" on the basis that collaboration is the antithesis of a fair and open democratic process. In other words, people were arguing either that community-based collaboration could solve intractable problems by improving civic engagement (Weber 2000) or that it would result in power over public lands devolving to the local level and private interests (Coggins 1998).

It became apparent that better understanding of the growing phenomenon of community-based collaboration was needed. Along with the Udall Center for Studies in Public Policy, and with support from the William and Flora Hewlett Foundation, the Institute for Environmental Negotiation at the University of Virginia convened this workshop, which was attended by critics, funders, facilitators, and community participants in collaborative efforts. The goal of the workshop was twofold: to try to understand why these efforts engendered controversy, and to identify a set of questions and a research agenda that stakeholders on all sides would see as legitimate and useful.

The participants did indeed articulate a common desire to learn more about these collaborative processes, and to do so in a way that would incorporate sound research methods, diverse ways of learning, and shared knowledge beyond academia. Because of that meeting and continued interest, the CBCRC was formed to provide a network for critics and supporters, researchers, community and environmental groups, government agencies, facilitators, and other interested individuals to share knowledge about community-based collaboration for environmental management. The CBCRC became a venue for identifying concerns, tracking new ideas and studies about community-based collaboration, and forming new research partnerships.

The CBCRC adopted a working definition of a community-based collaborative (CBC) that guided our work thereafter:

- Convened voluntarily from within the local community to focus on a resource management issue or planning involving public lands or publicly owned or regulated resources whose management impacts the physical, environmental and/or economic health of the local community;

- Brought together by a shared desire to influence the protection and use of natural resources through recommendations or direct actions that will impact the management of the resource;
- Membership that includes a broad array of interests, some of which may be in conflict; and
- A decision-making process that requires participation by local stakeholders.

Workshop participants also developed the CBCRC research agenda, *Assessing Research Needs* (Moote et al. 1999). Subsequent to the workshop, the CBCRC hosted five national workshops and funded thirteen research projects across the United States and Canada to foster research and learning about community-based collaboration. The CBCRC also developed the document titled *Protocol and Guidelines for Ethical and Effective Research of Community-Based Collaborative Processes* (2003) to foster effective and ethical research practice sensitive to the needs of the communities being studied. As this book goes to press, the CBCRC is examining ways to continue developing and disseminating knowledge, and is seeking a permanent home.

About the Book

This book synthesizes knowledge from conferences, research, and field experiences with community-based collaboration from a range of disciplines. Each chapter is written by a leading analyst and reflects the diversity and knowledge of the CBCRC's membership and of the field itself. We sought and received substantial input on the book's topics from CBC members, state and federal agency staff, mediators, researchers, and environmentalists. The book draws on findings from CBCRC-funded research projects as well as from existing research literature in diverse fields. It also suggests topics for future research.

Most of our authors are also engaged in community-based collaboration at the local level, enabling them to draw on both research and field-based experience. This book is thus distinct from others in the field in that it combines academic rigor with a grounding in lessons learned from community groups themselves.

We do not offer a recipe for when collaboration is appropriate, as this is covered in existing literature, such as *Collaboration: A Guide for Environmental Advocates* (Dukes and Firehock 2001). The contributors consider why people seek more collaboration to address community environmental issues, the social and political drivers that led to the CBC movement, whether these processes offer useful approaches for addressing and resolving environmental issues, and whether they improve mechanisms for integrating local knowledge and scientific information. They also address the new institutional roles fulfilled by CBCs and collaboratives' interactions with existing governance institutions. Finally, the book considers the future of the CBC movement and implications for democratic governance and environmental management for conveners, agencies, and participants.

Chapter 1 discusses the emerging field of community-based collaboration and provides a brief overview of the CBC movement and its implications for environmental management. We explain why community collaboration is an integral aspect of an emerging paradigm for environmental protection and management in the United States. Chapters 2 and 3 examine specific aspects of the integration of community knowledge and adaptive management. Chapter 4 discusses community collaboratives as new institutions and their relationships to existing structures of governance. Chapter 5 provides an overview of effective collaboration, with an emphasis on overcoming external barriers. Chapter 6 proposes "theoroids" that lay out best practices for collaboration. The final chapter looks at what this all means for governance and environmental management, and provides policy recommendations and directions for future research as well as for individuals.

We hope this book provides new ideas, provokes interesting dialogues, and leads to both increased understanding and better outcomes for communities and their environments.

The authors and editors wish to thank the many CBCRC participants for their contributions to our thinking. We particularly offer our appreciation to the members who served on the Steering Committee and those who attended a very engaging authors' retreat in Wintergreen, Virginia, as we began work on the manuscript.

We are grateful for the support of the William and Flora Hewlett Foundation and the foundation's program managers, Steve Toben and Terry Amsler, who offered invaluable guidance many times.

References

Coggins, George Cameron. 1998. "Of Californicators, Quislings, and Crazies: Some Perils of Devolved Collaboration." *Chronicle of Community* 2 (2): 27–32.
CBCRC. 2003. *Protocol and Guidelines for Ethical and Effective Research of Community-*

Based Collaborative Processes: Report of the Community-Based Collaboratives Research Consortium. Charlottesville, VA: CBCRC.

Dukes, E. Franklin, and Karen E. Firehock. 2001. *Collaboration: A Guide for Environmental Advocates.* Charlottesville, VA: University of Virginia, the Wilderness Society, and the National Audubon Society.

Moote, Ann, Alex Conley, Karen Firehock, and E. Franklin Dukes. 1999. *Assessing Research Needs.* Proceedings of the founding meeting of the Community-Based Collaboratives Research Consortium, Tucson, AZ.

Weber, Edward P. 2000. "A New Vanguard for the Environment: Grass-Roots Ecosystem Management as a New Environmental Movement." *Society and Natural Resources* 13 (3): 237–59.

1

The Community-Based Collaborative Movement in the United States

Karen E. Firehock

This chapter provides a brief description of the community-based collaborative (CBC) movement in the United States. It addresses what collaboration is, what CBCs are, why CBCs emerged in the United States, how they both solve and engender conflict, what CBCs contribute, how outcomes are measured, and what CBCs mean for environmental governance. This chapter thus sets the definitional and historical stage for later chapters in the book dealing with community knowledge, how CBCs can take an adaptive management approach, how they govern, building effective collaboratives, the theory of collaboration, and finally, the promise of collaboration and what the movement means for the future.

It is fair to question why community-based collaboration even matters. Why does the phenomenon warrant the attention of federal agencies, state and local governments, scientists, politicians, environmental and civic groups, and community members? The contributors to this book suggest that CBCs are worthy of attention primarily because they represent a quiet revolution in American environmental governance. They provide a unique forum for addressing complex environmental problems, a forum that is likely to become increasingly important in the future. CBCs may offer the best hope in cases where traditional resource management has failed because they bring together parties with diverse perspectives, knowledge, and interests, and they often include groups that have the capacity to implement solutions.

What Is Community-Based Collaboration?

Many terms have been used to describe the work of collaborative groups. Among them are *collaborative stewardship* (Burchfield 1998), *collaborative environmental management* (Randolph and Rich 1998), *community-based con-*

servation (Snow 1998, 254), *collaborative conservation* (Brick 1998), *community-based environmental protection* (U.S. EPA 1997), and *grassroots environmental management* (Weber 2000). *Cooperative conservation* is yet another term applied to these efforts at the 2005 White House Conference, "Faces and Places of Cooperative Conservation."

Since these descriptions also often include the notion of collaboration, it is worthwhile including a definition of that term. Potapchuck and Polk (1994) propose as a definition a locally based process in which parties who have a stake in the outcome of a problem (stakeholders) come together in a structured forum to engage in joint decision making. Gray (1989) defines collaboration as the joint ownership of decisions and collective responsibility for achieving the jointly agreed-upon objectives.

Some groups, such as the Policy Consensus Initiative (2010), have set standards for collaboration. The Policy Consensus Initiative suggests determining whether a group is truly collaborative based on the existence of the following standards:

- Jointly agreed-upon indicators of success or milestones for measuring progress.
- Mechanisms to monitor whether participants are contributing to meeting the jointly agreed-upon objectives.
- Jointly developed strategies and actions that spell out commitments, taking into account the differences among the participating groups and individuals.
- Contractual agreements or other provisions that describe roles and responsibilities for carrying out jointly agreed-upon objectives.
- Evidence of resource sharing or exchanges.
- Mechanisms for regular exchange of information and feedback about joint progress toward objectives.

This chapter adopts the definition of community-based collaboration advanced by the Community-Based Collaboratives Research Consortium (CBCRC) at a conference held in 1999 (Moote et al. 2000). The consortium's definition of a CBC is as follows: "(1) A group that has been convened voluntarily from within the local community to focus on a resource management issue(s) or planning involving public lands or publicly owned or regulated resources whose management impacts the physical, environmental, and/or economic health of the local community; (2) Was brought together by a shared desire to influence the protection and use of natural resources through recommendations or direct actions that will impact the management of the resource; (3) Has membership that includes a broad array of interests, some of which may be in conflict; and (4) Utilizes a decision-making process that requires participation by local stakeholders" (Moote et al. 2000, 2).

As suggested by this definition, what makes a CBC unique is not simply the sharing of decision making or the monitoring of outcomes but the diversity of the collaborative's membership. This diversity can aid the collaborative in problem solving. Since CBCs are made up of representatives of diverse stakeholder groups, participants in CBCs often are able to lend unique perspectives to framing problems and solutions. They may include fishers or ranchers, scientists, federal agencies, resource managers, and conservation groups. All of these groups can bring knowledge and experience to managing a resource.

CBCs are also diverse in scope and geography as well as in membership. The following examples demonstrate CBCs' diversity:

- The *Catron County Collaborative* in New Mexico found a collaborative solution after years of court gridlock over grazing. Ranchers had been distressed by being blocked from grazing, while environmentalists wished to restore the land. A solution developed collaboratively among the parties allowed a return of some grazing along with land restoration projects, allowing both sides to meet their needs (Smith 1998, 1–20).
- The *Applegate Partnership of Oregon* achieved collaboration between the community and agencies to better manage public and private lands within a 496,500-acre watershed. Not restricted to acting only within agency-defined land boundaries, the group was able to address stewardship activities on both public and private lands at the watershed scale, where change could be most effective (Firehock 1999).
- The *Rockfish River Forum* in Nelson County, Virginia, organized to address the impacts of sprawl-patterned development and river sedimentation. The group realized through stakeholder input over the nine months of the project that many other issues not within its original scope could also be addressed by the effort, such as stream habitat restoration, the creation of public access, environmental education, and the construction of a new river park to demonstrate habitat conservation principles (Firehock, personal experience).
- The *Northwest Colorado Stewardship*, working on a National Environmental Protection Act process on Bureau of Land Management (BLM) lands and off-highway vehicle uses, brought together multiple

participants not simply to argue about the condition of the resource but to monitor its condition and reach a shared understanding of what might be done to manage it (see chapter 3).

Why Did CBCs Emerge in the United States?

The collaborative movement is a uniquely American phenomenon that emerged late in the twentieth century. Although there is no national census of groups engaged in community-based collaboration for environmental protection, most researchers agree that the number is increasing (see chapter 4).

The growth of the CBC movement in the United States can be attributed to several factors: (1) settlement patterns that resulted in a patchwork of public and private land ownership; (2) the evolution of the American property rights movement and anger over restrictions emerging from endangered species rulings and other regulations, especially in the West; (3) the difficulty of managing for multiple objectives by large government bureaucracies across diverse ecological and social environments; (4) traditions of American democratic governance, including the right to participate in decisions that affect shared commons; (5) the inability of command-and-control technologies to solve pollution problems when decision makers and pollution sources are dispersed; and (6) communities' interest in seeking solutions that recognize community values.

The interwoven patterns of ownership among agencies, tribes, and private landowners in particular are a source of much conflict in the United States. The settlement patterns of the West led to a patchwork quilt of land ownership, with the original residents, Native Americans, relegated to leftover lands or forcibly removed to more remote territories. Many of the 569 federally recognized tribes manage their own lands, each according to its own distinct tribal laws, across thirty-five states. Federal lands include those administered by the National Park Service, the Bureau of Reclamation, the BLM, the U.S. Department of Agriculture's Forest Service, the National Fish and Wildlife Service, the Department of Energy, the U.S. military, and so on. States also administer their own lands and refuges. This complex land ownership pattern makes it difficult to manage western grasslands, forests, and rivers at a scale large enough to effectively include entire ecosystems. Moreover, in the eastern and Midwestern states, where most land is privately owned, there is just as much, if not more, complexity in managing ecosystems that stretch across multiple land tenures.

CBCs have emerged as one way to address the complex regulatory environment and to overcome the disparate patterns of ownership that add to the difficulty of managing land resources. Groups such as the Malpai Borderlands Group, described in chapter 2, have sought ways to voluntarily collaborate in the management of a vast rangeland ecosystem.

The expansion of community interest in environmental governance has also been fueled in part by the impacts of environmental regulations on individual property rights and the reach and power of those regulations. The property rights concern has been driven by controversial environmental decisions emanating from the Endangered Species Act, such as those concerning the snail darter fish in Tennessee, the California gnatcatcher, and the northern and Mexican spotted owls, in which large dam, development, or timber permit projects had to be suspended or altered. These cases and others have increased concern in some sectors about the reach of environmental laws and the powers held by administrators who implement them. These property rights concerns have spurred interest in how decisions are made and how the public is consulted about actions that affect them.

The U.S. Forest Service has faced challenges associated with its administrative mandate of multi-objective management. Although the Forest Service was originally created to secure a sustained timber supply for the country, its mission expanded over time to take into account the multiple values provided by forest resources. The Multiple-Use Sustained-Yield Act of 1960 codified the agency's multiple-use management objectives to explicitly include "outdoor recreation, range, timber, watershed and wildlife and fish purposes" (Kenney et al. 1998). The National Forest Management Act of 1976 sought to solve some of the difficulties inherent in managing lands for multiple uses by increasing opportunities for public input, yet the process has proved extremely difficult to implement (ibid.). Adding conflict and complexity to this situation, different U.S. administrations have sought to increase or restrict public participation and access to agency documents through various agency decisions, expanding or contracting participation based on political views of the moment.

In addition to changes in federal management approaches, the demand for more local control has been spurred by the perception that American governance is dominated by a large, centralized bureaucracy, characterized by rigid adherence to rules and regulations and afflicted with hierarchical chains of command that no longer work well. The complex demands of land management require agencies to be flexible and to empower citizens to participate as partners in governance (Osborne and Gaebler 1993).

CBCs represent an innovative form of governance by bringing additional stakeholders into the decision-making process. The question is whether this approach to governance is appropriate to managing lands held in trust by the government for the benefit of the public, whether or not that public resides near the resource in question or is directly affected by resource management decisions. In chapter 5, Walker and Senecah discuss the institutional challenges of collaborative land management.

A third factor contributing to the emergence of CBCs is an interest in reframing environmental issues so that problems are addressed more comprehensively. Participants in a dialogue may not be interested in collaborating if they think that problems have been framed in such a way as to exclude possible outcomes or solutions from the outset. For example, an issue that is highly value-laden may be reframed as technical, implying that only technical data can be used to make a decision and values do not have a place in the discussion. Public interests attempting to introduce values into the discussion may be labeled "irrational" and disempowered (Renn, Thomas, and Wiedemann 1995). Some collaborative groups, therefore, have formed precisely to broaden the scope of a problem and look for solutions that are more holistic. Since CBCs are not necessarily restricted to narrow problem definitions as an agency might be, they are often in a position to expand the scope of the problem solving and address the social and economic aspects of environmental problems. As an example of the broader issue scope possible through CBCs, Charles Curtin in chapter 2 discusses the Downeast Initiative in Maine, a collaborative concerned with the ecological decline of the groundfishery, the diversity of markets that support local fisheries, and the future of family-based businesses.

How Do CBCs Engender Conflict?

A number of concerns have been expressed about the roles of CBCs (Firehock 1999). There is concern that CBCs may exercise an inappropriate level of influence over a public resource, and that they lack the diversity of membership necessary to represent broader public interests. CBCs are sometimes thought to consist of self-appointed representatives who have no real accountability and to exclude members who might not agree with the majority. However, these concerns are not fundamentally different from those that may be expressed about an industry or an environmental group that has a distinct membership and is seeking to influence a land management agency.

The devolution of power from elected and public entities to nonelected local groups who are perceived as not accountable is a long-standing concern for some (see Coggins 1998) but not others. For example, while Weber (2000) acknowledges the issue of devolution inherent in grassroots ecosystem management, he does not share concerns about power and authority devolving to the local level. Indeed, the issue is more complex than a collision between the expertocracy at the federal level desperately clinging to power and local communities seeking to overturn regulation by exerting more local control over land resources. Some groups do, of course, seek to diminish federal authority, just as some bureaucrats do not see any value in engaging community perspectives in federal land management.

A number of researchers have noted that concerns over community roles increase when they affect publicly owned resources such as federal lands or rivers (Kenney 1999; Leach 2004). Conflicts can emerge between people who live on or near the resources in question and those who have an interest in that resource, such as a rancher protesting restrictions on grazing and an environmentalist who wants to see the landscape restored. Conflicts of this sort have often been described as the politics of place versus the politics of interest. Communities of place that depend on local physical resources may find themselves at odds with communities of interest that want to maintain existing regional or national federal land management agreements and policies. Critics suggest that local interests (communities of place) have undue influence simply through their ability to participate in local meetings while larger national or regional environmental groups (communities of interest) cannot (Leach 2004).

Another area of concern surrounding CBCs is how their membership is derived. In contrast to a government-appointed committee, in which stakeholder-based membership is defined by statute, ad hoc CBCs have more leeway to determine their membership. They may choose to include or exclude participants, and this may have consequences for the decision process and outcomes. The desire for greater inclusion at the local level may lead to conflicts over exclusion at other levels. For example, Timothy Duane (1997) leveled charges of exclusion of disparate interests in environmental decision making by the Quincy Library Group in California. He suggested that the group achieved exclusion either through intentional action, such as by preventing other groups from joining the dialogue, or through more indirect methods, such as by holding meetings at inconvenient times or places not accessible to all concerned parties. Thus, the question of who can and should participate in decisions that have an impact on both local land uses and publicly owned resources is at the heart of the conflict surrounding CBCs.

What Is CBCs' Key Contribution?

Despite concerns over how CBCs are formed and operate, they offer several unique elements for problem solving. They can be adaptive and flexible, they can work across political and ecological boundaries, they can help to ensure that solutions are implemented, and they can link social and technical issues. Collaboratives that employ consensus decision making may offer a framework in which creativity and adaptive response to change becomes the norm rather than the exception (Innes 2004).

In chapter 4, Melanie Hughes McDermott, Margaret Ann Moote, and Cecilia Danks present reasons for collaborative groups' successes and examine why some have been able to overcome seemingly intractable problems. High among the reasons is the unique ability of CBCs to dilute traditional power imbalances by using their "localness" and influence to change the way systems operate and redefine the rules of the game. Collaboratives can take a holistic approach because they are generally unhindered by rules outlining jurisdictional boundaries and are free to invite whomever they need to the deliberative table.

Based on the research of multiple groups and interviews I have conducted, the following benefits can be obtained by convening a collaborative group: (1) the creation of a community voice concerning the effects of federal decisions on local communities, (2) the provision of local knowledge about resources for the agency decision-making process, (3) posing of alternatives to traditional land management practices and policies, (4) an improved working relationship between and among agencies, the public, and businesses, (5) increased productivity of the decision-making processes through building community understanding and support for land management needs, (6) maintenance of the local, natural resource–dependent job base and related economies, and (7) a better balance of federal agency priorities with local community desires.

As noted earlier, CBCs can address issues at the level of the ecosystem and across political boundaries. For example, as Charles Curtin discusses in chapter 2, the Malpai Borderlands Group is comprised of ranchers who own 53 percent of the 880,000 acres they wish to manage, with the rest owned by state and federal agencies. By working collaboratively and expanding their areas of interest beyond individual holdings, ranchers can manage the rangeland at a scale needed to restore the grasslands. Similarly, the Applegate Partnership in southern Oregon is concerned with impacts from forestry, mining, and grazing within a 496,500-acre watershed that includes both federal and private lands, thus requiring management cooperation between public and private owners (Firehock 1999).

Collaborative groups may help resolve difficult problems implementing federal land management decisions successfully. Frank Fischer (2000) coined the term *expertocracy* to describe our current bureaucracy as dominated by experts who are leveraging greater influence over environmental decision making and policy, thus leading to a loss of power by the public.

Fischer and others have recommended greater local engagement as an antidote to this trend. Thomas Beierle and Jerry Cayford, Fischer, and Fiorino have championed the benefits of engaging the public in environmental decision making as a matter of course. Beierle and Cayford (2002, 75) suggest that "rather than seeing policy decisions as fundamentally technical with some need for public input, we should see many more decisions as fundamentally public with the need for some technical input," especially since values and interests are often, if not always, a component of environmental decisions.

A technocratic orientation alone is insufficient to solve environmental problems. Fiorino (1990) lays out substantive, normative, and instrumental reasons to engage the public in environmental decision making. Substantive reasons include the observation that citizens are often able to see problems, issues, and solutions that experts miss. A community's knowledge can inform and enrich environmental understanding of both the problem and its potential solutions. The community may also assist in framing the problem proposed to be addressed more holistically to include a broader set of issues (see chapter 2).

Fiorino explains that a normative reason to include the community in decision making is that technocratic orientations toward problem solving are incompatible with democratic ideals because they tend to ignore the value dimension of policy analysis, thereby disenfranchising the community. Finally, instrumental reasons advanced by Fiorino include the legitimization of citizens themselves, based on their participation and their ability to help implement solutions. Simply put, communities are more likely to assist in implementing ideas that meet their own goals.

Fiorino's concepts are backed up by Beierle and Cayford's (2002) study of the outcomes of 239 deliberative cases. This study found that the majority of the decisions provided better alternatives than those traditionally proposed. The authors attributed better outcomes in part to the fact that stakeholders were able to add new information, ideas, and analysis.

Brogden (2003a) suggests that the need to engage diverse knowledge sources in developing environmental decisions arises from the fact that decisions about future environmental outcomes can involve a great deal of uncertainty, both because of the complexity of environmental systems and because of the diversity of actors who may affect outcomes on the ground. Environmental complexity arises from the fact that processes affecting the environment vary in scale and duration, from catastrophic floods to chronic droughts. Actor diversity—the multiplicity of actors who may affect the system, such as legislators, landowners, or resource users—increases the potential for outcomes to be affected in ways that may be unanticipated. One way to reduce uncertainty is to diversify the knowledge base by including all the actors during the deliberative process who might affect the outcome. In that way, previously unanticipated concerns can be addressed during the process and resolved with all parties at the table. This results in less conflict later on, since concerns are anticipated during the process thereby lessening the likelihood that people will contest the outcomes (Fiorino 1990).

As self-convened groups, CBCs can expand the scope of the problem solving and redefine environmental problems as having social, economic, and ecological components as well. Unlike an agency required to follow a legislative mandate, a self-convened CBC may expand the scope and framing of the problem at hand. The Downeast Initiative collaborative group in Maine is exemplary in this regard. Whereas an agency-convened process might focus narrowly on regulatory questions of fish landings or reproduction numbers, the fishers in the Downeast Initiative were able to look more broadly at the sustainability of the fishery and their community, since both jobs and fish populations are intricately linked.

Challenges of Local Collaborative Management

For collaborative groups that want to exert greater influence over their ecosystems, the level of effort, degree of knowledge, and amount of time required to participate effectively can be daunting. For example, participants may have to research land development proposals or discharge permits, attend hearings, organize neighbors, or research complex technical issues. These tasks are time-intensive and require a commitment by many individuals to make the effort worthwhile. One reason community groups disband is that they must re-create the functions of a bureaucracy in order to participate effectively (Cortner and Moote 1998). For example, they may need to create databases for membership, develop communications such as newsletters, and conduct research and fundraising. A well-designed organizational structure may be important if the community hopes to influence already organized institutions, which have their own technical experts, studies, and financial resources.

Even agency-supported projects can demand tremendous effort of participants. In the Northwest Colorado Stewardship, when an agency requested that volunteers read and be familiar with a 1,700-page environmental impact study, one member abruptly left the group, and others expressed increasing frustration (Fernández-Giménez et al. 2005). Thus, it is important for agencies to consider the demands of time and resources that may be felt by community members who are volunteering their time.

The rise of CBCs signals a desire by communities to have far greater engagement in decision making about public and community resources, as well as the need to improve how agencies work together with the communities affected by agency decisions. The challenge for communities is that they may lack the expertise, resources, and membership diversity to take on the issues.

The challenge for agencies is whether they are equipped to initiate collaborative processes that engage a diversity of local interests. They may not be able to initiate or manage local collaborative processes even when there is support from their headquarters or national office. For example, a survey of BLM field offices found that, despite national support expressed in several policy documents, there was little material support—time, budget flexibility, or training—for staff to implement collaborative processes at the field level (Laninga 2004).

Unfortunately, increasing participation by diverse groups may result in unintended social repercussions. The agency manager who seeks to cooperate by joining or aiding a CBC may be considered co-opted. Similarly, a representative of an environmental group who cooperates with traditional adversaries, such as the logging industry may be deemed to have sold out (see Coggins 1998).

Measuring Outcomes of Community-Based Collaboration

Although a number of studies have evaluated the effects of community-based environmental protection, numerous difficulties arise in assessing outcomes. It can be difficult to use surveys of participants as a tool because they may give highly subjective results (Moote and Conley 2003). A group's own assessment of whether it has met its goals may similarly be highly subjective and may not link outcomes directly to group actions.

Attempts to compare case studies as a basis for drawing broader conclusions about success are also beset by difficulties. As Moote and Conley (2003) and others (Beierle and Cayford 2002; Yin 2002) point out, the high variation in case study methods makes cross-case analysis difficult. However, Beierle and Cayford (2002) have developed a method for systematically evaluating the case study literature for public participation. Their method may be useful for evaluating the growing case study literature concerning CBCs.

Evaluating outcomes is further complicated by problems with establishing cause and effect. A community decision-making body may be advisory to another entity, such as a federal agency, or may make decisions about projects over which it has no direct control, such as seeking to change range management practices on both private and public lands (a relevant example here is the Malpai Borderlands Group mentioned earlier). Regardless of how much control the group has over its decisions, it may not have much actual control over the environment or other factors it is seeking to influence, such as the local economy. A simple example is a fishery restoration plan that is thwarted not by failure of the group's actions but by a record drought that lasts several years. Similarly, a rangeland restoration project may fail because the price of beef declines, thus preventing the economic inputs needed to fund restoration, or an upstream air quality problem from a new emission source may negate community efforts to improve air quality locally.

The scale of time needed to address a problem also may be an issue. For example, a solution that has been instituted in an ecologically sound manner could take years to show results. These factors have all been framed in terms of complexity theory, which is applicable to problems that arise when multiple actors make multiple decisions and diverse inputs exist at various scales over various time frames (Gunderson and Holling 2002).

Brogden (2003a) suggests a potential way to evaluate CBC outcomes. She explains that CBCs operate in a complex system that both causes them to occur and at the same time constrains them. Thus, the problem of evaluating their outcomes is that they are functioning within a larger system with nonlinear dynamic properties. They are at the mercy of different actors and systems operating at varying scales and rates.

Drawing on the work of Gunderson and Holling, Brogden suggests that measuring the adaptive capacity and resilience of CBCs might be one way to understand how effective they are in achieving any desired environmental change. Does the CBC have the capacity to sustain membership, monitor outcomes, and change implementation plans if problems are discovered? Maria Fernández-Giménez and Heidi Ballard explore these questions in chapter 3.

Adaptive capacity of collaborative groups has been studied by two CB-CRC-sponsored research projects. Three rangeland collaboratives were evaluated by Fernández-Giménez and colleagues (2005), and applications for measurement indicators were used to assess the outcomes and potentials for the Diablo Trust by Muñoz-Erickson, Aguilar-González, and their colleagues (2005). Both studies found a gap in CBCs' ability to measure outcomes and to link those findings back to original assumptions and management actions.

Another CBCRC-sponsored study of the Malpai Borderlands Group demonstrated greater success at linking monitoring to management strategies since the group had the greatest technical capacity, including funded science investigators. It was able to implement large-scale controlled burns on more than 300,000 of the 880,000-acre project area and to measure the results of that work in terms of both increasing heterogeneity of the system and restoration of the grasslands (Curtin 2010).

One aspect that makes it difficult for CBCs to evaluate environmental change is that they often lack baseline or historical data about the condition of the resource they are seeking to influence. While many collaborative groups do their own monitoring (see chapter 3), they may not have historical trend data with which to compare their findings. Even federal agencies fall short on their ability to conduct adequate baseline condition assessments. Furthermore, the collection of data does not necessarily lead to better management. Although the Diablo Trust in Arizona collected additional data, it did not have a process in place for modifying group decisions based on new findings.

As Fernández-Giménez and Ballard explain in chapter 3, an adaptive management context can provide a feedback loop to help CBCs learn about the most effective or efficient management strategies and deploy those solutions that work best. Chapter 5 of this book examines factors that lead to successful outcomes for CBCs.

What Does This Mean for Environmental Governance?

An overarching question for some researchers is what CBCs mean for environmental governance. Are CBCs a sign of a more participatory democracy or are they a sign of failure by agencies and other public entities to reflect community goals and interests? The answer is both. These groups are proliferating across the United States because communities have come to realize that the only way to understand complex issues, to have local knowledge considered, and to tackle the intricate socio-ecological problems they face is to bring together disparate parties to work collaboratively toward a solution that all can live with. However, caution must be exercised in determining the appropriateness of using collaborative processes to address a local issue.

Groups such as the Quincy Library Group in California have sought to direct management strategies over two national forests that cover millions of acres (Firehock 1999). McDermott, Moote, and Danks (see chapter 4) ask whether a collaborative can really be considered local if it seeks to influence two million acres of land. On the other hand, as Charles Curtin discusses in chapter 2, the ability to manage an ecosystem at an appropriate scale has led to the success of the Malpai Borderlands Group, which now measures and monitors vast tracts (almost one million acres) of land and conducts restoration practices for grasslands on a scale at which it can actually be effective in addressing rangeland management needs.

Two remaining concerns for understanding CBCs are how to define a community, and what its bounds are. Should people who wish to use the courts to uphold environmental laws be excluded? Are some CBCs limited to only certain stakeholder groups in order to pursue a preconceived agenda rather than to promote genuine community debate? Do people form collaboratives to try to get around environmental restrictions, such as endangered species provisions or timber harvest restrictions? Anecdotally, yes. However, groups that seek to exclude those who might disagree with a proposed approach or that do not invite all voices to the table are not CBCs in the true spirit of cooperation, according to the definition used in this chapter.

CBCs should not exclude voices from the table or seek to manipulate data to paint a different picture of conditions on the ground. Moreover, the vast majority of collaboratives seem to be genuine community groups. Whatever the faults of a few, their overall perceived worth is such that the movement will continue to grow.

To return to the question of why collaborative groups are forming: they are seeking to change the power dynamics of a system that for too long has failed to provide adequate arenas for informed dialogue, debate, and deliberation, in which values can be recognized and discussed. Indeed, governments that work with CBCs have an important oversight role in ensuring that they do not become part of the problem of exclusion or disempowerment. In chapter 5, Gregg Walker and Susan Senecah discuss collaborative governance and issues surrounding CBCs as new institutions of governance, as well as the inherent challenges they face in doing so.

Some scholars, such as Cortner and Moote (1998), offer a hopeful vision for U.S. ecosystem management that entails four progressive outcomes: socially defined goals and objectives, holistically integrated science, adaptive institutions, and collaborative decision making. Other scholars, such as Gunderson and Holling (2002), echo this desire. They have called for a new foundation for renewal in order to build and sustain the capacity of people, economies, and nature for dealing with change. There is a new paradigm emerging for ecosystem management in the United States, one in which the role of the active citizen is critical. The challenge is how to balance the values of expertise and scientific knowledge in decision making with social consensus and civic action.

Areas in Need of Research

In each subsequent chapter we identify areas in need of further research. To better understand the field of community-based collaboration, we suggest a focus on the following activities:

1. Document and diagram collaborative group processes and then develop methodologies for facilitating best practices to allow for greater success. Some critics charge that "community collaborative groups exclude all parties" or that "community groups do not use good science." While some do and some do not, it would be very useful to better understand the scope of the groups currently operating and the diversity of processes and resources for scientific evaluation that are utilized. In short, there is a need for a national census of CBCs to document their true scope and diversity so that their societal and ecological role can be fully appreciated and analyzed.

2. Evaluate and establish more consistent processes for integrating community-based and scientific knowledge, making the values and assumptions behind both sources of knowledge more transparent, so that more informed decisions can be made. Agencies seeking to consult local groups would do well to conduct educational outreach to help the community prepare recommendations informed by the best science available. Community groups would also benefit from improved relationships with agencies so that they can learn how government processes work and consider ways that their local knowledge could help inform agency perspectives.

3. Measure whether and how CBCs are functioning as truly new institutions and the degree to which their collaborative function can bring diverse parties and knowledge sources together.

Answering the broad areas of inquiry noted above, as well as questions related to U.S. governance and theories of democracy, will take greater collaboration across research institutions, researchers in the social and natural sciences, local and federal agencies, and communities of interest and place. Answering these larger questions of democracy, civic participation, and avenues for cooperative natural resource management is key to understanding the CBC movement. These issues are addressed in the next several chapters, while chapter 7 gives our prescription for success.

Note

Two laws discussed in this chapter are the Multiple-Use Sustained-Yield Act (PL 86-517; approved June 12, 1960) and the National Forest Management Act (PL 94-588; approved August 17, 1974, as amended 1976).

References

Beierle, Thomas C., and Jerry Cayford. 2002. *Democracy in Practice: Public Participation in Environmental Decisions.* Washington, DC: Resources for the Future Press.

Brick, Phil. 1998. "Of Imposters, Optimists and Kings: Finding a Political Niche for Collaborative Conservation." *Chronicle of Community* 2 (Winter).

Brogden, Mette. 2003a. "Assessing Environmental Outcomes of Community-Based Collaboratives: What Research and Theory Streams Can Help Us?" September. Udall Center for Studies in Public Policy, University of Arizona. http://www.cb crc.org/2003speakerpapers/Mette%20Brogden.pdf (accessed December 1, 2005).

———. 2003b. "Assessment of Environmental Outcomes." In *The Promise and Performance of Environmental Conflict Resolution,* ed. Rosemary O'Leary and Lisa B. Bingham. Washington, DC: Resources for the Future Press.

Beierle, Thomas C., and Jerry Cayford. 2002. *Democracy in Practice: Public Participation in Environmental Decisions.* Washington, DC: Resources for the Future Press.

Burchfield, Jim. 1998. "Abandoned by the Roadside: The Long Road Ahead for Collaborative Stewardship." *Chronicle of Community* 3 (Autumn).

Coggins, George Cameron. 1998. "Of Californicators, Quislings and Crazies: Some Perils of Devolved Collaboration." *Chronicle of Community* 2 (2): 32.

Cortner, Hanna, and Margaret Ann Moote. 1998. *Politics of Ecosystem Management.* Washington, DC: Island Press.

Curtin, C. G. 2010. "The Ecology of Place and Natural Resource Management: Lessons from Marine and Terrestrial Ecosystems." In *The Ecology of Place: Contributions of Place-based Research to Ecological Understanding,* ed. I. Billick and M. Price. New York: Columbia University Press.

Duane, Timothy. 1997. "Community Participation in Ecosystem Management." *Ecology Law Quarterly* 24 (4).

"Faces and Places of Cooperative Conservation: Profiles in Citizen Stewardship." White House Conference on Cooperative Conservation. Saint Louis, MO, August 29–31, 2005.

Fernández-Giménez, María E., Bernardo Aguilar-González, Tischa Muñoz-Erickson, and Charles G. Curtin. 2005. "Assessing the Adaptive Capacity of Collaboratively Managed Rangelands: A Test of the Concept and Comparison of Three Rangeland CBCs." December. Unpublished manuscript.

Firehock, Karen E. 1999. "Evaluation of Community-Based Collaborative Approaches for Federal Lands Management." Master's thesis, University of Virginia.

Fiorino, Daniel J. 1990. "Citizen Participation and Environmental Risk: A Survey of Institutional Mechanisms." *Science, Technology and Human Values* 15 (2): 226–43.

Fischer, Frank. 2000. *Citizens, Experts and the Environment: The Politics of Local Knowledge.* Durham, NC: Duke University Press.

Gunderson, L. H., and C. S. Holling. 2002. *Panarchy: Understanding Transformations in Human and Natural Systems.* Washington, DC: Island Press.

Innes, Judith. 2004. "Consensus Building: Clarifications for the Critics." *Planning Theory* 3 (1): 5–20.

Kenney, Douglas S. 1999. "Are Community-Based Watershed Groups Really Effective?" *Chronicle of Community* 3 (Winter): 33–37.

Kenney, Douglas S., Gabriel D. Carter, and Joshua M. Kerstein. 1998. "Values of the Federal Public Lands." Boulder: University of Colorado School of Law, Natural Resources Law Center.

Laninga, Tamara J. 2004. "Collaborative Planning in BLM Field Offices: Where It's Happening and What It Looks Like." Master's thesis, University of Colorado. http://www.cbcrc.org/php-bin/grantsPublic.php?id=4 (accessed April 1, 2007).

———. 2005. "Collaboration and the Bureau of Land Management: Differential Adoption of Community-Based Approaches to Public Lands Planning in the West." PhD diss., University of Colorado.

Leach, William D. 2004. *Is Devolution Democratic? Assessing Collaborative Environmental Management.* Long Beach: California State University, Center for Collaborative Policy, August.

Moote, Margaret Ann, and Alex Conley. 2003. "Evaluating Collaborative Natural Resource Management." *Society and Natural Resources* 16:371–86.

Moote, Margaret Ann, Alex Conley, Karen E. Firehock, and Frank Dukes. 2000. *Assessing Research Needs: Summary of a Workshop on Community-based Collaboratives.* Udall Center Publications 00-5. Tucson: University of Arizona, Udall Center for Studies in Public Policy.

Muñoz-Erickson, Tischa, Bernardo Aguilar-González, Thomas D. Sisk, and Matthew R. Loeser. 2005. "Assessing the Effectiveness of the Holistic Ecosystem Health Indicator (HEHI) as a Monitoring Tool to Assess the Adaptive Capacity of Community-based Collaboratives." December. Unpublished manuscript, Cultural and Regional Studies Program, Prescott College, Prescott, AZ.

Osborne, David E., and Ted Gaebler. 1993. *Reinventing Government: How the Entrepreneurial Spirit Is Transforming the Public Sector.* Reading, MA: Addison-Wesley.

Policy Consensus Initiative. 2010. "What Is Collaborative Governance?" National Policy Consensus Center. http://www.policyconsensus.org/publicsolutions/ps_2.html (accessed March 3, 2010).

Potapchuk, William R., and Caroline Polk. 1994. *Building the Collaborative Community.* Washington, DC: National Institute for Dispute Resolution.

Randolph, John C., and Richard C. Rich. 1998. "Collaborative Environmental Management: An Emerging Approach and Experience in Virginia." *Virginia Issues and Answers* 5 (Summer): 12.

Smith, Melinda. 1998. *The Catron County Citizens Group: A Case Study in Community Collaboration.* Albuquerque: New Mexico Center for Dispute Resolution.

Snow, Donald. 1998. "A Politics Appropriate to Place." In *Writers on the Range,* ed. Karl Hess Jr. and John A. Baden. Niwot: University Press of Colorado.

U.S. Environmental Protection Agency. 1997. *Community-Based Environmental Protection: A Resource Book for Protecting Ecosystems and Communities,* 1-1. EPA 230-B-96-

003. September. Washington, DC: Environmental Protection Agency, Office of Policy, Planning and Evaluation.

Weber, Edward P. 2000. "A New Vanguard for the Environment: Grass-Roots Ecosystem Management as a New Environmental Movement." *Society and Natural Resources* 13:237–59.

Yin, Robert K. 2002. *Case Study Research, Design and Methods,* 3rd ed. Thousand Oaks, CA: Sage.

2

Integrating and Applying Knowledge from Community-Based Collaboratives
Implications for Natural Resource Management

Charles G. Curtin

This chapter discusses how community-based collaboratives (CBCs) integrate local, indigenous, and science-based approaches to gathering and using knowledge. This synthesis is exemplified by three case studies from marine and terrestrial systems in Africa and North America. The case studies underscore that collaborative approaches are more than a community development tool, representing a distinct departure from recent approaches to science and resource management.

As other contributors to this volume observe, CBCs can contribute much to society, in spheres as diverse as environmental restoration and social justice. Viewed through the narrow lens of the natural sciences, CBCs represent an opportunity to rescale conservation and science. Breaking out of the constraints of traditional agency and academic approaches, CBCs create hybrid social institutions that integrate social and ecological problem solving (Curtin 2011). Through a process dubbed "action research," communities and researchers learn from the actual process of collaborative conservation by conducting projects at the scale of management.

One benefit of the collaborative approach is the ability to integrate multiple kinds of knowledge. The synthesis of numerous cultural, traditional, and science-based approaches can be a powerful lever in expanding the problem-solving potential of science and policy (Curtin 2011). Such a synthesis also has fundamental implications for social justice because people often arbitrate conflicts over natural resource management through science. As the case studies demonstrate, however, when communities engage in the science- and policy-development process with local and science-based knowledge integrated into the research process, the relationship between resource users and resource managers can change. An evolving relationship built on trust and cooperation rather than conflict and litigation gives both sides credibility to engage more effectively in co-managing natural resources. At the same time, the science itself becomes more effective and relevant through matching the scale of the local system.

This chapter addresses three facets of the acquisition and use of knowledge by CBCs: (1) how community-based organizations integrate local, indigenous, and science-based forms of knowledge to advance their goals and values; (2) how different approaches to conservation and science influence natural resource management; and (3) how the synthesis of local and science-based knowledge leads to more effective management and research.

The Context for Cooperation: Cognition and Learning in Individuals and Organizations

Progress in natural resource management is largely a process of breaking down institutional barriers. These barriers are often psychological and social as much as structural (Lee 1993). In observing human behavior, social scientist Herbert Simon in pathbreaking work in the 1940s and 1950s developed the concept of "bounded rationality." Simon noted that humans have limited information-processing ability. Instead of considering all available alternatives when making decisions, we typically choose from a limited set of variables. Instead of choosing the best alternative, we make a satisfactory choice based on the perceptions at the time (Curtin 2011). Our perceptions are constrained by the social and institutional conditions we face and the institutional context within which we work. In other words, the social and institutional context defines the solution. Therefore, the process of problem solving is context dependent. Collaborative approaches at their core are about redefining the context within which decision making occurs.

Key to developing effective decision making is the process of learning. In this body of literature, people design actions to achieve certain outcomes and learn by watching whether their actions are effective. To do this, people hold maps in their heads of how to plan, fulfill, and review their actions (Argyris and Schon 1978). However, the practice of action often departs from the theory of action. In recognition of these fundamentally different facets of problem solving, scholars developed the concepts of single- and double-loop learning. The single-loop approach typically manifests in the plan-act-review-revise schema that has become the accepted norm of conventional decision making. This approach has several faults. First, it assumes the right question is asked to begin decision making and action. Second, it assumes the decision maker has relatively complete and accurate information. And third, it assumes control over or the ability to "manage" the system. In large complex systems, such as are found in many natural resource management situations, all these assumptions may be moot. In double-loop learning, by contrast, rather than rigidly pursuing predetermined policies, agents are able to create options for innovation by tightly coupling governance, policy, and science (i.e., action research). In what ecologist Simon Levin (1999) calls "tightening feedback loops," research and policy designers first ask whether the driving or "governing variable" has been explicitly integrated into the design process. If not, the policy may potentially succeed in the short term, but it will never be resilient in the face of change. Feedback loops must be created explicitly to allow actors in the system to learn from the process and to integrate the lessons learned into subsequent management and science.

The process of developing dynamic approaches to problem solving has been called "adaptive management" (Holling 1978). According to Lee (1993, 9), *"Adaptive Management* is an approach to natural resource policy that implies a simple command: policies are experiments; *learn from them"* (italics in original). Collaborative projects are often as much a social experiment as the research is a biological one. Command-control or conventional science-based approaches to problem solving sidetrack actors' ability to learn from the process and redefine the question in response to social feedback mechanisms.

Thus, a third schema is identified as triple-loop learning, or "learning to learn." In triple-loop learning, self-examination leads to changing not just the institutional design but also the core way actors perceive the problem and themselves (Peschl 2007). Restructuring the way a problem is perceived is crucial to finding durable solutions that are resilient in the face of change. Linking local and science-based knowledge integrates all three perspectives, but especially triple-loop approaches. This change in worldview can occur through bringing together diverse individuals, communities, or cultures in what has been termed "over-the-horizon" learning, in which practitioners see through others' experiences alternative futures and come to better anticipate the outcomes of their actions (Curtin and Western 2008).

The limitations to the way any actor's mind perceives problems mean that science and management are context dependent. Laying a solid foundation through developing common ground and a shared view of the problem is important for long-term success. Yet even in the most recent literature on the sociology and ecology of adaptive management, there is still a tendency to cling to traditional top-down approaches in which authorities (academic and agency) develop, largely in isolation, policies to be followed by local individuals and organizations, rather than trying to craft policies through a collaborative process. The bounds of traditional directive approaches are still in effect in much of practice, despite explicit attempts to change the process. Academics primarily write the literature, so the understanding of collaboration and management is still articulated primarily from the perspective of an outsider looking in rather than that of a participant actively engaged in the process.

Use of Knowledge by CBCs

From their beginnings, human communities and cultures have struggled with the question of how to sustain themselves in an ever-changing environmental and social milieu. Famine and flood, war and peace, ice ages and desertification, and countless other events and processes have shaped human ecology and culture (Diamond 2005). Although all species face the same struggle for existence, the ability to learn and culturally adapt sets the human species apart. Collecting, communicating, and storing knowledge has come to be tied ineluctably to what it means to be human.

Yet this knowledge revolution has come at a cost. As human roles and institutions have become ever more specialized, ecological and social systems have become increasingly brittle and prone to collapse (Holling 1986; Gunderson, Holling, and Light 1995). Centralized control of economic, ecological, or social systems has proved to be efficient in achieving short-term gains but ineffective in responding to the change that all systems go through. Recent examples of such problems run from the collective economies of the states of the former Soviet Union to the management of insect pests to water management in the Everglades (Gunderson, Holling, and Light 1995). A counterweight to the growth in centralized planning is greater individual and local community involvement in local land use and planning. This emerging hybrid approach to learning integrates community- and science-based approaches to gathering and using knowledge.

Types of Community Knowledge and Their Implications for Adaptive Management

Researchers and practitioners typically distinguish three fundamental kinds of community-based knowledge: *local, indigenous,* and *traditional* (Berkes and Folke 2002). Scholars use these categories to distinguish knowledge types, yet in reality, any given individual or community will integrate different approaches. *Local knowledge* is a generic term for knowledge created through observations of the local environment. *Indigenous knowledge* is local knowledge held by indigenous peoples, or local knowledge unique to a specific culture or society. *Traditional ecological knowledge* specifically refers to the cumulative body of knowledge and beliefs that are handed down through generations by cultural transmission (Berkes 1999).

Local and traditional ecological knowledge are both part of the cultural capital by which societies convert natural capital (resources and ecological services) into economic goods and services. Traditional and local resource management is based on local and traditional ecological knowledge and is considered distinct from Western (or conventional) resource management. Western resource management is based on Newtonian science and on the expertise of professional or government-based resource managers. Yet all cultures and societies have their own means of gaining knowledge that can be as powerful as, or more powerful than, Newtonian science-based approaches.

Natural resource analysts increasingly recognize that though the world is constrained by physical laws, all systems have emergent properties that are hard to predict or understand by applying Western scientific principles alone (Kauffman 2008). Local or indigenous knowledge is especially effective in generating an understanding of these emergent properties and processes.

Types of Ecological Knowledge and Their Implications for Adaptive Management

It is important first to distinguish between ecological knowledge and science, a term often used as a proxy for ecological knowledge. Science is not the generation of information but the explicit use of the scientific method. The method includes formulating and testing hypotheses and incorporating the knowledge gained from such testing into future questions and processes. Like case law, scientific precedents are built from rulings through peer-reviewed literature. In this way the scientific method is in essence institutionalized adaptation. Though widely recognized for centuries and taught to most elementary and high school students, this process has often been lost on even senior resource managers, who increasingly use the term "science" to denote anything that involves the collection of some kind of data. This is a critical issue in environmental problem solving because without some form of testing assumptions and integrating knowledge, there can be no adaptive process.

Though many areas of science address the adaptive management of natural resources, the ecological context forms an important backdrop for most natural resource–based collaboratives. Ecology is not a single monolithic science but a diverse field, composed of fundamentally different approaches to collecting and interpreting data. Each of these frameworks, or paradigms, influences the way knowledge is generated and used, and has important implications for how communities, agencies, NGOs, and researchers perceive and address environmental problems. There are many different forms of ecology, and studies often integrate different approaches within a single effort. However, we can divide ecology into three fundamental perspectives. The *community perspective* arose out of studies of plants in the late 1800s, in which systematic sampling methods allowed quantification of the abundance and distribution of individuals and populations. The *evolutionary perspective* uses evolution as an organizing theme to investigate the mechanisms that drive the organization of natural systems, especially animal populations. These are usually systems that exist in isolation from human action. The *ecosystem perspective* flows from a systems approach to problem solving and focuses less on the organism and more on interactions between organisms. The level of organization becomes the flow of energy and resources (Allen and Hoekstra 1992).

Though the specific organization of ecological thought can be debated, the core concept is that the types of conceptual or mechanical tools that are brought to the table determine the kinds of questions asked, and the kinds of question asked shape the potential answers. So not just ecological perspective but also institutional design influence the outcome of management and science. Agencies, scholars, and individual resource managers (not to mention countless others) have fundamentally different constraints and rewards that help shape their actions (Curtin 2002a). Not just integrating local knowledge but also getting the appropriate level of ecological investigation and governance into the process determines success in the collaborative process.

The rest of this chapter looks at how the interplay of knowledge, governance, and institutions influences the outcome of natural resource management. Though the examples—from the northeastern coast of North America to the plains of East Africa—may seem radically different, many of the underlying challenges are much the same. It is the commonalities of challenges and solutions and how they play out across different systems that is of the most value in illustrating how the synthesis of knowledge types can contribute to more effective natural resource management. These examples illustrate how collaborative, place-based approaches offer insights not obtainable through conventional academic or agency-based approaches.

Local Knowledge: Of Cod and the Coast

For nearly five centuries, fishers of European descent have plied the shores of North America and the banks off the Gulf of Maine in pursuit of cod and other bottom-dwelling groundfish species. This follows a four-thousand-year-old fishing tradition by aboriginal people. Decades before the Pilgrims founded the Massachusetts Bay Colony, semipermanent European fishing settlements were established all along the coastline of what is today Maine (Kurlansky 1997). These fishing grounds sustained local communities for centuries (Rich 1929; Ames 2004), coming to influence nearly every facet of coastal culture, ecology, and economy (Woodward 2004).

Groundfishing by Europeans in North America was originally conducted with hand lines from wind-powered sailing vessels. The purse seine came into use in the 1870s, and the first trawl vessel was introduced to New England in 1893. In the twentieth century technological advances and commercial demand caught up with the ecological constraints, and the fishery began a downward spiral (Wilson 1999). By the 1950s the Maine and Massachusetts fleets had depleted much of Maine's coastal groundfish stocks and eliminated large numbers of coastal spawning grounds. Vessels large enough to handle open water left the coastal shelf to fish the offshore banks, while small and midsized boats either left the fishery or shifted to whiting and redfish (Ames 2004).

Beginning in the 1960s, domestic and distant water fleets seriously reduced the remaining groundfish and herring stocks of the Gulf of Maine, Georges Banks, and the Canadian banks. By the early 1970s, both foreign and domestic catches had declined steeply. In response to these declines, in 1976 the United States created the National Marine Fisheries Service through the Magnuson-Stevens Fishery Conservation and Management Act. This legislation institutionalized federal control of fisheries, yet three decades and many amendments later, federal administration of fisheries has not resulted in recovery, and may even have compounded the problems (Wilson 2002, 2006).

Coastal ecosystems are now a shadow of their former selves. The huge diversity in fishes and marine mammals, evident from the archaeological record and the accounts of early explorers, is all but gone. The Gulf of Maine has declined from being one of the world's richest marine ecosystems to being one of the least diverse. The economic and social implications of the collapse of historical fisheries are masked by the boom in the fishery for a single species—the American lobster, *Homarus americanus*. The lobster catch has been at historic highs in recent years. All along the coast, the new wealth from the lobster boom is evident in bigger boats and new pickup trucks. Yet fishers and community leaders alike are increasingly concerned about a coastal economy largely dependent on a single species. They fear the devastating economic and social implications of a return to the lobster fishery closer to historical levels. No fishery has ever continued at consistently high levels. The key to survival of coastal communities and cultures has always been diversification. The current trend is toward increased capitalization and specialization on a single fishery. Many longtime observers of Maine fisheries see this specialization in the lobster fishery as a prelude to social and economic collapse. In harbors along the coast, in the statehouse, and even in Congress, there is increasing concern over the future of fishing in the Gulf of Maine, as well as increasing recognition that the answers may lie less with the National Marine Fisheries Service and centralized management of fisheries and more with the fishers themselves.

Information from fishers' understanding of stock structure suggests it is not the intensity alone but the scale of fishing that leads to problems with fisheries management. Starting in the mid-1990s, the former ground-fisherman and current lobsterman Ted Ames began a series of interviews with older fishers who had participated in the groundfishery (cod and other bottom-dwelling fish species) to document and locate historical fishing grounds and spawning sites (Ames 2004). Canadian researchers asked similar questions of retired fishers in the Bay of Fundy (Graham, Engle, and Recchia 2002). The investigators were able to create detailed maps of historical spawning sites in coastal waters, and occasionally to identify the decline in productivity of these sites over time.

This information is profoundly shifting the debate over fisheries management. Until recently, resource managers had assumed that fishery stocks were a large, undifferentiated mass distributed across the Gulf of Maine. The work of Ames and Graham (and others) tells a different story. Their charts indicate that groundfish stocks are localized spawning aggregations. If the stocks are local (as fishers have long believed, and as is increasingly supported by science), then management of the fishery is occurring at the wrong scale (Wilson 2006). Large reductions in fishing pressure can still lead to great pressure on isolated fish populations as a fast, mobile fleet of a few, relatively large (70-plus feet in length) and efficient boats can target the remaining local populations with devastating efficiency (Wilson 1999, 2002).

Though this local knowledge of fisheries, coupled with modern technologies, contributed to the fisheries collapse, it is now likely to play a significant role in the recovery. Armed with the insights provided by Ames's maps and genetic and population data (Taggart, Ruzzante, and Cook 1998; Robichaud and Rose 2004; Rosenberg et al. 2005), fishers and scientists are challenging current fisheries management. Starting in 2002, the Northwest Atlantic Marine Alliance (NAMA) led an effort to revise fisheries management under the amendment process in the Magnuson-Stevens Fishery Conservation and Management Act. These early efforts were important in defining the issues and galvanizing interest in rescaling fisheries management. Besides NAMA, organizations such as the Downeast Initiative and Midcoast Fishermen's Association are developing area-based comanagement and community-based stewardship of marine resources. Under various endeavors ranging from NAMA's Fleet Vision Project to science-based workshops and gatherings, a consensus is developing on the need to rescale fisheries management (Wilson 2002; Crocker 2008). Diverse groups of researchers are now interacting to work across disciplines and break down institutional barriers. These changes are all a direct outgrowth of the fishers' insights that approaches to fishing caused the problem and that changing fishers' behavior is critical to the solution.

One of the key insights of fisheries conservationists Ted Ames and former Maine Commissioner of Marine Resources Robin Alden is the need to have programs grounded in a core set of guiding principles that keeps programs on track. In the fisheries programs of NAMA during the early strategic planning sessions, and later during the strategic implementation phase of the Downeast Initiative, the initial guiding principles provided a framework for the synthesis of local, historical, and science-based knowledge. Governance design and principles provided a structure for dispensing that knowledge and a series of benchmarks for ensuring that the program goals were met. Though these principles are not binding and frequently were violated or altered later in the life of the organization, they provided a common unifying context that can generate unity of purpose if adequately delineated and followed.

Despite these insights and the strong institutional design of the place-based fisheries organizations, the fishing stocks continue to decline, and the lessons of place-based management exhibited by the lobster fishery go largely unheeded. At present, the nexus of commercial and scientific interests exhibited by the New England Council of the National Marine Fisheries Service and larger fleets in southern Maine and Massachusetts continue to challenge the increasing ecological and social evidence of the need for change in governance implied by decades of local knowledge, but a pilot program of area management in eastern Maine does appear to be going forward. Place-based approaches are gaining momentum, but the lobster fisheries appear to have leveled off or declined following a decade of growth, while traditional fin fisheries continue their downward spiral. It is an open question whether collaborative place-based approaches will catch on in time to save a four-hundred-year tradition of fishing on the coast. This example is perhaps most informative in illustrating that despite well-documented evidence, asymmetries in policy design frequently result in failures in policy and planning (see, e.g., Norberg and Cumming 2008).

Indigenous and Traditional Ecological Knowledge: The Maasai and Community-Based Conservation

Home to some of the world's last great herds of migratory mammals, the plains of East Africa offer a glimpse of the vast diversity that once covered the planet. Ironically, these last great herds are associated with the cradle of human civilization, where human life evolved in East Africa in tandem with a collection of wildlife that continues today. The experience of the developing world offers an important contrast to North American and European approaches to conservation and land tenure, with East Africa serving as a laboratory for innovation that has strongly influenced collaborative approaches in Western conservation.

When Europeans developed the great parks and game preserves of East Africa, the conservation planning frequently embodied the Victorian-era ideal of man apart from nature. Colonial powers and later African governments removed indigenous peoples from their lands to create "preserves" for wildlife (Western 1997). Starting in the 1960s it became clear that removal of local people from parks was counterproductive (Western, Wright, and Strum 1994; Western 2000). Researchers increasingly recognize that these indigenous practices were not apart from but an important part of nature (Lemons, Victor, and Schaffer 2003). Perhaps most important, however, by removing people from their traditional homelands to promote wildlife for colonial hunters and later ecotourists, wildlife managers inadvertently turned an asset into a liability. Rather then viewing wildlife as their "second cattle," to be protected and hunted only in times of hardship, the Maasai and other pastoral cultures instead came to view wildlife as "white man's cattle" and the parks as *"Shamba la Bibi,"* or the "Women's Farm" (in reference to the British queen) (Bohlen 1993; Western 1997). Elephant and rhino numbers plummeted as *shiftas* (Somali bandits) slaughtered them for the ivory trade. There was no longer an incentive to protect wildlife.

This situation led to a triple threat to East African ecology and culture. The wildlife was in decline from poaching, the ecosystem was in decline from too many elephants in protected areas and too few in areas accessible to poachers, and local people's crops and therefore livelihoods were imperiled. Meanwhile, cattle were threatened from conflicts with wildlife and the loss of historical grazing habitats as former range areas were turned into parks and preserves.

Eventually, conservationists and communities realized the only way to reverse this downward spiral was to reconnect people and wildlife. This was only possible through actively engaging local people in the conservation process. As a result of this response, many of the pioneering efforts in collaborative or community-based conservation occurred in eastern and southern Africa (Western 1997, 2000; Adams and Hulme 2001; Murphee 2004; Nelson and Ole Makko 2005).

As relative newcomers to collaborative approaches to conservation, Europeans and North Americans have much to learn from the experience of more than forty years of collaborative conservation in Africa and across the developing world. High population densities, low standards of living, and modest economic resources mean that collaboration is frequently the only option for sustaining natural and social systems (Lemons, Victor, and Schaffer 2003).

More than forty years of landscape-level conservation in East Africa shows that engaging local people in the planning process is essential for developing durable approaches to conservation. The Maasai's four-thousand-year history of coexisting with wildlife in East Africa has much to teach those who practice European approaches to conservation in respect to maintaining viable ecosystems in arid and semi-arid landscapes. The most important lesson is that reserve design cannot be effective without considering the needs of the pastoral communities that once were contained within and now surround the protected lands. People are an integral part of the underlying biodiversity (e.g., Curtin and Western 2008) and thus have to be considered in the overall functioning of the system. A final lesson to be drawn is that effective conservation projects must be large-scale and dynamic to be able to encompass the inherent variability of the system.

The experience of the Maasai provides an example of how indigenous knowledge can be an indicator of environmental conditions. The Maasai have a pastoral culture based on milk production. Through observing milk quality, the Maasai have developed a powerful assay of environmental change. Milk quality and productivity closely track environmental variables, so the Maasai have a daily index of environmental quality. In response to environmental variability as detected in daily milkings, the Maasai have developed a nomadic culture that tracks the rainfall and the nutrient flush in vegetation. The Maasai and their cattle, like the wildlife, move in response to environmental conditions. And like the wildlife, the Maasai follow the "green-up front," where vegetation first responds to rainfall and their cattle can gain an energy bonus beyond that from grazing at random (David Western, personal communication 2002; Western et al. 2009). Thus, by following their cattle, the Maasai have tapped into the underlying richness of the Serengeti and other rangelands of East Africa.

Conventional Northern European approaches to grazing do not match the Maasai's ability to track the richest plant resources, while the scale of ranching is usually too small to incorporate environmental variation. There are large benefits from this knowledge, both for improving western range management and for designing preserves and conservation areas. Arid and semi-arid environments vary significantly from year to year in both rainfall abundance and distribution. Though daily milking is unlikely to be a useful strategy in Western rangelands, the Maasai example demonstrates that in these environments, wildlife and cattle need to be managed at much larger scales then has been practiced in recent decades.

The Maasai also hold some areas in reserve to have back-up resources in times of drought. Their approach differs from grazing reserve approaches developed in North America in being dynamic and not requiring a fixed location (Curtin 2005). The *olopololi* is a preserve that shifts across the landscape in response to rainfall and wildlife patterns (Western and Manzolillo Nightingale 2005). Along with this dynamic approach, the Maasai use wetlands and wildlife as backup reserves of forage and food in drought. In wetter periods the wetlands are allowed to recover, and the Maasai keep cattle away from them.

The concept of dynamic reserves may now be largely unworkable in landscapes where land ownership patterns are fixed or fences block migration. But this concept provides an especially useful example for other large open systems such as the marine environments, where a lack of fixed ownership means that dynamic approaches are still possible.

The four-thousand-year history of the coexistence of pastoralists and wildlife in East Africa illustrates the potential benefits of the interaction of local knowledge and conservation (Curtin and Western 2008). The reemergence of this type of place-based conservation in East Africa in the decades since independence shows that changing economic incentives and wildlife laws can lead to benefits for wildlife, people, and the land (Western 1997).

The Malpai Borderlands Group: Community-Based Adaptive Management in Action

In the next case study the nexus of local and science-based knowledge is explored in the North American context through an examination of the work of the Malpai Borderlands Group. In contrast to the Maasai of East Africa, who face intense pressure to subdivide communally held lands, some North American ranchers are exploring approaches to reconnecting landscapes by using science as a community-building tool to promote large-scale conservation and management (Curtin and Western 2008). The following discussion points up the complementarity of local and science-based approaches, resulting in more effective science and stewardship.

On a windswept ridge in southwestern New Mexico the perspective extends south far into Mexico. In the foreground miles of rangeland stretch into the distance, while on the horizon the Sierra Madre rises up from the south. To the north, the Rocky Mountains descend south out of the Gila Wilderness. Less obvious to a viewer on this ridge but equally important to the landscape are the Great Plains grasslands adjoining the region from the northeast, and the Chihuahua and Sonoran Deserts coming in from the southeast and southwest. This is arguably the most biologically diverse region in North America (Gelbach 1981; Brown and Kodric-Brown 1995), with some of the greatest diversity of plants and animals found anywhere north of the tropics.

Yet this area's prominence in the conservation literature and the national media is not so much for its biodiversity but for the efforts of a small group of ranchers and their partners to preserve this wild and unique place. This area is home to the Malpai Borderlands Group, a rancher-led CBC working to preserve over one million acres of "working wilderness" (Page 1997; Curtin 2002a; Sayre 2005). The work of the Malpai Borderlands Group is noteworthy because this group, like similar CBCs across the continent, is changing the way people undertake conservation and resource management.

The Malpai Borderlands Group was formed in 1994 to facilitate the development of collaborative partnerships among agency land managers, researchers, and the ranching community. The group's official formation followed years of informal discussions on how to sustain ranching and preserve open landscapes, discussions that often took place on the porch of the Malpai Ranch on the Mexican border in southeastern Arizona. A primary goal of the Malpai Borderlands Group and its collaborators is to develop an adaptive management program for ranching and other traditional land uses based on a foundation of peer-reviewed science. The specific goal is to sustain and restore the 356,131-hectare (880,000-acre) Malpai planning area and adjoining landscapes (Curtin 2002a; Sayre 2005).

External pressures facing the ranching community include unprecedented climatically driven vegetation change (Brown, Valone, and Curtin 1997; Swetnam and Betancourt 1998; Curtin and Brown 2001), external development pressures, and changes in resource economies. These pressures ultimately led the ranching community to seek collaborative approaches to landscape conservation (Curtin, Sayre, and Lane 2002; Curtin 2005). Integrated conservation and research programs in the Mexico-U.S. borderlands demonstrate how partnerships between pastoral communities and researchers can benefit the local community and expand the scale and scope of science and land management (Curtin 2002a).

The Indirect Effects of Knowledge: Power and Process in Natural Resource Management

Communities in the American West have long been at odds with the federal government. For the Malpai Borderlands Group, the community's efforts initially arose out of concern for restoring fire to their landscape. Borderlands rancher Bill Miller once summed up the federal approach to fire management as "Spending hundreds of thousands of dollars to prevent a fire that could do thousands of dollars of good, to prevent destroying property worth a few hundred dollars."

Not only were the local ranchers incensed by the waste, they were frustrated by a sociopolitical system in which they were increasingly powerless to control the fate of the public lands they had been entrusted to manage. This frustration served as a catalyst for change. They worked to alter their situation not by threats or litigation, as has often been the case, but by developing a science-based knowledge system similar to that used by the agencies. Partnering with conservation organizations such as The Nature Conservancy, a diverse set of researchers, and the agencies themselves, the ranchers leveled the playing field and become an active partner in the stewardship of lands. In the process, they brought resources and expertise to the equation that not even the agencies had (Curtin 2002a, 2005).

What sets the Malpai Borderlands Group's efforts apart from those of many CBCs is that the group uses the "best available science," coupled with input from long-time ranchers, to guide its conservation and management efforts. Science in the borderlands draws on all three fundamental approaches to ecology, in addition to geology, history, and numerous other disciplines. Vegetation monitoring and experimental research programs integrate community and systems approaches to examine the dynamic interactions of key processes.

Studies of threatened and endangered species draw from the population biology perspective. Based on this science, a management program is now in place to conserve the numerous threatened and endangered species, ranging from Chiricahua leopard frogs (*Rana chiricahuensis*) to jaguars (*Panthera onca*). The process of drawing expert opinion into the management of threatened and endangered species, combined with proactive approaches to their conservation, has become a hallmark of the group's approach, one that has involved communities on both sides of the Mexico-U.S. border (Curtin 2002a).

As The Nature Conservancy's John Cook, co-director during the formative years of the group, said, "Live by the sword, die by the sword." By this he meant the group would invest in science-based management, for better or for worse. This represented a significant change in approach for a community noted for its self-reliance and distrust of outsiders and where conservationist and scientists were more often than not viewed with suspicion. Yet this leap of faith has come to serve the Malpai Borderlands Group well, not just influencing the group's stewardship activities but also giving credibility to everything the group undertakes (Curtin 2002a).

The Malpai Borderlands Group could have reached out only to rangeland ecologists, who are the traditional partners of ranchers and who could have given them direct input into their livestock management practices. Instead, they collaborated with scientists, who had more of a systems perspective and who could offer insights into how the whole system functioned rather than limit their advice to specific management questions. A focus on the whole rather than on specific pieces has typified the group's approach ever since.

At the same time, the science community has also taken a leap of faith. Collaboration with local communities is not without risk. In the early 1990s, at the height of the debate over public-lands grazing in the West, even ecologists with international reputations took heat from colleagues for being associated with ranchers. For junior researchers, association with ranchers was nearly academic suicide in many disciplines. But with the success of the Malpai Borderlands Group, which produced a superb experimental system, a spirit of cooperation on the part of ranchers attracted many scientists. The researchers who have invested in the borderlands and its ranching community generated one of the largest and most ambitious monitoring and research programs anywhere (Curtin 2002a, 2005, 2008). This illustrates that nontraditional, community-based approaches to science and conservation can contribute significantly to increasing ecological knowledge of both pure and applied questions.

The Importance of the Socioeconomic Context: Integrating Community- and Science-Based Knowledge in the Borderlands

An appreciation of the importance of temporal and spatial scale and the dynamics of large-scale systems has transformed ecology and natural resource management over the past several decades (Allen and Starr 1982; Allen and Hoekstra 1992; Gunderson, Holling, and Light 1995; Levin 1999). Researchers have increasingly recognized that long-term, large-scale studies are essential for understanding natural systems and for generating knowledge relevant to management (Carpenter 1996; Schindler 1998; Weins 2002). Expanding the scale of inquiry has resulted in more effective linkages between biological and socioeconomic systems. In essence, changes in scale shift the perception, and therefore the boundaries, of the problem (e.g., Lee 1993). The integration of biological and social perspectives is now increasingly recognized as essential for natural resource management (Holling 1986; Gunderson, Holling, and Light 1995; Berkes and Folke 1998;Wilson 2006).

Nonetheless, conservation and management still typically ignore the larger socioeconomic context in which systems are embedded. The Malpai experience shows that by revising institutional frameworks through community–science partnerships, resource users, scientists, and resource managers can rescale the scope and scale of conservation and management, making it more relevant in addressing both basic and applied questions (Curtin 2005, 2011).

The Malpai Borderlands Group example is noteworthy because it is one of the few examples of the use of a common vision (or ecological model) to guide stewardship based on integrating local and science-based knowledge (Curtin 2005, 2008). The process demonstrates that this integration resulted not in a dumbing down of the science, as some might suppose, but in a gain in rigor and complexity rarely obtained through science-based processes alone. The collaboration with the ranching community in turn allowed researchers access to a large-scale experimental system that facilitated direct experimental testing of the underlying assumptions of the model, providing an important adaptive component to the overall management system.

A Hierarchical Framework

The problem facing the conservation and research community in the borderlands was how to distill a nearly million-acre ecosystem with a vast number of variables into a coherent model or joint vision of the system. This meant that ranchers and researchers needed to integrate community- and science-based approaches to collecting and applying knowledge. This occurred through many informal meetings and long hours in the saddle discussing the needs of the land and its people.

Interactions between ranchers and researchers resulted in a hierarchical approach (e.g., Allen and Starr 1982) to understanding the driving variables of and measurable constraints on the ecology of the borderlands. Though perhaps novel for scientists at the time, a hierarchical approach that cut across scales and integrated different federal and state jurisdictional spheres came naturally to borderlands ranchers, who had always had to balance diverse issues across scales in the course of managing grazing lands The fundamental insight the ranchers brought to the table was the need to pay attention to process rather than pattern. Conservation biologists were still asking what minimum area was required to preserve viable populations. The ranchers and their scientific collaborators turned the logic on its head and instead asked, how large an area do you need to preserve a functioning ecosystem? (Curtin 2002a). From this simple realization it followed that fire was the key integrator of all other variables in the system. Fire created the diverse landscape the ranchers knew they needed to preserve their livelihood, and thus their communities and culture, whereas subdivision threatened the very fabric of their existence by potentially compromising their ability to manage fire and preserve landscape-level diversity. Even a few small inholdings of a few acres with a cabin or a trailer have ramifications that stretch far beyond the boundaries of individual property owners by making the ability to plan coordinated, cross-boundary fire management much more difficult and expensive (Curtin 2003).

Implications for Adaptive Management and Research

The fundamental implication of a dynamic, place-based approach is that natural communities are inherently a continuum of vegetation associations that shift through space and time in response to multiple interacting variables. The shifts are caused by both environmental variation and human action (e.g., Cooper 1926; Whittaker 1956). It follows that successful management for sustainable land use must be based on investigation and management of these interactions. This is a significant contrast to previous approaches. Too much of conservation, management, and research persists in focusing on single-factor solutions (Holling and Meffe 1996; Curtin 2002b). Depicting the interaction of climate, grazing, and fire illustrates how conservation and land management solutions must address how multiple variables interact. Understanding the interaction of these processes therefore requires a hybrid approach that integrates community, evolutionary, and systems ecology by drawing on the relevant portions of each paradigm. This integration of ecological paradigms is coupled with interactions with the local ranching community that provide both insights into what is key to understand about the system and what it takes to keep the science relevant.

The second implication of the dynamic hierarchical approach is that conservation, management, and research resources should be focused on those areas where the system can easily change state. In areas where existing soil and vegetation have already considerably declined, conservation and management are more difficult without massive inputs of capital and labor. Between these two extremes is a transition area where system function is beginning to decline but the system has not yet degraded to the point that it is unrecoverable. It is in this transition area that the system is likely to exhibit the largest response to restoration efforts and research is likely to be the most informative.

At the same time, if natural processes are maintained, a dynamic mosaic of ecosystems can be sustained or restored. Preserving the natural process against climatic gradient (Swetnam and Betancourt 1998; Curtin and Brown 2001) suggests that these landscapes often must be actively managed to sustain the structure and function of the seminatural matrix (Curtin, Sayre, and Lane 2002; Brown, Curtin, and Braithwaite 2003). These are therefore the areas on which to focus conservation action and the primary locations to carry out management, restoration, or research efforts.

Validation of Place-Based and Socio-Ecological Feedbacks in the Adaptive Process

Though much of the ranching community intuitively understands the approach undertaken in the U.S.-Mexican borderlands, this local knowledge does not have standing without empirical testing. At the same time, testing long-held beliefs leads to increased knowledge and insight among the ranching community (Curtin 2008). Articulating beliefs and testing them empirically creates a positive cycle of experimentation and learning. Science in the borderlands in essence uses a hypothetical-deductive approach. The hypotheses are not solely from ecological theory but also reflect ranchers' questions and perceptions.

In addition to several hundred vegetation monitoring plots distributed across the landscape (Curtin 2002a, 2003), two landscape-level experiments examined how response variables in ecotones interact between major vegetation communities. At 1,687 m (5,400 ft), the McKinney Flats Project on the Gray Ranch in southwestern New Mexico examines the effects of disturbance on a grassland-shrub transition within an 8,800-acre experimental site by focusing on the implications of the interactions in the model of core variables—grazing, fire, and climate(Curtin 2002a, 2005, 2008). At 1,812 m (5,800 ft) on the Cascabel Ranch, 50 km (32 miles) northwest of McKinney Flats at the savanna-woodland transition, watershed studies have examined the role of fire on hydrology and savanna restoration (Christensen 2002; Curtin 2002a, 2003). These studies focus on the interactions of the driving variables outlined in the hierarchical analysis and landscape model. The hierarchical approach taken here examines interactions across scales, from the socioeconomic perspective that bounds the entire million-acre planning area, to monitoring plots nested in several habitats across the planning area (Curtin 2002a, 2003), to the landscape-level experiments at the boundary between ecotones. The focus has remained not on the individual management of specific ranches (this would be considered invasive by much of the ranching community) but on the larger issues of how disturbance and climatic variation affect the overall ecosystem. This broader focus allows individual land managers to learn from the research without threatening individual ranchers' privacy or property rights.

One of the factors that set the Malpai Borderlands Group apart from other collaboratives is the heavy emphasis on research. A research emphasis is important to the adaptive process because it allows rigorous testing of underlying assumptions. This testing has yielded several surprising results about how herbivores (grazing animals) and climate interact, results that are changing the way the borderlands ranchers perceive their landscape (Curtin 2005, 2008). Especially noteworthy is the role disturbances such as grazing and fire can play in the post-drought recovery of grassland ecosystems (Curtin 2008).

In contrast, monitoring largely confirms the status quo. It allows one to track environmental change but has little predictive power concerning future change because there are no ideas (i.e., hypotheses) being formally tested. As stated by borderlands rancher and Malpai Borderlands Group executive director Bill McDonald, "Monitoring vegetation often seems to be a really expensive way to measure rainfall." Nor does monitoring have enough scientific replication to tease out how various processes work. In the borderlands, the monitoring plots are used to supplement the understanding produced by the more intensive research plots.

Directions for Future Research

This chapter has highlighted the value of integrating community- and science-based knowledge and perceptions from the outset to develop more effective collaborative processes. All else being equal, a stake in the process by local people and a sense of involvement are frequently the major variables separating policy success from failure (Curtin 2011). This theme is common to all the examples given in this chapter and will be revisited from a diversity of perspectives throughout the rest of this book.

The preceding discussion illustrates that researchers need to work toward the integration of different disciplines. Science is often as much a social process as a biological one. The relevance of research is largely a reflection of the social system in which it is embedded.

Collaborative approaches provide a means of creating a social context within which the scale of conservation and science can be expanded. In contrast, the scientific literature mainly recommends approaches to management that may pay lip service to institutional change but more often support existing top-down institutional structures. The crux of the problem is getting input into the process at the beginning of the design phase rather then as a comment on completed management designs (Curtin 2011).

The examples from fisheries and rangelands both illustrate the importance of using local and community-based knowledge to focus and refine basic science approaches. The act of engaging communities in the scientific process both increases the quality of the science and gives communities standing in the process. As the Malpai Borderlands Group example illustrates, knowledge can be power. Engagement in the research process does not just improve the science, it provides credibility for all facets of the CBC's work.

Despite the widespread acceptance of the importance of monitoring and science for CBCs, the case studies from the 2006 White House Conference on Cooperative Conservation (see the discussion in chapter 5) underscore that out of hundreds of projects, only a few extensively integrate science. A final question is how monitoring and research can be made more widely available to CBCs. In the following chapters, these issues and the larger question of the role of CBCs in natural resource management are addressed through discussions of monitoring, social structure, and the institutions that promote and sustain collaborative approaches.

Conclusions

CBCs rarely attempt landscape-level research because of its cost, but, as discussed in the next chapter, improvements in design and the explicit testing of specific hypotheses can improve monitoring studies and increase their relevance to resource management. The key point now is that conventional experimental research approaches that operate at small scales for short durations or that hold treatments constant while manipulating one variable miss much of the dynamics of a system. Yet research at a scale that involves manipulation of hundreds of cattle, more than 25 km of fence, the development of new water sources, and active management of fire will almost certainly require creating partnerships to develop and sustain landscape-level management. Research at scales relevant to conservation and management therefore almost by definition means integrating human land use, management, and resource users by including the socioeconomic context in the research design.

The hierarchical approach presented above provides an empirically supported conceptual tool for distilling complex landscapes into their fundamental ingredients based on the intersection of local, community-, and science-based knowledge systems. Capturing the bare essence of a system is invaluable for developing a shared vision of landscape processes to establish common ground among parties with diverse interests and expectations. The process described emerged from the intersection of local and scientific knowledge, demonstrating the compatibility of these different systems as frameworks for understanding environmental change. Developing new socioeconomic systems through partnerships of diverse individuals and organizations facilitates sustainable land use through conservation, management, and research at scales that are hard to obtain through conventional agency or academic approaches alone, thereby expanding the ability to learn for all parties involved (Curtin 2011).

Community- and science-based learning are fundamentally different in their approach to the acquisition and use of knowledge. In traditional societies, individual or community-based knowledge is gathered through years of observation and communicated primarily by word of mouth. In science-based approaches, while verbal interactions play a role, it is written papers that document the progress of change. Scientists use the existing literature much as attorneys use the existing body of case law, to create hypotheses and craft arguments. In each of these approaches something is lost, but something is also gained. The observational practices of individuals and communities lack the validation and self-testing process of Newtonian science (e.g., Kauffman 2008). At the same time, science can only address those questions that can be accurately measured or manipulated. Individuals and communities cannot readily test assumptions or questions in ways that evolutionary ecologists can. On the other hand, the Maasai are able to think more holistically about their ecosystem and respond to changes immediately, without waiting for complicated data, peer review, or publication. The hypothetical-deductive approach, powerful as it is, would be of limited utility in assessing the huge number of interacting variables affecting a fisher's decision about where to fish or the Maasai's decision about where to graze. Humans have a vast capacity for pattern detection that guides much of our daily lives and integrates a range of complexity unobtainable through science. However, these perceptions are often clouded by bias or incomplete information. Yet this is the case with all human endeavors. As the sections on the science of ecology illustrate, science is also a reflection of perception, with different physical or conceptual tools leading to different questions, answers, and ultimately management outcomes.

In natural resource management, community- and science-based approaches need each other. Individual longtime observers can observe patterns, ask questions, and respond to answers in ways unavailable to science. Science can test assumptions and measure outcomes with much greater resolution than is possible using an observational approach. The Malpai Borderlands Group's experience revolves around seeking a synthesis of these fundamentally different knowledge types, illustrating the power and insight that can stem from an integrated approach. The integrated approach rests on finding common ground among the different perspectives and constraints faced by ranchers, researchers, and land managers. In closing the loop between action and reaction, management and learning, in an increasingly uncertain world, it is hard to envision an effective adaptive process that does not rest on a synthesis of different knowledge types and a healthy dose of humility on all sides.

In conclusion, the one factor that unifies effective collaborative approaches is a focus on system function among the communities and their scientific collaborators. This is distinct from existing management systems, which often direct research and management in ways inconsistent with local and even scientific knowledge. In essence, the top-down control that formerly characterized many natural resource management systems lacked the feedback process to facilitate iterative decision making responsive to environmental or social change (Gunderson, Holling, and Light 1995; Holling and Meffe 1996; Berkes and Folke 1998; Levin 1999; Ostrom et al. 2002). Community-based science is the process of developing the essential feedback system between resource users, scientists, and resource managers. As stated by ecologist Simon Levin, "Tightening feedback loops leads to empowerment, giving people incentives for environmentally beneficial behavior" (1999, 204). Developing an adaptive framework to critically evaluate the structure and function of ecosystems is a key ingredient for effective adaptive management. Integrating local and community knowledge, scientific knowledge, and the scientific method is an essential part of the process of developing the necessary feedback loops to promote effective environmental policy and action.

Note

Work was supported by the Hewlett Foundation through the Community-Based Collaboratives Research Consortium. Additional support came from the Gordon and

Betty Moore Foundation and the U.S. Department of Agriculture, Forest Service, Rocky Mountain Research Station. The results are a reflection on twenty years of conservation and research and were influenced by countless experiences and individuals. I especially want to recognize the influence of T.H.F. Allen, J. H. Brown, J. C. Cairns, J. Cook, C. S. Holling, S. L. Light, B. McDonald, D. Western, and J. Wilson, all of whom I have had the privilege of working with and who have profoundly influenced my thinking.

References

Adams, W. M., and D. Hulme. 2001. "If Community Conservation Is the Answer in Africa, What Is the Question?" *Oryx* 35:93–99.

Allen, T.F.H., and T. W. Hoekstra. 1992. *Toward a Unified Ecology.* New York: Columbia University Press.

Allen, T.F.H., and T. B. Starr. 1982. *Hierarchy: Perspectives for Ecological Complexity.* Chicago: University of Chicago Press.

Ames, E. P. 2004. "Atlantic Cod Structure in the Gulf of Maine." *Fisheries* 29:10–28.

Argyris, C., and D. Schon. 1978. Organizational Learning: A Theory of Action Prospective. Reading, MA: Addison-Wesley.

Berkes, F. 1999. *Sacred Ecology: Traditional Ecological Knowledge and Resource Management.* Ann Arbor, MI: Taylor and Francis.

Berkes, F., and C. Folke. 1998. *Linking Social and Ecological Systems.* Cambridge: Cambridge University Press.

———. 2002. "Back to the Future: Ecosystem Dynamics and Local Knowledge." In *Panarchy: Understanding Transformations in Human and Natural Systems,* ed. L. H. Gunderson and C. S. Holling. Washington, DC: Island Press.

Bohlen, J. T. 1993. *For Wild Places: Profiles in Conservation.* Washington, DC: Island Press.

Brown, J. H., C. G. Curtin, and R. W. Braithwaite. 2003. "Management of the Seminatural Matrix." In *How Landscapes Change: Human Disturbance and Ecosystem Fragmentation in the Americas,* ed. P. G. A. Bradshaw and P. A. Marquet, 328–42. Heidelberg: Springer-Verlag.

Brown, J. H., and A. Kodric-Brown. 1995. "Biodiversity in the Borderlands." *Natural History* 105:58–61.

Brown J. H., Valone T. J., and Curtin C. G. 1997. "Reorganization of an Arid Ecosystem in Response to Local Climate Change." *Proceedings of the National Academy of Sciences of the USA* 94:9729–33.

Carpenter, S. R. 1996. "Microcosm Experiments Have Limited Relevance for Community and Ecosystem Ecology." *Ecology* 77:677–80.

Christensen, J. 2002. "Environmentalists Hail the Ranchers: Howdy, Partners." *New York Times,* Science Times, September 10, D3.

Cooper, W. S. 1926. "The Fundamentals of Vegetation Change." *Ecology* 7:391–413.

Crocker, M. 2008. *Sharing the Ocean.* Fredrick, MD: Tilbury House Publishers.

Curtin C. G. 2002a. "Integration of Science and Community-based Conservation in the Mexico-US Borderlands." *Conservation Biology* 16:880–86.

————. 2002b. "Livestock Grazing, Rest, and Restoration in Arid Landscapes." *Conservation Biology* 16:840–42.

————. 2003. "Fire as a Landscape Restoration and Management Tool in the Malpai Borderlands." In *National Congress on Fire Ecology, Prevention, and Management, Proceedings*, ed. K.E.M. Galley, R. C. Klinger, and N. G. Sugihara, 1:79–87. Tallahassee, FL: Tall Timbers Research Station.

————. 2005. "Complexity, Conservation, and Culture in the Mexico/U.S. Borderlands." In *Natural Resources as Community Assets: Lessons from Two Continents*, ed. B. Child and M. West Lyman, 237–58. Monona, WI: Sand County Foundation; Aspen, CO: Aspen Institute.

————. 2008. "Emergent Properties of the Interplay between Climate, Fire, and Grazing in Desert Grasslands." *Desert Plants*, vol. 24. Tucson: University of Arizona Press.

————. 2011. *The Science of Open Spaces*. Washington, DC: Island Press.

Curtin, C. G., and J. H. Brown. 2001. "Climate and Herbivory in Structuring the Vegetation of the Malpai Borderlands." In *Vegetation and Flora of La Frontera: Vegetation Change along the United States–Mexico Boundary*, ed. C. J. Bahre and G. L. Webster, 89–94. Albuquerque: University of New Mexico Press.

Curtin C. G., N. F. Sayre, and B. D. Lane. 2002. "Transformations of the Chihuahuan Borderlands: Grazing, Fragmentation, and Biodiversity Conservation in Desert Grasslands." *Environmental Science and Policy* 5:55–68.

Curtin, C. G, and D. Western. 2008. "Rangelands as a Global Conservation Resource: Lessons from Cross-Cultural Exchange between Pastoral Cultures in East Africa and North America." *Conservation Biology* 22:870–77.

Diamond, J. 2005. *Collapse: How Societies Choose to Fail or Succeed*. New York: Viking Press.

Gehlbach, F. G. 1981. *Mountain Islands and Desert Seas: A Natural History of the US-Mexico Borderlands*. Austin: Texas A&M Press.

Graham, J., S. Engle, and M. Recchia. 2002. *Local Knowledge of Local Stocks: Atlas of Groundfish Spawning in the Bay of Fundy*. Antigonish, NS: St. Francis Xavier University, Centre for Community-based Management, Extension Department.

Gunderson, L. H., Holling C. S., and Light, S. S. 1995. *Barriers and Bridges to the Renewal of Ecosystems and Institutions*. New York: Columbia University Press.

Holling, C. S., ed. 1978. *Adaptive Environmental Assessment and Management*. New York: John Wiley and Sons.

————. 1986. "Resilience of Ecosystems: Local Surprise and Global Change." In *Sustainable Development of the Biosphere*, ed. W. C. Clark and R. E. Munn, 292–317. Cambridge: Cambridge University Press.

Holling, C. S., and G. K. Meffe. 1996. "Command and Control and the Pathology of Natural Resource Management." *Conservation Biology* 10:328.

Kauffman, S. A. 2008. *Reinventing the Sacred: A View of Science, Reason, and Religion*. New York: Perseus Books.

Kurlansky, M. 1997. *Cod: A Biography of the Fish That Changed the World*. New York: Walker and Co.

Lee, K. N. 1993. *Compass and Gyroscope: Integrating Science and Politics for the Environment*. Washington, DC: Island Press.

Lemons J., R. Victor, and D. Schaffer. 2003. *Conserving Biodiversity in Arid Regions.* Dordrecht: Kluwer Academic.

Levin, S. A. 1999. *Fragile Dominion: Complexity and the Commons.* Reading, MA: Perseus Books.

Murphee, M. 2004. "Communal Approaches to Natural Resource Management in Africa: From Whence and Where?" Paper presented at the Breslauer Symposium on Natural Resource Issues in Africa, Center for African Studies. Berkeley: California Digital Library, Berkeley Electronic Press. http://escholarship.ucop.edu/uc/search?entity=cas_breslauer http://repositories.cdlib.org/cas/breslauer/murphee2004a.

Nelson, F., and S. Ole Makko. 2005. "Communities, Conservation, and Conflicts in the Tanzanian Serengeti." In *Natural Resources as Community Assets: Lessons from Two Continents,* ed. B. Child and M. West Lyman, 122–45. Monona, WI: Sand County Foundation; Aspen, CO: Aspen Institute.

Norberg, Jon, and Graeme Cumming, eds. 2008. *Complexity Theory for a Sustainable Future.* New York: Columbia University Press.

Ostrom, E., T. Dietz, N. Dolsak, P. C. Stern, S. Stonich, and E. U. Weber, eds. 2002. *The Drama of the Commons.* Washington, DC: National Academy Press.

Page, J. 1997. "Ranchers Form a 'Radical Center' to Protect Wide-Open Spaces." *Smithsonian,* June, 50–60.

Peschl, M. F. 2007. "Triple-Loop Learning as Foundation for Profound Change, Individual Cultivation, and Radical Innovation: Construction Processes beyond Scientific and Rational Knowledge." *Constructivist Foundations* 2:136–45.

Rich, W. H. 1929. "Fishing Grounds of the Gulf of Maine." In *Report of the US Commissioner of Fisheries for 1929,* Appendix III. Washington, DC: U.S. Bureau of Fisheries.

Robichaud, D., and G. A. Rose. 2004. "Migratory Behavior and Range in Atlantic Cod: Inference from a Century of Tagging." *Fish and Fisheries* 5:185–214.

Rosenberg, A. A., W. J. Bolster, K. E. Alexander, W. B. Leavenworth, A. B. Cooper, and M. G. McKenzie. 2005. "The History of Ocean Resources: Modeling Cod Biomass Using Historical Records." *Frontiers in Ecology and Evolution* 3:84–90.

Sayre, N. 2005. *Working Wilderness.* Tucson, AZ: Rio Nuevo Publishers.

Schindler, D. W. 1998. "Replication versus Realism: The Need for Ecosystem-Scale Experiments." *Ecosystems* 1:323–34.

Swetnam, T. W., and J. L. Betancourt. 1998. "Mesoscale Disturbance and Ecological Response to Decadal Climatic Variability in the American Southwest." *Journal of Climate* 11:3128–47.

Taggart, C. T., D. E. Ruzzante, and D. Cook. 1998. "Localised Stocks of Cod (*Gadus morhua* L.) in the Northwest Atlantic: The Genetic Evidence and Otherwise." In *The Implication of Localized Fishery Stocks,* ed. I. Hunt von Herbing, I. Kornfield, M. Tupper, and J. Wilson, 65–90. New York: Northeast Regional Agricultural Engineering Service.

Weins, J. A. 2002. "Central Concepts and Issues in Landscape Ecology." In *Applying Landscape Ecology in Biological Conservation,* ed. K. J. Gutzviller, 3–21. New York: Springer-Verlag.

Western, D. 1997. *In the Dust of Kilimanjaro.* Washington, DC: Island Press.

———. 2000. "Conservation in a Human Dominated World." *Issues in Science and Technology,* online. Spring. www.issues.org/16.3/western.html.

Western, D., and D. L. Manzolillo Nightingale. 2005. "Keeping the East African Rangelands Open and Productive." *Conservation & People: A Technical Bulletin of the African Conservation Centre* 1:1–8.

Western, D, R. Groom, and J. Worden. 2009. "The Impact of Subdivision and Sedentarization of Pastoral Lands on Wildlife in an African savanna Ecosystem." *Biological Conservation* 142:2538–46.

Whittaker, R. H. 1956. "Vegetation of the Great Smoky Mountains." *Ecological Monographs* 26:1–80.

Wilson, J. 1999. "Economic Impacts of Maine's Fisheries." Unpublished report to the Department of Marine Resources. School of Marine Resources, Orono, ME.

———. 2002. "Scientific Uncertainty, Complex Systems, and the Design of Common Pool Institutions." In *The Drama of the Commons,* ed. E. Ostrom, T. Dietz, N. Dolsak, P. C. Stern, and E. U. Weber. Washington, DC: National Academy Press.

———. 2006. "Matching Social and Ecological Systems in Complex Ocean Fisheries." *Ecology and Society* 11:1–21.

Woodward, C. 2004. *The Lobster Coast: Rebels, Rusticators, and the Struggle for the Forgotten Frontier.* New York: Viking Press.

3

How CBCs Learn
Ecological Monitoring and Adaptive Management

María E. Fernández-Giménez and Heidi L. Ballard

The previous chapter described how local knowledge and scientific research could play powerful roles in developing and maintaining effective community-based collaboratives (CBCs). CBCs use local knowledge to form project goals, ask meaningful questions, gather and interpret information about the surrounding ecosystem, and learn whether their management actions are having an effect. In partnership with researchers, a few CBCs have used science to test their understanding of how ecosystems work. In this chapter we examine how CBCs learn about the ecology of their region and the impacts of their activities on it through formal ecological monitoring and adaptive management, an organized cycle of intentional "learning by doing." We ask why and how CBCs use ecological monitoring and adaptive management to advance their objectives, and how these activities contribute to learning and applying new knowledge to management.

To start, we discuss why ecological monitoring and adaptive management are important to CBCs, and define these terms as we use them in this chapter. We then review current knowledge about CBCs' monitoring and adaptive management activities, drawing on both published accounts and case studies from our experiences. Next, we report on the challenges that CBCs face in implementing effective ecological monitoring and adaptive management and discuss potential strategies for addressing them, although barriers to and strategies for collaboration are mostly developed in chapter 4. Finally, we consider the social implications of ecological monitoring, and conclude by suggesting future directions for CBCs, agencies, and researchers to enhance monitoring capacity and cooperation within and among CBCs and among CBCs, agencies, and researchers.

Why Do CBCs Monitor?

One obvious reason for CBCs to monitor is to assess progress toward meeting ecological goals and objectives. Monitoring in an adaptive management context can also help CBCs learn about the most effective or efficient management strategies (such as the effects of a salvage logging operation, discussed later in the example of the Public Lands Partnership) and answer questions about how the ecosystem works (how climate change affects a desert rangeland ecosystem in the Malpai borderlands). CBCs' deliberate efforts to monitor and evaluate their progress in turn can help build internal accountability and external credibility (Harding and Moote 2005; see also McDermott, Moote, and Danks this volume). For example, both funders and skeptics of collaboration want to know whether the environmental outcomes of collaboration are an improvement over the results of conventional resource management approaches.

Ecological monitoring can also have social consequences. When CBCs involve diverse stakeholders with differing values and knowledge about the land, collaborative or multiparty monitoring can help participants gain greater respect for and understanding of each other's perspectives. It can also forge a shared understanding of the ecosystem and its response to natural and human-caused events. The previous chapter provided an excellent example of the way that ranchers, agency staff, and scientists in the Malpai Borderlands Group developed a shared conceptual model of the ways that grazing, fire, and rainfall affected vegetation dynamics in the borderlands. Joint monitoring by stakeholders can sometimes help resolve controversial issues (see the example of the Public Lands Partnership, below), or at least clarify and distinguish questions of fact from value-based differences. In sum, monitoring by CBCs can advance learning about the ecosystem, specifically about management impacts, and can foster collaborative learning among participants about their diverse views, values, and knowledge (Daniels and Walker 2001; Guijt 2007).

Many CBCs have social and economic goals as well as goals for the ecological condition of their landscapes. Thus, socioeconomic monitoring can also play an important part in CBC efforts to track progress toward meeting goals. Socioeconomic monitoring involves a different set of processes than ecological monitoring, so we do not address it in this chapter. However, many CBCs are specifically concerned with the relationship between a healthy ecosystem and a healthy, economically vibrant community, and may therefore be especially well suited to develop integrated monitoring programs involving both ecological and socioeconomic variables. Several manuals (Moseley and Wilson 2002; Ecological Restoration Institute 2004;

Yaffee 2004) and other examples (Danks, Wilson, and Jungwirth 2002; Christoffersen et al. 2004; Muñoz-Erickson 2004) are available to help community-based groups develop integrated systems of monitoring their progress.

Case 1. Public Lands Partnership: Monitoring to Resolve Conflict and Learn about Management Effectiveness

In the late summer of 2002, a wildfire swept through the foothills of the Rocky Mountains in western Colorado, scorching more than 50,000 acres of oak and ponderosa pine woodlands. In hopes of providing surrounding communities with some economic benefit from this event, the Forest Service scheduled a salvage timber sale on a portion of the burned area. Regional environmental groups objected, but a local CBC, the Public Lands Partnership (PLP), saw the sale as an opportunity to advance its twin goals of improving local livelihoods while restoring the health of the forest. The PLP facilitated a dialogue with the concerned environmental groups, which eventually agreed not to appeal the salvage sale if monitoring were implemented to discover whether the logging was harmful, helpful, or benign in its ecological impacts. The PLP invited scientists nominated by diverse interests within the group to help the PLP clarify its monitoring objectives, identify appropriate indicators, and create a monitoring protocol the citizens' group could implement on its own. With the help of two monitoring consultants hired by the group, the PLP collected baseline data before the logging occurred, and continued monitoring after logging. Replicated monitoring plots were located in both logged and unlogged areas of the burn, as well as in an unburned, unlogged area. University researchers engaged in a participatory research relationship with the group analyzed the initial data (PLP 2004).

Why Collaborative Adaptive Management?

Two significant trends in natural resource management have emerged in the past twenty-five years. The first is the move from centralized, technocratic top-down management toward the decentralization and democratization of decision making about natural resources, as seen in the proliferation of grassroots and agency-initiated CBCs (Wondolleck and Yaffee 2000; Brunner et al. 2002; Weber 2003). The second, described in depth in the previous chapter, is the shift away from a "command-and-control" paradigm of resource management toward an adaptive ecosystem management approach that recognizes the complexity and uncertainty of ecological systems and strives to maintain rather than limit natural variability (Holling and Meffe 1996; Pahl-Wostl 2007). In the past decade these two movements fused, leading to an emergent management paradigm we call *collaborative adaptive ecosystem management.* CBCs embody this fusion as they work to learn about, document, and manage changes in the natural resources they care about using ecological monitoring and adaptive management.

Adaptive management is a process for learning by doing in which monitoring plays a key role. Adaptive management is potentially important for CBCs, for several reasons. First, the process of planning for adaptive management, when done well, can foster collaborative learning and the integration of diverse knowledge sources, advancing the common CBC goals of developing a shared understanding of and vision for the ecosystem. Second, adaptive management provides stakeholders who hold differing views of ecosystem function or of what constitutes an appropriate management strategy a credible way to test their conflicting hypotheses that does not force them to a consensus decision (Habron 2003). Third, a strong adaptive management planning process makes it more likely that monitoring efforts will yield useful information and that CBCs will apply this information to improve future management. Finally, successful collaborative adaptive management provides a mechanism for self-regulation within a socio-ecological system.

As discussed in chapter 2, adaptive management fosters multiple-loop learning that leads participants to go beyond observing the consequences of their actions and to question governing assumptions. At the scale of a community, region, or even the globe, the absence of monitoring and structured mechanisms for learning and self-adjustment can lead to missed signals of impending degradation and eventually to environmental crises that negatively affect individual and community health and well-being. By setting out intentionally to learn from managing and monitoring ecosystems, CBCs that use an adaptive management approach promote self-correcting behavior in socio-ecological systems, apply collective learning in a local system, and advance the twin goals of improving ecological conditions and strengthening community well-being and resilience.

What Is Ecological Monitoring?

We define ecological monitoring as the repeated observation over time of some ecosystem characteristic, with the goal of tracking changes in and interpreting the status of that characteristic in relation to management objectives and activities. For example, a watershed council might monitor water temperature in a stream to help determine whether riparian plantings are shading and cooling it and improving habitat for fish. Monitoring includes both observations (e.g., rating water turbidity on a 1-10 scale) and measurements (e.g., measuring water temperature with a thermometer). The main qualities that distinguish monitoring from more casual forms of observation are (1) the intentional design of monitoring observations to answer specific questions related to management and (2) the process of formally documenting and analyzing observations.

Several different types of ecological monitoring are common in land management, and distinguishing among them helps illustrate why CBCs may use different types of monitoring at different times. An inventory characterizes the current amount, condition, and location of a natural resource. CBCs sometimes use inventory data as a baseline for future monitoring. Implementation monitoring assesses whether individuals or groups completed planned actions. Effectiveness monitoring is used to find out whether the desired ecological outcomes were achieved because of management. Validation (sometimes called verification) monitoring uses monitoring data to evaluate hypotheses about ecosystem behavior (i.e., to validate, verify, or reject hypotheses) (Busch and Trexler 2003).

Our focus in this chapter is on formal ecological monitoring by CBCs because of its importance in natural resource management generally and adaptive management specifically. However, many natural resource users informally monitor the places and resources they use and possess a wealth of experiential knowledge (Niamir 1995; Berkes 1999; Fernández-Giménez 2000; Huntington 2000; Ballard and Huntsinger 2006). This local ecological knowledge and those who hold it can and do contribute to the design of formal ecological monitoring by CBCs in various ways (Armitage 2003; Berkes 2004; Moller et al. 2004; Ballard et al. 2008; Fernández-Giménez, Ballard, and Sturtevant 2008). For example, informal observations often generate questions that formal monitoring can help answer. Local knowledge also can help identify locally appropriate and feasible monitoring indicators. For example, in the Northwest Colorado Stewardship's off-highway vehicle (OHV) monitoring project (discussed below), one OHV user explained the importance of modifying the original monitoring design to include a transect running lengthwise down the OHV trail to document the increase in ridges caused by OHV traffic, which might be associated with increased erosion. The enhanced use and integration of diverse knowledge sources is one way in which monitoring by CBCs may differ from conventional ecological monitoring carried out by natural resource agencies, consultants, or researchers.

Case 2. The Northwest Colorado Stewardship: Multiparty
Monitoring Sets the Stage for Adaptive Management

In the spring of 2004, the Bureau of Land Management (BLM) told the newly formed collaborative group, the Northwest Colorado Stewardship (NWCOS), of its plan to revise the BLM's Resource Management Plan (RMP) for the one-million-acre Little Snake Resource Area in northwestern Colorado, and invited NWCOS to participate in the planning process. The BLM and some NWCOS participants were excited about the prospect of incorporating adaptive management into the RMP revision, but it quickly became clear that group members disagreed on the meaning of "adaptive management." To clarify the definition of adaptive management and help NWCOS and the BLM explore the potential for adaptive management in the Little Snake Resource Area, Colorado State University (CSU) researchers presented an informational workshop on adaptive management, followed by a hands-on workshop to guide interested NWCOS members through a hypothetical adaptive management planning process for OHV use. A small group of NWCOS participants was eager to continue learning about monitoring and adaptive management, and wanted to get something "real" done on the ground. With technical assistance from CSU, the OHV monitoring work group outlined monitoring objectives and indicators and designed a sampling protocol for a baseline monitoring study of OHV impacts in Sand Wash, a popular off-road recreation area.

The group realized early in the process that it would not be able to answer some of its key questions because of limited technical and financial resources, but decided to move forward with a more modest monitoring scheme that addressed two main questions: (1) How do soil, vegetation cover, and invasive species vary on trails with different use levels (high, medium, low, and off-trail control sites)? (2) How do OHV impacts on vegetation, soils, and invasive plants change with increasing distance from the trail? The group, which included OHV enthusiasts, a rancher, an oil-and-gas industry representative, wildlife and wilderness advocates, concerned citizens, and a BLM recreation planner, agreed on a way to classify trails into use categories based on their local knowledge and joint observations. The group then randomly selected four trails from each use category and four off-trail control sites for its baseline monitoring study. Nine group members participated in the field sampling, which took place over five days in the spring of 2005 and was supervised by a CSU graduate student.

Analysis of the first year's monitoring data provided some preliminary answers to the group's questions but also pointed to some of the challenges of multiparty monitoring by community groups, including inconsistency in data quality among observers. The group also experienced some difficulties effectively communicating its monitoring objectives and protocols to other NWCOS and community members, primarily because members lacked the technical background to explain the sampling strategy. The group modified the monitoring protocols slightly for its second year of data gathering, including adding a new indicator suggested by a community member. The BLM also increased its participation by agreeing to purchase trail counters that would make it possible to measure the actual use levels on each sampled trail, and by providing additional assistance in field sampling. Group members are working to recruit new volunteers from the local high school and community college. The group continued collecting data though 2009, and hopes that this baseline data-gathering effort will help inform the development of an adaptive management plan for OHV use in the future (Bishop 2005).

What Is Adaptive Management?

In the face of growing awareness of the complexity and unpredictability of ecosystems, the need for reliable information about the consequences of management actions is ever greater, yet credible and predictive knowledge about ecosystem behavior seems increasingly elusive. Holling (1978) suggested that applying the principles of scientific experimentation to the implementation of resource management policies and practices could speed up learning and improve the quality of knowledge while still meeting societal objectives for management by supplying ecological goods and services. The knowledge gained from these management experiments could in turn be used to select the most effective management strategies to meet objectives.

Many agencies, scientists, and CBCs have gravitated toward the general concept of adaptive management, yet they often use conflicting or confusing definitions of this term. Nyberg (1998, 2) provides the following definition of adaptive management, which we rely on in our discussion: "Adaptive management is a systematic process for continually improving management policies and practices by learning from the outcomes of operational programs. Its most effective form—'active' adaptive management—employs management programs that are designed to experimentally compare selected policies or practices, by evaluating alternative hypotheses about the system being managed."

Some agencies, however, use the term adaptive management to refer to a process of performance- or outcome-based management, which differs from that provided by Nyberg (1998) or Holling (1978). For example, the BLM defines adaptive management as "a system of management practices based on clearly defined outcomes, monitoring to determine if management actions are meeting outcomes, and, if not, facilitating management changes that will best ensure that outcomes are met or to re-evaluate the outcomes" (U.S. Department of the Interior 2003, 1). In short, the BLM focuses solely on achieving desired outcomes (performance) from management actions. In our view, this emphasis misses the fundamental premise of adaptive management, which is the tandem focus on *learning* about socio-ecological systems while improving management effectiveness.

There are two basic approaches to implementing adaptive management, which differ mostly in the degree to which the principles of experimental design are applied. We refer to them as "active" and "passive" adaptive management (Walters and Holling 1990; Nyberg 1999), and CBCs may choose to use one or the other, depending on their particular objectives and constraints. Active adaptive management involves trying several alternative management actions simultaneously at different locations with similar environmental conditions to see which is most effective. For example, a prairie restoration project might try seeding in one area, burning in another, a combination of seeding and burning in a third area, and leaving a fourth area as an untreated control. To distinguish management effects from other changes in the environment, baseline monitoring measurements should be taken before management treatments are applied, and then monitoring should continue after management is implemented. The use of multiple treated and untreated areas and measuring before and after the treatment are hallmarks of a strong experimental design that enable managers to distinguish the ecological effects of management from the influences of confounding factors such as variable weather patterns and environmental differences between sites. The knowledge gained from active adaptive management is often more reliable and more broadly applicable than information gained from a single location, or from posttreatment measurements only. Active adaptive management, however, may not always be possible for CBCs limited by space or funding. Passive adaptive management involves testing only one management practice at a time, but if well thought out, it still provides an effective alternative to command-and-control management. Ideally, passive adaptive management still incorporates the other elements of experimental design (before-and-after measurements, replications, and controls), but in reality, it is not always possible to include all of these design elements.

The Adaptive Management Process

There are six steps in an idealized adaptive management process: assess, design, implement, monitor, evaluate, and adjust (Nyberg 1999). Since several sources provide a useful summary of each of these steps (e.g., Nyberg

1999; Murray and Marmorek 2003), we will not repeat them here. Instead we will focus on three key steps—assessment, design, and monitoring. The important point is that adaptive management is an iterative and flexible cycle of learning by doing, coupled with documentation of and reflection on the results of management actions. Recent discussions of community-based adaptive management particularly emphasize learning as both a process and an outcome (Armitage 2005; Folke et al. 2005; Guijt 2007). Resource managers or CBCs apply their learning by changing management actions or objectives as needed, and by continually modifying and improving understandings of ecosystem behavior and responses to management.

Resource managers, including CBCs, often overlook the assessment and design phases of adaptive management in the rush to implement and monitor alternative management treatments, which can lead to problems in interpreting and applying results later. The assessment phase involves describing and bounding the management problem or situation, defining management objectives, and identifying possible management choices. An important aspect of assessment, especially when adaptive management is implemented in a collaborative setting, is finding out and documenting participants' current understanding of the socio-ecological system. Like the ranchers of the Malpai Borderlands Group described in chapter 2, many interested stakeholders already have an implicit mental model of how the ecosystem works, but it is seldom discussed, written down, or drawn on paper for others to see. For example, members of the Watershed Research and Training Center in Hayfork, California, all knew that fire was the main driver of change in their ecosystem and the focus of their management. Only recently, however, have they developed a precise statement of what they believe constitutes a healthy forest. An explicit conceptual model or system diagram can help participants visualize their current understanding, highlight assumptions, and pinpoint knowledge gaps, uncertainties, and disagreements. These areas of uncertainty or conflict may then become the focus of learning and can be used as the basis for developing alternative hypotheses about how the system works. For example, researchers working in partnership with the Diablo Trust (discussed below) helped the group rephrase conflicting claims about grazing impacts as competing hypotheses that could be tested using a management experiment. Conceptual models, developed collaboratively and represented visually, can also help participants understand the linkages between the social and ecological components of the system (for examples of system models, see Bishop 2005; Poole and Berman 2000).

Similarly, it is critical that participants collaboratively develop and clearly document management objectives. Monitoring cannot be effective if it is not clear what needs to be monitored to determine management effectiveness or answer key questions about the system's behavior. Sometimes a CBC may not have enough information to set measurable management objectives. For example, a CBC may not know what an appropriate target level of perennial grass cover should be to meet a particular wildlife habitat objective, or it may not know how much erosion represents a critical threshold for soil loss. In these cases, CBC members may agree to set a preliminary range of acceptable values, based on the best available knowledge, that will be reevaluated as more is learned about the system through ongoing monitoring.

The design phase of adaptive management involves developing an adaptive management and monitoring plan. In this step, different possible management actions are considered (e.g., seeding versus burning in a prairie restoration), and one or more are selected. This is the phase in which management "experiments" are designed and monitoring protocols are specified, evaluating the trade-offs between scientific rigor, practicality, and cost. Careful design of management experiments and monitoring protocols is often skipped over or rushed through, resulting in projects that fail to provide unambiguous and reliable results. The thoughtful design of components that allow for learning and comparison in a project need not necessarily add extra time to the process. For example, once the preferred method of forest thinning for fuels reduction has been selected, a CBC can decide to allow one or more small areas to be left alone, providing control stands against which to compare the results of thinning.

Monitoring is the crux of adaptive management but is often the weakest link in the process. Adaptive management can encompass all types of monitoring—baseline, implementation, effectiveness, and validation—but our main focus here is on effectiveness and validation monitoring, since these forms most directly assess the effects of CBC management activities. Often the same data are used both to assess management effectiveness and to evaluate hypotheses about ecological systems.

CBCS are often concerned about the distinction between monitoring and research. The main difference between these activities is the purpose of data collection. Managers collect monitoring data to track resource conditions over time to inform management decisions, while researchers collect data to answer questions about how an ecosystem works. Monitoring designs are usually less rigorous than research designs, making it difficult to establish cause-and-effect relationships. Monitoring is often specific to a single location on the ground, whereas research strives for broad generalizations about system behavior that can be extrapolated beyond the sites where data were collected. One reason for this continuing tension is the recent trend toward making monitoring more scientifically rigorous (Elzinga, Salzer, and Willoughby 1998; Herrick et al. 2005), as well as the increasing interest in adaptive management, which in its active form strives to apply rigorous experimental design to management. Not every CBC may want to generalize the information it gathers to broader areas, but as networking among groups increases, this may become a more desirable and attainable goal. As discussed in this chapter, and as many community-based organizations have experienced (Fernández-Giménez, Ballard, and Sturtevant 2008), the tensions between rigor, utility, and practicality are central to monitoring in collaborative adaptive management.

Case 3. The Diablo Trust: The Role of Researchers in Collaborative Research and Monitoring

Since 1997, researchers from Northern Arizona University and Prescott College have worked closely with the Diablo Trust on an ecological experiment that examines how different livestock grazing treatments affect grassland biodiversity and ecosystem function. The researchers followed a series of steps to guide the collaborative group through the process of turning conflicting claims into testable research hypotheses.

The steps were as follows: (1) study the controversy, understand the conflict; (2) restate contradictory claims as questions or hypotheses; (3) discuss questions and hypotheses with all parties; (4) get "buy-in" on the research approach from the affected parties; (5) design research through an open process; (6) initiate the study and guard scientific independence; and (7) maintain channels of communication and provide regular updates. This first ecological research effort led to another project aimed at selecting key ecological and social indicators for an integrated monitoring framework for the Diablo Trust. The researchers used a similar process to set up the monitoring framework, including creating a conceptual model, conducting interviews with stakeholders, and convening multiparty monitoring workshops to refine and test the indicators.

From these experiences there emerged several lessons about how researchers can work effectively on collaborative research and monitoring projects with CBCs. First, establishing a working relationship based on trust between the researchers and the Diablo Trust was key to the long-term viability of both projects. A candid and trusting relationship helped clarify differences over values and information and aided stakeholders in overcoming fears about the misuse of scientific information by others. Second, the challenging but vital process of incorporating stakeholder input into research and monitoring design not only helped maintain trust but also ensured and demonstrated the independence of the scientific process. This independence in turn benefited the entire group by increasing credibility. Finally, active involvement in research and monitoring design helped stakeholders gain ownership of results and motivated them to use scientific information in making management decisions (Sisk et al. 1999; Muñoz-Erickson and Aguilar-González 2003).

Learning to Learn: Collaborative Adaptive Management and Monitoring in CBCs

Initially, adaptive management was viewed as a means of bringing science and management together, for the mutual benefit of researchers and managers. The public was largely left out of the discussion. More recently, with the rise of ecosystem management and collaboration, the value of involving multiple stakeholders in adaptive management has become clear (Bormann et al. 1999; Kusel et al. 1996; McLain and Lee 1996; Folke et al. 2005). Stakeholders are critical to defining management objectives, and their diverse knowledge and experiences can contribute to assessment, management implementation, monitoring, and evaluation. Further, as we discussed earlier, adaptive management and ecological monitoring have many potential benefits for CBCs, particularly CBCs that are working to learn about the ecological effects of their management activities.

Nevertheless, what are CBCs really doing? Since various types of monitoring and adaptive management have different purposes, processes, and outcomes, what kinds of monitoring and adaptive management are CBCs using? How might CBCs' monitoring and adaptive management activities affect the future of collaboration and natural resource management more broadly? We attempt to answer these questions by first reviewing the scant literature on CBCs involved in processes related to ecological monitoring and collaborative adaptive management (Conley 2003; Muñoz-Erickson 2004; Bishop 2005; Pierce Colfer 2005; Mutimukuru, Kozanayi, and Nyirenda 2006). We then turn to the growing research on adaptive management more generally, the vast literature on volunteer monitoring and citizen science, and preliminary data we have gathered from eight groups in the western United States.

We are guided in our discussion of current knowledge by the following set of questions: (1) How prevalent is ecological monitoring in CBCs? (2) Are CBCs using an explicit adaptive management approach or monitoring without a commitment to adaptive management? (3) Are CBCs that use adaptive management implementing active or passive approaches? (4) Over what spatial and temporal scales are CBCs implementing monitoring and adaptive management? (5) Do CBCs that monitor develop an explicit system model and state clear management objectives? (6) What kinds of monitoring are CBCs doing—implementation, effectiveness, or validation? (7) What kinds of monitoring indicators and measures are CBCs using? (8) Who designs, implements, analyzes, and interprets monitoring by CBCs? (9) How are CBCs using the information they get from monitoring?

How Prevalent Is Ecological Monitoring by CBCs?

Several large-scale surveys of CBCs show that many CBCs conduct some type of ecological monitoring. In a survey of a random sample of forty-four watershed partnerships, Leach, Pelkey, and Sabatier (2002) found that 41 percent of all the groups surveyed conducted some monitoring. The proportion increased to 80 percent of groups four to six years old and 62 percent of groups more than six years old. Fernández-Giménez and colleagues (2004) found that fifty-one of fifty-five surveyed rangeland collaboratives in Arizona were involved in monitoring. Cline and Collins (2003) found that water quality monitoring was among the most common small activities of the sixty volunteer organizations they surveyed (of which forty-two were watershed associations), and watershed studies and information gathering were among the most common large activities carried out. Sixty of the 108 CBCs in the database of the Community-Based Collaboratives Research Consortium conduct some type of environmental outcomes monitoring (CBCRC 2005). It should be noted that the existing data on monitoring in CBCs came mainly from watershed groups (except for data in the study by Fernández-Giménez et al.) and may not be representative of efforts by CBCs working on other natural resource or environmental issues. In addition, despite the prevalence of monitoring, monitoring was rated relatively low in importance as a factor contributing to success in a survey of watershed councils (Leach, Pelkey, and Sabatier 2002). Interestingly, how-to manuals for community-based monitoring outnumber reports on the results and use of monitoring by CBCs (Moseley and Wilson 2002; Savage 2003; Ecological Restoration Institute 2004; Pilz, Jones, and Ballard 2005).

Do CBCs Adopt an Explicit Adaptive Management Approach? Is It Active or Passive, and Over What Temporal and Spatial Scales Is It Used?

Based on our fieldwork in the western United States, we have found that many CBCs explicitly pursue adaptive management approaches. Several of these have implemented some form of active adaptive management, usually at a relatively small spatial scale (tens to hundreds of hectares) and short time frame. For example, the PLP is carrying out monitoring in Burn Canyon to assess whether areas that are salvage logged show different short- and long-term trends in understory species cover and diversity than areas that burned but were not logged. Wallowa Resources in northeastern Oregon tested the effectiveness of different types of fencing around aspen stands for promoting aspen regeneration and landbird conservation (Sallabanks 2000). Other groups are trying to monitor at a landscape scale, but usually with a passive adaptive management approach. For example, with help from Northern Arizona University, the Diablo Trust in Flagstaff, Arizona, is carrying out a long-term, landscape-scale ecological and social monitoring program that will inform a passive adaptive management approach to managing livestock and wildlife on 426,000 acres of private, state, and public rangelands (Diablo Trust 1999; Muñoz-Erickson 2004; see example in case 4, Coos Watershed Association, below). NWCOS in Craig, Colorado, carried out a retrospective adaptive management study and gathered baseline data for future passive or active adaptive management of OHV use on BLM lands in lower Sand Wash Basin, a 5,600-square-mile area of high-desert rangelands in northwestern Colorado (Bishop 2005). The Coos Watershed Association (CWA) of Charleston, Oregon, monitors a number of factors related to stream temperature, as well as stream temperature itself, to help assess the effectiveness of individual restoration projects and the overall effectiveness of the group's restoration program across the watershed (CWA 2002; Souder 2005). These few examples illustrate that diverse CBCs have made an explicit commitment to adaptive management, and that adaptive management and monitoring are being carried out at several different spatial-temporal scales.

Case 4. Coos Watershed Association: Using a Conceptual Model to Guide Adaptive Management and Monitoring

The CWA undertakes many restoration-related activities, and wanted to implement an effectiveness monitoring program that would enable it to assess both the effectiveness of individual restoration projects and the effectiveness of its overall restoration program. The group's overall assessment and monitoring goal is to "develop information on aquatic resources in the Coos watershed so we can understand their status and trends in relation to our restoration programs." In addition, the group wanted to be able to test and assess promising restoration and monitoring techniques while controlling for natural variation and cycles: it made an explicit commitment to adaptive management. To identify key monitoring indicators, the group relied on an existing process-based system model published in the scientific literature. The group used this model to decide what data to collect. Between 1993 and 2000, the association's monitoring staff collected pretreatment baseline data and posttreatment data on three types of in-stream habitat enhancement projects, large wood placement, boulder weir construction, and culvert replacement, on thirty-one streams. In addition, several untreated control reaches were sampled. The projects were implemented in 1995–98, but in 1996 a hundred-year flood occurred, which also had dramatic effects on many of the treated streams. Monitoring showed that stream reaches with in-stream structures were associated with improved pool area and pool complexity but not with increased pool depth, as hypothesized. Culvert replacement projects also showed mixed results. The monitoring resulted in a set of recommendations for improved restoration project implementation, as well as suggestions for more effective monitoring (CWA 2002; Souder 2005).

Do CBCs Develop and Use an Explicit System Model?

Some CBCs have developed explicit system models to guide their monitoring and adaptive management, but the use of such models is not yet common. CBCs that have developed explicit system models include the Muleshoe Ecosystem Management Planning team in Tucson, Arizona (U.S. Department of the Interior 1998), the Diablo Trust (Muñoz-Erikson, Loesser, and Aguilar-González 2004), the Watershed Research and Training Center in Hayfork, California, the CWA (Poole and Berman 2000), and NWCOS (Bishop 2005). These models range from the all-encompassing and integrative model of the socio-ecological system developed by the Diablo Trust (see Muñoz-Erikson, Loesser, and Aguilar-González 2004 for examples of models) to issue-specific models such as those developed by the Watershed Center to guide a forest thinning project and by NWCOS to develop a monitoring plan for OHV use (see Bishop 2005 for examples of models). Some models, such as the ecological process model used by the CWA to develop its stream monitoring protocols (see Poole and Berman 2000 for examples of models), are detailed and science-based. Other models, such as the model of the effects of fire and grazing on upland vegetation developed by the Muleshoe Ecosystem Management Planning team, are more general but still grounded in ecological research (see U.S. Department of the Interior 1998 for examples of models). The NWCOS developed its models based solely on stakeholder input. These models integrated diverse knowledge sources and perspectives, including those of resource professionals, users, and other interest groups.

We do not know how many CBCs have explicit models and how useful or important they are to the success of monitoring and adaptive management in CBCs. However, related research on cognitive mapping in education (Novak 1998), environmental conflict resolution (Daniels and Walker 2001), adaptive management (McLain and Lee 1996), ecosystem monitoring (Maddox, Polani, and Unnasch 1999; Ogden, Davis, and Brandt 2003), and system modeling (Heemskerk, Wilson, and Pavao-Zuckerman 2003) suggests that such models can be useful. The University of Michigan Ecosystem Management Initiative is training many CBCs in the use of a self-evaluation tool that incorporates a situation mapping exercise resulting in a graphic depiction of the group's objectives, assets, threats, and strategies (Yaffee 2004). Two of the groups we studied, the Watershed Research and Training Center and NWCOS, used this guide effectively to develop multi-party monitoring plans for forest thinning and OHV use, respectively.

Most CBCs have broad goals and vision statements and some have more specific ecological objectives or restoration principles, but few have articulated quantifiable desired outcomes that can be monitored. Occasionally, specific quantifiable objectives are stated and clearly linked to a system model (such as the Muleshoe Ecosystem Management Plan and the Watershed Research and Training Center Post Mountain Thinning Project). The lack of clear management and monitoring objectives is not limited to CBCs. Rather, it is indicative of much ecological monitoring on public and private lands (Fernández-Giménez, Ruyle, and Jorstad McClaran 2005; Tear et al. 2005).

What Kinds of Monitoring Do CBCs Do, and What Kinds of Indicators Are Measured?

CBC monitoring includes implementation, effectiveness, and validation monitoring, although most groups we know of focus on effectiveness. The range of indicators monitored by CBCs is as diverse as the environments they steward. Ecological attributes monitored include water quality and temperature; soil characteristics; vegetation structure, cover, and composition; invasive plant occurrences; and wildlife and fish populations, to name a few. The CWA used an existing ecological process model to develop the indicators the association used to monitor its stream restoration activities. In addition, some groups, such as the Diablo Trust, integrate both ecological and socioeconomic variables into a comprehensive monitoring program. Some groups also conduct social or economic monitoring. Where monitoring is conducted by volunteers, the indicators are relatively easy to understand and the measures are relatively simple to implement. Some groups struggle with narrowing down the number of indicators and measures to use. A key question for these groups is, what is the right number of questions to ask?

Who Does the Monitoring in CBCs?

Critics of CBCs raise concerns about whether such collaborative groups are inclusive enough of the wide variety of community members, agencies, and nonprofits interested in their work. Answering the question of who does the monitoring in CBCs may shed light on this issue, as monitoring can be a vehicle for inclusion in CBC processes. In the groups we have studied, a technical expert is usually involved in helping design CBC monitoring projects. Sometimes the expert is in-house, but frequently a scientist or resource professional is brought in from outside the group to assist and work together with CBC members and citizen volunteers. Often the process of designing monitoring—including identification of monitoring questions, indicators, and measures—is a collaborative process involving multiple stakeholders. However, there are also instances in which an outside or in-house expert designs a monitoring system alone for the CBC. Similarly, volunteers, consultants, and partner scientists all conduct or take part in field monitoring efforts for CBCs.

As with design of monitoring, some CBCs involve members in gathering data in the field, while others hire professional monitoring consultants to gather and analyze the data. There is much discussion about multiparty monitoring, and many manuals to guide such efforts, but we found no data to indicate the prevalence of multiparty monitoring compared to monitoring by CBC consultants, staff, or partner agencies alone. Similarly, rather little is known about the effectiveness and benefits of multiparty monitoring for CBCs (Kusel et al. 2000; Bliss et al. 2001; Bishop 2005).

How Are CBCs Using What They Learn from Monitoring and Adaptive Management?

For most groups, it is too early to tell whether CBCs are effectively closing the loop and using the information gained from monitoring to inform future management decisions. However, there is evidence to suggest that some groups are doing this. For example, the Watershed Research and Training Center studied the effects of different slash treatments on soil characteristics and erosion potential in an early forest thinning project and is now applying this information to the design of another community-based restoration project (Everett 1999; Danks 2002). The CWA used data from effectiveness monitoring of salmon habitat improvement projects to recommend changes in the design of future projects, as well as to adjust its monitoring protocols (Banks et al. 2001). The PLP is using what it learned about monitoring design in the Burn Canyon Project to help an adaptive management planning and monitoring process on a larger-scale habitat restoration project (PLP 2004). NWCOS revised its monitoring protocols based on its baseline data and collected four additional years of data (through 2009). The OHV working group hopes these data will help inform an adaptive management plan for OHV use in the next several years (Bishop 2005).

CBC Challenges and Pathways to Progress in Monitoring and Adaptive Management

The cases we refer to above illustrate that some CBCs are committed to an adaptive management approach to resource stewardship and are making strides toward institutionalizing adaptive management. These examples and many others also point to the many hurdles on the path to realizing the promise of collaborative adaptive management. These challenges include monitoring design and data-gathering obstacles, internal and external institutional barriers, and impediments to disseminating and applying learning from monitoring. In this section we discuss these barriers and some of the strategies CBCs have used to address them.

Design and Data Barriers and Strategies

In the literature on volunteer and community-based monitoring, a lack of clear monitoring objectives, rigorous design, or objective measurements and inconsistent data quality are commonly reported problems that can lead to low data credibility and utility (Nicholson, Ryan, and Hodgkins 2002; Vaughan et al. 2003; Whitelaw et al. 2003; Gouveia et al. 2004). These barriers often stem from inadequate technical expertise to guide monitoring design and implementation. On the other hand, the use of indicators that are technical and poorly understood or irrelevant to local people and decision makers also is problematic (Gasteyer and Flora 2000). Similarly, when data are not available within the time frame for decision making, they become superfluous (Maguire 2003; Vaughan et al. 2003). Finally, lack of baseline (i.e., pretreatment) data often makes it difficult or impossible to determine what changes occurred or can be attributed to management actions (Bormann et al. 1999; Banks et al. 2001).

Many of the above challenges can be traced to the assessment and design phases of adaptive management, which are often overlooked in the rush to go out and gather data (table 3.1). We believe it is worthwhile for CBCs to invest the necessary time and human resources in the design phase to develop an adaptive management and monitoring plan that will work well, be broadly supported and understood by CBC participants, and be credible to outside interests and agencies. This phase can also serve as an important collaborative learning opportunity for participants and a means of incorporating local knowledge.

First, it is important to begin with a shared understanding of how the ecosystem functions. Key stakeholders and decision makers should be involved at the beginning in developing a clear system model that depicts their shared understanding of the ecological issue and highlights gaps in knowledge or conflicting assumptions. For example, the Diablo Trust, working closely with researchers from Northern Arizona University, turned differing ideas of how their ecosystem worked into a conceptual model from which they developed testable hypotheses. Stakeholders should also take part in identifying the major questions that monitoring is to address and in developing locally meaningful indicators directly relevant to decision making.

Some CBCs have staff or participants with strong scientific backgrounds to help explain the trade-offs involved in designing field monitoring protocols. For example, technical expertise in sampling may be needed to help the group explore the benefits and costs of a random sampling approach compared with subjectively locating monitoring plots. Similarly, it is important to discuss the scientific rigor necessary to meet the group's objectives. Occasionally qualitative assessments may be enough, while in other cases measurements that are more objective are required. If a CBC lacks the in-house expertise to help it make these decisions, it should seek an outside scientific adviser. The level of rigor and generalizability required for monitoring will depend on the group's monitoring objectives. These objectives in turn may be driven by the degree of controversy associated with the proposed management or monitoring, outside scrutiny, or the need to produce scientifically credible data. It is important whenever possible to collect baseline data before changes in management are implemented. However, when management is already under way, it is sometimes possible to conduct a retrospective study or to document local knowledge about historical conditions (Bormann et al. 1999).

While concerns about data quality must be taken seriously, there are measures that CBCs can take to ensure the data gathered are of high quality. Volunteer or contract monitoring crews should be well trained, provided

Table 3.1 Project design and data barriers to implementing monitoring and active management, and strategies to overcome them

Barriers	Suggested strategies
• Management objectives are unclear, immeasurable, or absent. • Indicators are not relevant to local people or decision-makers. • CBC participants lack understanding or don't buy in. • Monitoring design lacks rigor. • No technical expertise is available to guide design. • Data lack quality, objectivity, or credibility. • No baseline data are available. • Data are not timely for decision-making.	• Invest in the assessment and design phases of active management. • Involve stakeholders (including decision-makers) in creating a system model and developing measurable indicators. • Write clear, quantifiable management objectives that reflect shared goals. • Seek outside technical and scientific expertise when needed, while building internal science capacity. • Consider level of rigor and objectivity needed. • Consider both short- and long-term data needs. • Collect baseline data whenever possible. • When no baseline data are available, consider retrospective study or documentation of local knowledge about historical conditions.

with clear protocols and ground rules for data collection, and supervised by a knowledgeable leader (Pilz, Jones, and Ballard 2005). If many different individuals will be collecting data, it is advisable to select monitoring methods that are objective and repeatable among multiple observers. Certain tasks, such as those that require accurate species identification of plants, may need more trained and experienced monitoring crews (Brandon et al. 2003). Recently, several studies have been conducted that compared data gathered by volunteers to those collected by professionals (Canfield et al. 2002; Nicholson, Ryan, and Hodgkins 2002; Brandon et al. 2003). For some types of variables and methods, data gathered by volunteers were less accurate or more variable, but for others there was little difference (Lopez and Dates 1998; Canfield et al. 2002; Nicholson, Ryan, and Hodgkins 2002; Brandon et al. 2003). Several studies have found that despite the challenges of relying on volunteer monitors, volunteers make an invaluable contribution to developing long-term data sets over many sampling points (Brown, Krasny, and Schoch 2001; Brandon et al. 2003; Greve et al. 2003; Boylen et al. 2004; Bruhn and Soranno 2005; Danielsen et al. 2008).

Institutional Barriers and Strategies

Institutional barriers to monitoring and adaptive management include both obstacles within the CBC and those external to it. Internal challenges often include inadequate funding and waning volunteer interest in and commitment to monitoring (Byron and Curtis 2002; Whitelaw et al. 2003) (table 3.2). Monitoring designs developed without input from key stakeholders or that privilege science over local or traditional knowledge may lack buy-in from stakeholders (Kusel et al. 1996, 2000; McLain and Lee 1996). When stakeholders perceive that monitoring results may negatively affect their ability to access or use resources (Allen et al. 2001; Habron 2003) or may reflect poorly on the CBC's effectiveness, they may resist developing and implementing monitoring that is closely tied to management decision making. In some groups, participants may be reluctant to change in response to new information. For example, they may be hesitant to consider revising management objectives or altering management strategies based on monitoring data.

Some strategies for addressing these challenges include continually seeking and rewarding participation by a broad base of stakeholders. To combat apathy toward and fears about monitoring, it is important to clarify why monitoring is being conducted, how it can help advance the CBC's mission, and how data will be used. Stakeholder concerns about data confidentiality should be taken seriously and every effort made to arrive at clear, written agreements about data ownership, confidentiality, and the way data will be used and displayed. For example, it may be important to assure private landowners that data gathered on private land will only be analyzed and reported in aggregate form, and that individual properties will not be identified as either problem areas or biodiversity hot spots (Allen et al. 2001).

External barriers include the lack of commitment to adaptive management generally on the part of public agencies, and reluctance to take risks through experimentation (McLain and Lee 1996; Stankey and Shindler 1997; Moir and Block 2001; Stankey et al. 2003; Stankey, Clark, and Bormann 2005). Agencies may also be skeptical or resentful of CBC monitoring efforts (see table 3.2). For both agencies and CBCs internally, a decision space for adaptive management should be discussed early during the design phase (McDermott, Moote, and Danks 2005). For example, if for legal reasons there is no scope for adjusting management in response to monitoring data, then an adaptive management approach is not appropriate. The BLM has published an "adaptive management filter" to help managers determine whether adaptive management is a suitable approach to address a particular management issue. Further, even agency offices that desire to

Table 3.2 Institutional barriers to implementing monitoring and adaptive management, and strategies to overcome them

Internal issues

Barriers	Suggested strategies
• Long-term funding and commitment to monitoring are lacking. • Not enough volunteers are available or volunteers are not sufficiently committed. • Representative participation is lacking in multiparty monitoring. • Science is privileged over local knowledge. • Participants fear that data may be used to harm them. • Participants fear change. • Institution lacks flexibility to respond to new information.	• Involve all stakeholders over long term. • Clarify how data will be used to make decisions. • Incorporate local, traditional, and experiential knowledge in all phases of AM and monitoring, especially design and interpretation phases. • Address concerns about data confidentiality and application. • Clarify decision space and flexibility to change management strategies and objectives during the design phase.

External and interorganizational issues

Barriers	Suggested strategies
• Public agencies lack commitment to adaptive management. • Agencies are reluctant to take risks. • Agencies resent or are skeptical of CBC adaptive management and monitoring efforts. • Legal barriers to adaptive management exist. • Agencies have weak collaborative capacity and a culture that is resistant to change. • CBCs don't coordinate monitoring efforts or collect comparable data.	• Involve agencies and other groups in monitoring design. • Seek external review of monitoring design. • Encourage networking and peer learning among CBCs that work in the same bioregion or ecosystem type or are addressing similar management issues. • Work toward regional monitoring protocols for specific ecosystem types and management objectives.

incorporate collaborative adaptive management into their regular planning and management processes may have no protocols and few examples to draw on. For example, the Little Snake Resource Area, working with NW-COS, struggled to determine how adaptive management could be incorporated into its area RMP (Bishop 2005), which is primarily geared toward allocating land uses across the landscape rather than prescribing specific management actions or strategies. Finally, as many studies have pointed out, collaboration generally is not part of agency culture, and many agencies lack an understanding of how to engage constructively in collaborative planning and management with CBCs (McDermott, Moote, and Danks 2005, this volume).

Agency and interest-group skepticism about CBC monitoring may be reduced by encouraging their participation in monitoring design. For the PLP, environmental groups were invited to nominate an external technical adviser to help design and review the monitoring protocols. Proponents of the controversial salvage logging proposal suggested a different expert. With the help of these external advisers, the group eventually developed a sampling design and monitoring protocol that all participants found acceptable.

Communication and Application Barriers and Strategies

Many adaptive management efforts fail to close the loop and complete the adaptive management cycle. In CBCs, there are often two weak links in the adaptive management cycle: (1) communicating the results of monitoring back to the group and larger community and (2) applying results to future management (table 3.3). A strong argument for including a broad cross-section of CBC participants in monitoring design, data gathering, and interpretation is that community members are likely to be the most effective conduits of information to other CBC members and to the larger community.

Two strategies can help guarantee that monitoring data are evaluated and acted on. First, attention in the design phase to clear objectives, trigger points (predetermined thresholds in key ecosystem attributes that "trigger" a management action), and anticipated responses to triggers will help ensure that appropriate actions are taken in response to monitoring findings. Second, creating and institutionalizing a transparent, structured process for regular review, evaluation, and decision making on monitoring results will also help this process. Sometimes this process may be informal, at other times it will be more formal. An example of an informal but regular and institutionalized review of monitoring data is the Empire-Cienega Biological Planning Team's twice-yearly meetings (Conley 2003). At least once a year this multi-stakeholder planning group reviews rangeland monitoring data from the 42,000-acre Las Cienegas National Conservation Area. It considers this information along with other scientific data and reports from state and federal agency managers and the grazing permittee to plan grazing management during the coming year.

At the regional and even national scales, CBCs may miss opportunities to enhance their learning and document positive environmental impacts by taking a piecemeal, group-by-group approach to monitoring. Although

Table 3.3 Communication and application barriers to implementing monitoring and active management, and strategies to overcome them

Barriers	Suggested strategies
• Monitoring results are not communicated back to group or community. • Feedback links from monitoring to management are weak.	• Involve stakeholders in monitoring design, data gathering, and interpretation phases. • Develop clear and measurable management objectives, trigger points, and anticipated responses during the design phase. • Develop a transparent, structured process for regular review, evaluation of, and action on monitoring results.

monitoring objectives are specific to each project and group and its socio-ecological context, many CBCs are addressing the same management issues in comparable landscapes, often with similar strategies. For example, many groups in the western United States are working on restoring historical stand structures and natural fire regimes to forests where fire has been unnaturally excluded or suppressed for the past century. Similarly, many watershed councils in the Pacific Northwest are working on stream and riparian restoration projects. Networking and peer learning among CBCs working in the same bioregion or ecosystem type or addressing similar management issues should be encouraged. Consistent but adaptable monitoring protocols for specific ecosystem types and management objectives (leading to comparable data gathered in many locations for diverse projects) can help CBCs demonstrate their environmental impacts regionally while increasing the precision and power of monitoring efforts and strengthening learning by gathering data over many sampling points using consistent protocols. In the southern Rocky Mountains and Colorado Plateau regions, the community-based monitoring protocols for ponderosa pine forests are a good example of one such effort (Savage 2003). Although no meta-analysis of data has yet been conducted to our knowledge, many communities are using a similar protocol, enhancing the potential to compare across groups.

The Social Implications of Ecological Monitoring

As we noted earlier, monitoring by CBCs has the potential to provide social as well as ecological benefits. Monitoring and adaptive management are not simply technical activities that yield data. They are also social processes with social results (Fernández-Giménez, Ruyle, and Jorstad McClaran 2005; Fernández-Giménez, Jorstad McClaran, and Ruyle 2005). The value of bringing stakeholders together to observe the ecological features of important places has long been recognized by technical experts who work closely with landowners and resource users (Sundt 2002). A recent survey of grazing permittees and land management agency employees in Arizona confirmed this long-held hunch (Fernández-Giménez, Ruyle, and Jorstad McClaran 2005; Fernández-Giménez, Jorstad McClaran, and Ruyle 2005). Most land management agency employees and a significant number of grazing permittees felt that joint agency-permittee monitoring improved relationships between ranchers and agencies. In the same study, many agency and rancher focus-group participants valued multi-stakeholder monitoring-related activities such as workshops, field tours, and demonstrations because they led to increased mutual respect, understanding, and knowledge sharing. In a review of three pilot all-party monitoring projects, Kusel and colleagues (2000) came to similar conclusions, asserting that the collaborative aspect of all-party monitoring is as important as the data collection and citing the role of monitoring in building human, cultural and social capital. Bliss and colleagues (2001, 148–49) agree:

> By engaging citizens to work together on shared objectives, monitoring can help build "social capital," cooperative, interdependent relationships that comprise the foundation of community. Social capital that comes through an increasing community awareness of problems and promises strengthens existing institutions and builds new social networks. Other examples of building social capital include identifying and engaging volunteers, creating new agency connections, building leadership skills and responsibilities, brokering solutions to persistent conflicts, and identifying overlooked or unrecognized resource values.

Less has been written about the social costs or risks of multiparty monitoring, or monitoring in a collaborative setting. The Arizona study cited above (Fernández-Giménez, Ruyle, and Jorstad McClaran 2005) found that in a few cases, joint permittee-agency monitoring led to worse instead of better relationships between the parties. As with collaboration more generally, studies are needed that help identify when collaboration, and collaborative monitoring, lead to improved relationships and when they contribute to declines in trust and cooperation. The literature on joint fact-finding, defined as a "process in which parties with differing interests work together to develop a shared information base for making decisions" (Andrews 2002, 7), may provide some guidance on when multiparty monitoring is likely to succeed and when it is not (Ehrmann and Stinson 1999; Andrews 2002). Specifically, Ehrmann and Stinson (1999) suggest that joint fact-finding is not appropriate where large power imbalances exist among stakeholders, a fair process is unlikely, or the process is forced on participants.

Recommendations for CBCs

Although we have relatively few accounts in the scientific literature of CBC monitoring and adaptive management, we do know that many CBCs are carrying out some ecological monitoring, and that a number of them aspire to set up active or passive adaptive management. In several instances, CBCs are leaders in adaptive management, creating opportunities for innovative management and monitoring that would otherwise not occur. Because of their nongovernmental status and their credibility with private landowners, CBCs may sometimes be able to achieve adaptive management where agencies have failed or been slow. Recent CBC monitoring experiences and the longer-term record of successful volunteer monitoring efforts suggest that CBCs have the potential to make significant contributions to their own knowledge base through monitoring, as well as contributing to improved overall understanding of ecological systems and their response to different management actions.

The reported challenges of volunteer monitoring suggest that CBCs that plan to monitor should set up partnerships with scientists and natural resource professionals or build internal science capacity. This technical expertise, whether internal or external, can help CBCs make informed choices about monitoring objectives and protocols and build the monitoring capacity and confidence of participating stakeholders. At the same time, CBCs should recognize the value of nonscientist stakeholder participation in developing conceptual models of the ecosystem, identifying appropriate monitoring indicators, and interpreting monitoring results, and should seek participation from a broad range of knowledge sources. Involving volunteers in gathering data can be an effective way of leveraging limited monitoring resources while meeting educational goals and helping to build relationships in the community. However, volunteer monitors must be well trained and supervised, and care must be taken to maintain their enthusiasm and commitment over the long term.

CBCs working in similar ecosystems or addressing similar environmental problems should consider forming monitoring networks to share data and learning. Although monitoring must be tailored to the objectives and needs of each group, often monitoring designs can be slightly changed to increase the comparability among groups. CBCs could share monitoring results to help learn whether certain management actions have similar results in similar and different ecosystems, or not. For example, several CBCs in the western states are working on the most effective small-diameter wood removal treatments for fuels reduction. Sharing information about monitoring protocols and design as well as results could eliminate much of the trial and error groups face now. Creating such networks should speed learning, strengthen the reliability and generalizability of results, and help CBCs demonstrate their impacts at a broader spatial scale than was previously possible.

Our focus in this chapter has primarily been on monitoring environmental changes and outcomes; however, social and economic monitoring is equally important, and some CBCs have implemented socioeconomic monitoring programs (Danks 2002; Christoffersen et al. 2004; PLP 2004). Ultimately, everyone is interested in better understanding the relationship between a community's social and economic well-being and the health of its ecosystems. Thus, not only should both ecological and socioeconomic data be gathered, these data should be integrated and interpreted together. The Holistic Ecosystem Health Indicators advanced by Muñoz-Erickson and Aguilar Gonzáles (2003; Muñoz-Erickson 2004) strive for this kind of integrated monitoring.

Recommendations for Agencies

Collaboration and adaptive management are still new to many agencies, and long-time employees often lack the skills or will to embrace such new approaches. However, many agency employees try very hard to make collaboration and adaptive management work within the rigid structures of their organizations. At a policy level, agencies must do more to build the capacity for collaboration among their staff, and to reward staff who work successfully with CBCs on management and monitoring. Similarly, where adaptive management is being proposed, clear guidelines are needed for agency staff on how to carry it out, and the appropriate spatial and temporal scales for implementation.

Agency staff on the "front lines" of collaboration should communicate clearly and transparently with CBCs about such issues as decision space, agency resources for monitoring and collaboration, and expectations or concerns about data quality and use. We strongly recommend that when CBCs are involved in monitoring on agency-managed lands, the agency and the CBC have a clearly documented agreement about monitoring protocols and data use. Nothing sours collaboration faster than an agency that declines to use data that volunteers spent weeks or months collecting. We recognize that agency budgets are shrinking and resources for monitoring are scarce. Agencies should realize the potential benefits that monitoring by CBCs can bring to their programs. Even in an era of declining funding for land management, agencies can help leverage the assistance they receive from CBCs by committing to assist and support these efforts at whatever level is feasible—for example, a week of time for a seasonal technician, use of field equipment, or training on species identification. Most CBCs have far fewer resources than their agency partners. Finally, publicly acknowledging and rewarding the contributions of citizens and CBCs to monitoring and adaptive management goes a long way to building good will and making collaboration successful over the long term. For specific guidelines for implementing all of the above suggestions, see Pilz, Jones, and Ballard (2005).

Recommendations for Researchers

Like agencies, many researchers, particularly those in the physical and natural sciences, are new to collaboration and community-based research. They may be brought in as outside experts to advise the CBC on monitoring design, or they might begin contact with the CBC to carry out research with the group. In any case, researchers should realize that they are seldom the first scientists the group has had contact with and that many CBCs have had negative experiences with scientists in the past who disregarded local knowledge or never returned the results to the community.

Scientists should not expect to have instant credibility with a collaborative group, regardless of their relationship to the CBC. Rather, they must work to gain the group's trust. For example, researchers at Northern Arizona University and Prescott College have worked since 1997 with the Diablo Trust on research about the effects of alternative livestock grazing practices on biodiversity and ecosystem function. Trust building is enhanced by the ability to listen, to communicate science clearly and simply without being patronizing, and the willingness to accept the legitimacy of other ways of knowing.

Researchers can help CBCs gain technical capacity in monitoring and adaptive management, as well as encouraging them to reflect critically on their progress and embrace the learning process. Outside scientific consultants should also realize the financial and staffing limits of CBCs when making monitoring recommendations and discuss candidly with the group the strengths and drawbacks of possible monitoring designs in accuracy, precision, and efficiency.

Directions for Future Research

Many of the basic descriptive questions about CBCs' monitoring activities remain unanswered in any broad or deep way. For example, we know little about the kind or intensity of monitoring undertaken by CBCs, the monitoring indicators and measures used, and how or whether groups apply monitoring data to future management decisions. Our knowledge of the social context of monitoring in CBCs is also slight. To what extent is monitoring by CBCs a collaborative effort? How important is the collaborative aspect of monitoring to the quality and utility of monitoring, and to the social outcomes of the CBC? We have suggested in this chapter, based on a few studies, that monitoring has important social dimensions, but this question has been little explored by researchers (Fernández-Giménez et al. 2008).

The limited data available suggest that many CBCs conduct some ecological monitoring. Does the prevalence of monitoring by CBCs suggest that CBCs are filling a gap in monitoring conducted by public land management agencies and technical service providers on private lands? Alternatively, are CBC monitoring efforts complementary to those of agencies? Similarly, we might ask whether CBCs are able to innovate in adaptive management where agencies are limited by institutional or resource constraints.

The main underlying reason for ecological monitoring remains assessing progress toward defined ecological objectives. Individual CBCs want to know whether they are moving closer to achieving their goals for ecological restoration or sustainability. At a broader scale, policymakers, funders, and researchers want to know whether CBCs as a new class of institutions for governing natural resources are having a positive effect at regional to national scales. While there are many challenges to addressing the latter question (Brogden 2003; Conley and Moote 2003; Moseley 2003), not least the lack of comparable, long-term ecological data, the emphasis that many CBCs have placed on monitoring is encouraging. In the near term, the presence of effective monitoring and adaptive management may serve as an interim criterion for assessing the ecological impacts of CBCs, based on the assumption that groups with well-defined monitoring and adaptive management programs are poised to learn and respond to new knowledge in a way that will help restore and sustain complex and variable ecosystems.

Over the longer term, the ability of CBCs and researchers to answer the broader question of CBCs' contribution to environmental stewardship will require effective long-term ecological monitoring, the development of monitoring networks among CBCs using comparable protocols, cooperative and participatory research that engages university and agency-based scientists along with CBCs and citizen scientists, a willingness to incorporate all types of knowledge, and the ability to balance scientific rigor with locally meaningful and management-relevant indicators.

As McDermott, Moote, and Danks point out in the next chapter, monitoring is but one indicator of successful collaboration, and an indirect indicator at that. Nevertheless, we argue, CBCs committed to monitoring and adaptive management stand the best chance of transforming human relationships with the land, because these activities nurture our reflective natures and make it more likely that we will question the governing assumptions that so often have led to unsustainable use of natural resources.

References

Allen, W., O. Bosch, M. Kilvington, D. Harley, and I. Brown. 2001. "Monitoring and Adaptive Management: Resolving Social and Organizational Issues to Improve Information Sharing in Natural Resource Management." *Natural Resources Forum* 25:225–33.

Andrews, C. J. 2002. *Humble Analysis: The Practice of Joint Fact-Finding.* Westport, CT: Praeger.

Armitage, D. R. 2003. "Traditional Agroecological Knowledge, Adaptive Management and the Socio-politics of Conservation in Central Sulawesi, Indonesia." *Environmental Conservation* 30 (1): 79–90.

———. 2005. "Adaptive Capacity and Community-Based Natural Resource Management." *Environmental Management* 35 (6): 703–15.

Ballard, H. L., M. E. Fernández-Giménez, and V. E. Sturtevant. 2008. "Integration of Local Ecological Knowledge and Conventional Science: A Study of Seven Community-based Forestry Organizations in the USA." *Ecology and Society* 13 (2): 37.

Ballard, H. L., and L. Huntsinger. 2006. "Salal Harvester Local Ecological Knowledge, Harvest Practices and Understory Management on the Olympic Peninsula, Washington." *Human Ecology* 34 (4): 529–47.

Banks, J., E. Kolkemo, J. Colby, and J. Souder. 2001. *Effectiveness Monitoring of Large Wood, Boulder Weirs, and Culvert Replacement Projects in Selected Streams in the Coos Watershed.* Charleston, OR: Coos Watershed Association.

Berkes, F. 1999. *Sacred Ecology, Traditional Ecological Knowledge, and Resource Management.* Philadelphia: Taylor and Francis.

———. 2004. "Rethinking Community-Based Conservation." *Conservation Biology* 18 (3): 621–30.

Bishop, D. 2005. "Collaborative Adaptive Management and Participatory Monitoring: Case Studies of the Northwest Colorado Stewardship." Master's thesis, Colorado State University.

Bliss, J., G. Aplet, C. Hartzell, P. Harwood, P. Jahnige, D. Kittredge, S. Lewandowski, and M. L. Soscia. 2001. "Community-based Ecosystem Monitoring." *Journal of Sustainable Forestry* 12 (3–4): 143–67.

Bormann, B. T., J. R. Martin, F. H. Wagner, G. W. Wood, J. Alegria, P. G. Cunningham, M. H. Brookes, P. Friesema, J. Berg, and J. R. Henshaw. 1999. "Adaptive Management." In *Ecological Stewardship: A Common Reference for Ecosystem Management*, ed. N. C. Johnson, A. J. Malk, W. T. Sexton, and R. Szaro. Oxford: Elsevier Science.

Boylen, C. W., E. A. Howe, J. A. Bartkowski, and L. W. Eichler. 2004. "Augmentation of a Long-Term Monitoring Program for Lake George, NY, by Citizen Volunteers." *Lake and Reservoir Management* 20 (2): 121–29.

Brandon, A., G. Spyreas, B. Molano-Flores, C. Carroll, and J. Ellis. 2003. "Can Volunteers Provide Reliable Data for Forest Vegetation Surveys?" *Natural Areas Journal* 23 (3): 254–61.

Brogden, M. 2003. "The Assessment of Environmental Outcomes." In *The Promise and Performance of Environmental Conflict Resolution*, ed. O.L.R. Bingham and L. B. Bingham. Washington, DC: Resources for the Future Press.

Brown, W. T., M. E. Krasny, and N. Schoch. 2001. "Volunteer Monitoring of Nonindigenous Invasive Plant Species in the Adirondack Park, New York, USA." *Natural Areas Journal* 21 (2): 189–96.

Bruhn, L. C., and P. A. Soranno. 2005. "Long Term (1974–2001) Volunteer Monitoring of Water Clarity Trends in Michigan Lakes and Their Relation to Ecoregion and Land Use/Cover." *Lake and Reservoir Management* 21 (1): 10–23.

Brunner, R. D., C. H. Colburn, C. M. Cromley, R. A. Klein, and E. A. Olson, eds. 2002. *Finding Common Ground: Governance and Natural Resources in the American West*. New Haven, CT: Yale University Press.

Busch, D. E., and J. C. Trexler. 2003. "The Importance of Monitoring in Regional Ecosystem Initiatives." In *Monitoring Ecosystems: Interdisciplinary Approaches for Evaluating Ecoregional Initiatives*, ed. D. E. Busch and J. C. Trexler. Washington, DC: Island Press.

Byron, I., and A. Curtis. 2002. "Maintaining Volunteer Commitment to Local Watershed Initiatives." *Environmental Management* 30 (1): 59–67.

Canfield, D. E., C. D. Brown, R. W. Backmann, and M. V. Hoyer. 2002. "Volunteer Lake Monitoring: Testing the Reliability of Data Collected by the Florida LAKEWATCH Program." *Lake and Reservoir Management* 18 (1): 1–9.

CBCRC. 2005. Community-Based Collaboratives Research Consortium Project Database, www.cbcrc.org.

Christoffersen, N., J. Tanaka, B. Sorte, J. Overson, and E. Kohrman. 2004. *Social and Economic Monitoring in the Blue Mountains: Grant, Union, and Wallowa Counties as Case Studies. The Impact of Restoration and Stewardship Projects in Northeast Oregon with an Emphasis on National Fire Plan Contracts*. Enterprise, OR: Wallowa Resources, with Oregon State University, Grande Ronde Model Watershed Program, and the Blue Mountains Forest Plan Revision Team.

Cline, S. A., and A. R. Collins. 2003. "Watershed Associations in West Virginia: Their Impact on Environmental Protection." *Journal of Environmental Management* 67:373–83.

Conley, A. T. 2003. "Learning from the Land, Learning from Each Other: Case Studies of Collaborative Management in Arizona Rangelands." Master's thesis, University of Arizona.

Conley, A., and M. A. Moote. 2003. "Evaluating Collaborative Natural Resource Management." *Society and Natural Resources* 16:371–86.

CWA. 2002. *Willanch Creek Project Effectiveness Monitoring and Stream Temperature Study 1997–2002.* Charleston, OR: Coos Watershed Association.

Daniels, S. E., and G. B. Walker. 2001. *Working through Environmental Conflict: The Collaborative Learning Approach.* Westport, CT: Praeger.

Danielsen, F., N. D. Burgess, A. Balmford, P. F. Donald, M. Funder, J.P.G. Jones, P. Avlivioa, D. S. Balete, T. Blomley, J. Brashares, B. Child, M. Enghoff, J. Fjeldsa, S. Holt, H. Hubertz, A. E. Jensen, P. M. Jensen, J. Massao, M. M. Mendoza, Y. Ngaga, M. K. Poulsen, R. Rued, M. Sam, T. Skielboe, G. Stuart-Hill, E. Topp-Jorgensen, and D. Yonten. 2008. "Local Participation in Natural Resource Monitoring: A Characterization of Approaches." *Conservation Biology* 23 (1): 31–42.

Danks, C. 2002. "Role of Communities in Adaptive Management: A Case from North America." In *Adaptive Management: From Theory to Practice,* ed. J. Oglethorpe. Cambridge: IUCN.

Danks, C., L. J. Wilson, and L. Jungwirth. 2002. *Community-based Socioeconomic Assessment and Monitoring of Activities Related to National Forest Management.* Hayfork, CA: Watershed Research and Training Center.

Diablo Trust. 1999. *Diablo Trust Area Range Management Plan and Proposed Action.* Flagstaff, AZ: Diablo Trust.

Ecological Research Institute. 2004. *Handbook One: What Is Multiparty Monitoring?* Flagstaff, AZ: Ecological Restoration Institute.

Ehrmann, J. R., and B. L. Stinson. 1999. "Joint Fact-Finding and the Use of Technical Experts." In *The Consensus Building Handbook,* ed. L. Susskind, S. McKearnan, and J. Thomas-Larmer. Thousand Oaks, CA: Sage.

Elzinga, C. L., D. W. Salzer, and J. W. Willoughby. 1998. *Measuring and Monitoring Plant Populations.* BLM Technical Reference 1730–1. Denver, CO: Bureau of Land Management.

Everett, Y. 1999. *"Chopsticks" Small Diameter Thinning Ecological Monitoring Project Final Report.* Hayfork, CA: Watershed Research and Training Center.

Fernández-Giménez, M. E. 2000. "The Role of Mongolian Nomadic Pastoralists' Ecological Knowledge in Rangeland Management." *Ecological Applications* 10 (5): 1318–26.

Fernández-Giménez, M. E., H. L. Ballard, and V. E. Sturtevant. 2008. "Adaptive Management and Social Learning in Collaborative and Community-based Monitoring: A Study of Five Community-based Organizations in the Western U.S." *Ecology and Society* 13 (2): 4.

Fernández-Giménez, M. E., S. Jorstad McClaran, and G. Ruyle. 2005. "Arizona Permittee and Land Management Agency Attitudes toward Rangeland Monitoring by Permittees." *Rangeland Ecology and Management* 58:344–51.

Fernández-Giménez, M. E., S. LeFebre, A. Conley, and A. Tendick. 2004. "Collaborative Management of Arizona's Rangelands." *Rangelands* 26 (6): 24–30.

Fernández-Giménez, M. E., G. Ruyle, and S. Jorstad McClaran. 2005. "An Evaluation of Arizona Cooperative Extension's Rangeland Monitoring Program." *Rangeland Ecology and Management* 58 (1): 89–98.

Folke, C., T. Hahn, P. Olsson, and J. Norberg. 2005. "Adaptive Governance of Socio-Ecological Systems." *Annual Review of Environment and Natural Resources* 30:441–73.

Gasteyer, S., and C. B. Flora. 2000. "Measuring ppm with Tennis Shoes: Science and Locally Meaningful Indicators of Environmental Quality." *Society and Natural Resources* 13:589–97.

Gouveia, C., A. Fonseca, A. Camara, and F. Ferreira. 2004. Promoting the Use of Environmental Data Collected by Concerned Citizens through Information and Communication Technologies." *Journal of Environmental Management* 71:135–54.

Greve, A. I., J. C. Loftis, J. B. Brown, R. R. Buirgy, and B. Alexander. 2003. "Design and Implementation of a Cooperative Water Quality–Monitoring Program in Colorado's Big Thompson Watershed." *Journal of the American Water Resources Association* 39 (6): 1409–18.

Guijt, I. 2007. "Strengthening Learning in Adaptive Collaborative Management: The Potential of Monitoring." In *Negotiated Learning: Collaborative Monitoring in Forest Resource Management,* ed. Irene Guijt. Washington, DC: Resources for the Future Press.

Habron, G. 2003. "Role of Adaptive management for Watershed Councils." *Environmental Management* 31 (1): 29–41.

Harding, K., and M. Moote. 2005. "Appendix B. Monitoring and Evaluation." In *Social Science to Improve Fuels Management: A Synthesis of Research on Collaboration,* ed. V. E. Sturtevant, M. A. Moote, P. Jakes, and A. S. Cheng. General Technical Report GTR-NC-257. St. Paul, MN: U.S. Department of Agriculture, Forest Service, North Central Research Station.

Heemskerk, M., K. Wilson, and M. Pavao-Zuckerman. 2003. "Conceptual Models as Tools for Communication across Disciplines." *Conservation Ecology* 7 (3): 8 (online).

Herrick, J. E., J. W. Van Zee, K. M. Havstad, L. M. Burkett, and W. G. Whitford. 2005. *Monitoring Manual for Grassland, Shrubland and Savanna Ecosystems.* Las Cruces, NM: U.S. Department of Agriculture, Agricultural Research Service, Jornada Research Station.

Holling, C. S. 1978. *Adaptive Environmental Assessment and Management.* Toronto: Wiley.

Holling, C. S., and G. K. Meffe. 1996. "Command and Control and the Pathology of Natural Resource Management." *Conservation Biology* 10:328–37.

Huntington, H. P. 2000. "Traditional Ecological Knowledge of the Ecology of Belugas *Delphinapterus leucas,* in Cook Inlet, Alaska." *Marine Fisheries Review* 62 (3): 134–40.

Kusel, J., S. C. Doak, S. Carpenter, and V. E. Sturtevant. 1996. "The Role of the Public in Adaptive Ecosystem Management." In *Sierra Nevada Ecosystem Project: Final Report to Congress,* vol. 2, *Assessments and Scientific Basis for Management Options.* Davis: University of California, Centers for Water and Wildland Resources.

Kusel, J., L. Williams, C. Danks, J. Perttu, L. Wills, D. Keith, and Lead Partnership Group. 2000. *A Report on All-Party Monitoring and Lessons Learned from the Pilot Projects: Forest Community Research and The Pacific West National Community Forestry Center.*

Leach, W. D., N. W. Pelkey, and P. A. Sabatier. 2002. "Stakeholder Partnerships as Collaborative Policymaking: Evaluation Criteria Applied to Watershed Management in California and Washington." *Journal of Policy Analysis and Management* 21 (4): 645–70.

Lopez, C., and G. Dates. 1998. "The Effects of Community Volunteers in Assessing Watershed Ecosystem Health." In *Ecosystem Health,* ed. D. Rappoport, R. Costanza, P. R. Epstein, C. Gaudet, and R. Levins. Oxford: Blackwell Science.

Maddox, D., K. Polani, and R. Unnasch. 1999. "Evaluating Management Success: Using Ecological Models to Ask the Right Monitoring Questions." In *Ecological Stewardship: A Common Reference for Ecosystem Management*, ed. N. C. Johnson, A. J. Malk, R. Szaro, and W. T. Sexton. Oxford: Elsevier Science.

Maguire, L. A. 2003. "Interplay of Science and Stakeholder Values in Neuse River Total Maximum Daily Load Process." *Journal of Water Resources Planning and Management* 129 (4): 261–70.

McDermott, M. H., M. A. Moote, and C. Danks. 2005. "How Community-based Collaboratives Overcome External Institutional Barriers to Achieving Their Environmental Goals." Charlottesville: University of Virginia, Community-Based Collaboratives Research Consortium.

McLain, J. R, and R. G. Lee. 1996. "Adaptive Management: Promises and Pitfalls." *Environmental Management* 20 (4): 437–48.

Moir, W. H., and W. M. Block. 2001. "Adaptive Management on Public Lands in the United States: Commitment or Rhetoric." *Environmental Management* 28 (2): 141–48.

Moller, H., F. Berkes, P. O'Brian Lyver, and M. Kislalioglu. 2004. "Combining Science and Traditional Ecological Knowledge: Monitoring Populations for Co-management." *Ecology and Society* 9 (3): 2 (online).

Moseley, C. 2003. "Constrained Democracy: Evaluating Community-based Conservation Using Environmental Outcomes." Paper presented at the conference, "Evaluating Methods and Environmental Outcomes of Community-based Collaborative Processes," Snowbird, UT, September 14–16.

Moseley, C., and L. Wilson. 2002. *Multiparty Monitoring for Sustainable Natural Resource Management*. Eugene, OR, Hayfork, CA: University of Oregon Ecosystem Workforce Program and Watershed Research and Training Center.

Muñoz-Erickson, T. 2004. "Evaluating the Ecological and Social Outcomes of Collaborative Management: Ecosystem Health Indicators for Monitoring Effectiveness." Master's thesis, Northern Arizona University.

Muñoz-Erickson, T., and B. Aguilar-González. 2003. "The Use of Ecosystem Health Indicators in Evaluating Ecological and Social Outcomes of Collaborative Approaches to Management: The Case Study of The Diablo Trust." Paper presented at the conference, "Evaluating Methods and Environmental Outcomes of Community-based Collaborative Processes," Snowbird, UT, September 14–16.

Muñoz-Erickson, T., M. Loesser, and B. Aguilar-González. 2004. "Identifying Indicators of Ecosystem Health for a Semiarid Ecosystem: A Conceptual Approach." In *The Colorado Plateau: Cultural, Biological and Physical Research*, ed. I. C. van Ripper and K. L. Cole. Tucson: University of Arizona Press.

Murray, C., and D. Marmorek. 2003. "Adaptive Management and Ecological Restoration." In *Ecological Restoration of Southwestern Ponderosa Pine Forests*, ed. P. Freiderici. Washington, DC: Island Press.

Mutimukuru, T., W. Kozanayi, and R. Nyirenda. 2006. "Catalyzing Collaborative Monitoring Processes in Joint Forest Management Situations: The Mafungautsi Forest Case, Zimbabwe." *Society and Natural Resources* 19 (3): 209–24.

Niamir, M. 1995. "Indigenous Systems of Natural Resource Management among Pastoralists of Arid and Semi-arid Africa." In *The Cultural Dimension of Development*, ed.

D. M. Warren, L. J. Slikkerveer, and D. Brokensha. London: Intermediate Technology Publications.

Nicholson, E., J. Ryan, and D. Hodgkins. 2002. "Community Data—Where Does the Value Lie? Assessing Confidence Limits of Community Collected Water Quality Data." *Water Science and Technology* 45 (11): 193–200.

Novak, J. D. 1998. *Learning, Creating and Using Knowledge: Concept Maps as Facilitative Tools in Schools and Corporations.* Mahwah, NJ: Lawrence Erlbaum.

Nyberg, B. 1998. "Statistics and the Practices of Adaptive Management." In *Statistical Methods for Adaptive Management Studies, Land Management Handbook 42,* ed. V. Sit and B. Taylor. Victoria, BC: Ministry of Forests.

———. 1999. *An Introductory Guide to Adaptive Management for Project Leaders and Participants.* Victoria, BC: Forest Service.

Ogden, J. C., S. M. Davis, and L. A. Brandt. 2003. "Science Strategy for a Regional Ecosystem Monitoring and Assessment Program: The Florida Everglades Example." In *Monitoring Ecosystems: Interdisciplinary Approaches for Evaluating Ecoregional Initiatives,* ed. D. E. Busch and J. C. Trexler. Washington, DC: Island Press.

Pahl-Wostl, C. 2007. "The Implications of Complexity for Integrated Resources Management." *Environmental Modelling and Software* 22:561–69.

Pierce Colfer, C. J. 2005. *The Complex Forest: Communities, Uncertainty, and Adaptive Collaborative Management.* Washington, DC: Resources for the Future Press.

Pilz, D., E. T. Jones, and H. Ballard. 2005. *Manager's Manual for Participatory Biological Monitoring Projects.* Portland, OR: Institute for Culture and Ecology.

PLP. 2004. *Managing to Learn, Learning to Manage, Burn Canyon Salvage Logging.* Delta, CO: Public Lands Partnership.

Poole, G. C., and C. R. Berman. 2000. "An Ecological Perspective on In-stream Temperature: Natural Heat Dynamics and Mechanisms of Human-Caused Thermal Degradation." *Environmental Management* 27 (6): 787–802.

Sallabanks, R. 2000. *Non-game Landbird Conservation and the Restoration of Aspen and Ponderosa Pine Habitat in Wallowa County, Northeast Oregon.* Report prepared for Wallowa Resources, Enterprise, Oregon. Eagle, ID: Sustainable Ecosystems Institute.

Savage, Melissa. 2003. *Multiparty Monitoring and Assessment Guidelines for Community Based Restoration in Southwestern Ponderosa Pine Forests.* Santa Fe, NM: Forest Trust.

Sisk, T. D., T. E. Crews, R. T. Eisfeldt, M. King, and E. Stanley. 1999. "Assessing Impacts of Alternative Livestock Management Practices: Raging Debates and a Role for Science." In *Proceedings of the Fourth Biennial Conference of Research on the Colorado Plateau.* U.S. Geological Survey / FRESC Report Series USGSFRESC / COPL / 1999 / 16.

Souder, J. 2005. "Defining the Role of Local Organizations in Assessments and Monitoring: The Coos Watershed Association's Emerging Strategy." PowerPoint presentation, Coos Watershed Association, Charleston, OR.

Stankey, G. H., B. T. Bormann, C. Ryan, B. Shindler, V. Sturtevant, R. N. Clark, and C. Philpot. 2003. "Adaptive Management and the Northwest Forest Plan: Rhetoric and Reality." *Journal of Forestry* January / February: 40–46.

Stankey, G. H., R. N. Clark, and B. T. Bormann. 2005. *Adaptive Management of Natural Resources: Theory, Concepts, and Management Institutions.* General Technical Report PNW-GTR-654. Portland, OR: U.S. Department of Agriculture, Forest Service, Pacific Northwest Research Station.

Stankey, G. H., and B. Shindler. 1997. *Adaptive Management Areas: Achieving the Promise, Avoiding the Peril.* General Technical Report PNW-GTR-394. Portland, OR: U.S. Department of Agriculture, Forest Service, Pacific Northwest Research Station.

Sundt, P. 2002. "The Statistical Power of Rangeland Monitoring Data." *Rangelands* 24 (2): 16–20.

Tear, T. H., P. Kareiva, P. L. Angermeier, P. Comer, B. Czech, R. Kautz, L. Landon, D. Mehlman, K. Murphy, M. Ruckelshaus, J. M. Scott, and G. Wilhere. 2005. "How Much Is Enough? The Recurrent Problem of Setting Measurable Objectives in Conservation." *BioScience* 55:35–49.

U.S. Department of the Interior. 1998. *Final Muleshoe Ecosystem Management Plan and Environmental Assessment.* BLM/AZ/PL-98/024. Tucson, AZ: U.S. Department of the Interior, Bureau of Land Management, Tucson Field Office.

————. 2003. *Procedures for Implementing Adaptive Management Practices.* OEPC PEP—Environmental Statement, Memorandum no. ESM03-6. Washington, DC: U.S. Department of the Interior.

Vaughan, H., G. Whitelaw, B. Craig, and C. Stewart. 2003. "Linking Ecological Science to Decision-making: Delivering Environmental Monitoring Information as Societal Feedback." *Environmental Monitoring and Assessment* 88:399–408.

Walters, C. J., and C. S. Holling. 1990. "Large-Scale Management Experiments and Learning by Doing." *Ecology and Society* 71 (6): 2060–68.

Weber, E. P. 2003. *Bringing Society Back In.* Cambridge, MA: MIT Press.

Whitelaw, G., H. Vaughan, B. Craig, and D. Atkinson. 2003. "Establishing the Canadian Community-Monitoring Network." *Environmental Monitoring and Assessment* 88:409–18.

Wondolleck, J. M., and S. L. Yaffee. 2000. *Making Collaboration Work: Lessons from Innovation in Natural Resource Management.* Washington, DC: Island Press.

Yaffee, S. L. 2004. *Measuring Progress: A Guide to the Development, Implementation, and Interpretation of an Evaluation Plan.* Ann Arbor: University of Michigan, School of Natural Resources and Environment, Ecosystem Management Initiative.

4

Effective Collaboration
Overcoming External Obstacles

Melanie Hughes McDermott, Margaret Ann Moote, and Cecilia Danks

Community-based collaboratives (CBCs) have been lauded for their ability to bring together diverse, often conflicting interests to address intractable environmental and resource management problems collectively. At the same time, CBCs are criticized for spending years in discussion and negotiation without being able to demonstrate significant improvements in environmental conditions. Both participants in and observers of CBCs have observed that, despite years of hard work, many such efforts still fall short of achieving the desired environmental outcomes, such as improved water quality, wildlife habitat, or rangeland or forest health.

The literature has documented well the many internal challenges collaboratives face getting people to the table and dealing with internal disputes and process issues once they are at the table. Yet in many cases, even though they are able to resolve those issues and come to internal agreement on needed actions, something still blocks many CBCs from implementing them. Often, this occurs when CBCs encounter external institutional obstacles—obstacles that exceed the scale of their influence or that are held in place by disproportionate power. These obstacles include externally imposed impediments deriving from established social, political, and economic practices, policies, legal forms, and organizations.

This chapter examines the external institutional obstacles encountered by CBCs in their efforts to improve environmental conditions and identifies ways in which CBCs have overcome these obstacles. Specifically, this chapter addresses the following questions: (1) What external institutional obstacles do CBCs encounter that affect their ability to achieve environmental goals? (2) In cases where CBCs have overcome external institutional obstacles and begun to reach some of their environmental goals, what strategies have enabled them to do so?

The material in this chapter is drawn from research conducted in three phases. First, from a comprehensive review of the broader literature on collaboration, we identified and analyzed thirty multicase (minimum of five cases each), empirical comparative studies of CBCs. We then conducted a series of semistructured interviews with key informants to capture current practitioner knowledge that might not yet be reflected in the literature. Finally, we conducted in-depth interviews of participants in seven case studies of CBCs that had successfully overcome one or more external obstacles to achieving their environmental goals. The subjects of our seven cases are the Downeast Initiative (Maine), the Elizabeth River Project (Virginia), the Jobs and Biodiversity Coalition (New Mexico), the Public Lands Partnership (Colorado), Trinity River Restoration (California), Wallowa Resources (Oregon), and White Mountains Restoration (Arizona). For this chapter we integrated findings from the literature, key informant interviews, and case studies, rather than identifying the multiple sources for each statement, unless it is a direct quotation or reference. For citations to the publications analyzed, key informant interviews, or case studies, the full research report by McDermott, Moote, and Danks (2006) is available online in the open access *CBCRC Journal*.

The Challenge of Documenting Environmental Outcomes

To identify effective strategies, we sought out cases and studies of CBCs that had achieved some positive environmental outcomes. We discovered, however, that whereas many groups had made progress toward their environmental goals, few CBCs have been able to document measurable and attributable improvements in environmental variables, such as improved water quality or the sustained return of a fish species to a stream. This deficit is in part due to intrinsic difficulties in measurement, in distinguishing clear trends amid environmental variability, and in ascribing causality. Moreover, the end goal of environmental change may take many years to manifest in a measurable way. Many CBCs have documented intermediate outcomes that are expected to result in positive environmental change in the longer term. Such outcomes include acres of wetland, wildlife habitat, and forests restored, as well as educational and policy changes with anticipated positive effects on environmental conditions.

Many CBCs also engage in monitoring and evaluation, which are expected to provide an indirect benefit to the environment by allowing collaborative members and resource managers to learn about changing ecological conditions and the specific impacts of the ecological interventions they undertake (see chapter 3). Yet another outcome indirectly linked to environmental improvement is the formal and informal networks of communication and collaboration built through repeated interaction among stakeholders. These relationships build social capital and political will, which can be of assistance in implementing the projects, programs, and policy changes developed or advocated by CBCs. Our research confirms that many CBCs are achieving one or more of these types of outcome. Moreover, we found that a number of CBCs have identified and pursued bold and important environmental goals.

Nonetheless, serious questions remain in many cases as to the ability of CBCs to tackle the most critical environmental problems, particularly those that are large in scale or that threaten the existing distribution of power. The environmental achievements of CBCs are constrained not only by the need to reach consensus but also by what can be implemented. The barriers we identified are largely barriers to implementation rather than collective decision making. For this study, we analyzed in some depth seven cases in which CBCs were able to overcome these obstacles and achieve measurable environmental effects.

Factors Affecting Success

We chose to focus on external institutional obstacles to CBCs' success in achieving goals because, while CBCs are by definition local, in many cases both the roots of the problems they address and the potential solutions extend far beyond the locality. A number of CBCs have expressed frustration when they have done the hard work of reaching local consensus only to be stopped by obstacles that appear beyond their reach. Of course, "local" is a relative concept. For a collaborative to be community-based, the participating geographic communities should live in close proximity to the resource of concern and be directly affected by the condition of the resource and the conditions of access to it. In sparsely populated areas, such as those adjacent to public lands, the area covered by a CBC could exceed two million acres.

Not all obstacles to achieving environmental outcomes are external to CBCs. Indeed, CBCs face formidable internal obstacles to bringing diverse parties together, working collectively, and reaching consensus. The literature on collaborative governance has identified a number of characteristics of CBCs that contribute to the failure of a collaborative effort. These include unclear or differing expectations and goals, narrow or unbalanced representation, lack of mutual respect among participants, participants' unwillingness to compromise or take risks, and lack of organizational structure. Chapters 5 and 6 in this book discuss these and other internal factors in detail. Any of these variables can affect a collaborative's ability to realize measurable environmental outcomes.

A number of success-enabling factors have repeatedly been cited in the literature (e.g., Wondolleck and Yaffee 2000; Leach and Pelkey 2001; Schuett, Selin, and Carr 2001; Koontz et al. 2004; Sabatier et al. 2005). In general, they fall into three, somewhat overlapping categories: external sources of support, access to resources, and the internal features, or capacities, of collaboratives. The first category, external sources of support, includes active support from elected officials and agency heads, including the direct involvement of key decision makers in the collaborative, along with legal authority, supportive policies and laws, and community involvement. The second category, access to resources, includes an adequate and stable source of funding, adequate staffing, and access to and active exchange of information. The third category, the capacity of the CBC to act, includes features such as effective leadership, trust among the participating parties, and social capital—particularly social networks that facilitate information flows, identify knowledge gaps, and create nodes of expertise. In this chapter we describe how specific strategies related to each of these factors are deployed in ways that effectively overcome external institutional barriers.

In this chapter we begin by delineating the nature of the external institutional obstacles that CBCs commonly encounter that impede their ability to achieve their environmental goals. The following section—and the bulk of this chapter—examines an issue that most published work does not directly address, namely, what particular strategies have some CBCs employed to deflect, duck, work around, reform, or eliminate these external obstacles? Finally, we address lessons learned and implications for CBCs, policymakers, and researchers.

External Obstacles to CBCs' Success

Based on our analysis of the comparative literature, interviews with key informants, and our case studies, we have identified six types of external institutional obstacles CBCs commonly encounter:

- Obstructive laws and regulations.
- Agency capacity and culture.
- Lack of financial and human resources.
- Resistance from powerful parties.
- Lack of authority and legitimacy.
- Large-scale political-economic factors.

These barriers on the path to environmental change have in common that they exceed the scale of the community or reflect power disparities.

Obstructive Laws and Regulations

Laws and regulations, particularly federal administrative, environmental, and natural resource laws and their implementing regulations, are frequently cited as obstacles causing procedural delays to project implementation. The National Environmental Policy Act, for example, is the subject of common complaint for delaying projects with several months to years of environmental review (e.g., Leach and Pelkey 2001). Recent studies and our interview respondents note that consultations, appeals, and lawsuits under the Endangered Species Act can greatly delay or even halt collaborative projects (e.g., Moote and Becker 2003.) The Federal Advisory Committee Act (FACA) is also frequently cited as a barrier to collaboration as well: compliance with FACA can be onerous, yet the vague language of the act has left some agency personnel unwilling to participate in a group that is not FACA-chartered (Huntington and Sommarstrom 2000; Kenney 2000).

On the other hand, a number of participants in CBC groups state that laws and regulations are not a primary obstacle for the CBCs they work with; rather, they report, the obstacle is a lack of understanding of the constraints imposed—or the opportunities provided—by specific policies. Some cite the use (or misuse) of laws and regulations as the obstacle. In other cases, CBCs find themselves "caught in the wrong authority" because they have attempted to use a legal mechanism inappropriate to their task. However, collaboratives have at times found themselves in situations in which, in the words of one key informant, "what we wanted to do wasn't permissible by Federal legislation . . . so we had to try to change the national laws."

Agency Capacity and Culture

Scientific management achieved through hierarchical bureaucracies that aim for consistent, science-based decision making and planning was considered a very positive, progressive innovation in American resource management (Hays 1959). A resource or environmental agency that made decisions based on science and was responsive to a central authority rather than local influence was an improvement over the common practice of market-led extraction to the point of resource exhaustion or even extinction of species. However, the same bureaucratic features that contribute to scientific management inhibit agency responsiveness to CBC efforts. The frequent result has been lengthy, inflexible, and overly bureaucratic procedures, a culture of risk aversion, a propensity to reward efficiency rather than creativity, limited discretion allowed to field staff, and a lack of incentives for collaboration and innovation. These propensities have been formalized through rigid and prescriptive planning and budgetary cycles and formats (Gray 1989; Carr, Selin, and Schuett 1998; Imperial and Hennessey 2000; Kenney 2000; Curtis, Shindler, and Wright 2002). Large bureaucracies have difficulty working at the community scale, in part because of administrative or congressional pressure to maximize quantitative targets (e.g., number of acres treated). Another commonly reported difficulty is the transfer of a key agency participant in a CBC midstream in the collaborative process, forcing members to build new relationships and bring the replacement person up to speed (Wondolleck and Yaffee 2000). If she or he is not receptive, progress may grind to a halt.

Further challenges arise from overlap and conflicts among different government agencies, including differing priorities and data management inconsistencies (Coughlin et al. 1999; Imperial and Hennessey 2000; Leach and Pelkey 2001; Takahashi and Smutny 2001). Equally important, government agencies may fail to understand that collaboration means not only building common understanding and support for proposed projects but also inviting others to be part of the planning for programs and projects. A lack of clarity about the CBC's "decision space" can lead to expectations that agency decision makers are simply going to accept collaborative groups' final decisions (Moote and Becker 2003).

Finally, it is worth noting that while federal and state natural resource management agencies are often singled out, local units of government can impose obstacles of their own to CBCs. Anticollaboration gatekeepers, restrictive zoning, demanding permitting processes, staffing and budget shortfalls—all these can pose hurdles that CBCs must negotiate around or knock down.

Lack of Financial and Human Resources

Adequate time, money, and staffing are critically scarce resources for most CBCs (e.g., Kenney et al. 2000; Schuett, Selin, and Carr 2001; Dopplet, Shinn, and Johnson 2002; Lubell 2004). Some funding is available to initiate collaborative activities, but otherwise most available funds are linked to specific projects and management targets. It is difficult to obtain funds for ongoing work and core administrative and personnel expenses (Born and Genskow 2000; Imperial and Hennessey 2000; Moote and Becker 2003). Furthermore, without core resources it is difficult to attract more. Not only do proposals take (often unpaid) time to develop and administer but also, as one CBC coordinator explained, "Our greatest need is consistent funding, and especially consistent funding that does not require nonexistent matches."

Usually, at most only a few nongovernmental participants in a collaborative are paid as project or nonprofit staff. Citizen members grow weary of the endless hours of volunteer time demanded of them, particularly when government employees or national interest group personnel generally are compensated for their time and travel to attend meetings, go on field trips, and other forms of participation. Burnout is especially a problem when it claims leaders, whose loss means a loss of continuity, relationships, and knowledge that can set the whole process back. As one CBC participant we interviewed lamented, "Time is a barrier—people are willing to give time, but they start wearing out after 9–10 years. . . . Collaboration is nobody's job. It's an extra. . . . Other interest groups have staff and ongoing support."

Budget and staffing cuts have imposed serious constraints on the capacity of federal agencies to fulfill their charges to manage natural resources and protect the environment. The challenge becomes even greater when agents are asked to support, participate in, and implement collaborative efforts on top of completing their traditional tasks. Moreover, collaborative efforts often come up with projects or priorities that are outside the agencies' current targets, budgets, structure, and ways of doing business. As one key informant summed it up, "On public land, the biggest factor affecting whether or not CBCs can achieve their ecological goals on the ground is the extent to which the plans or projects agreed upon by the CBC coincide with plans and budgets of the agencies."

Resistance from Powerful Parties

By virtue of their very localness, CBCs generally lack political power outside, and at times inside, their local sphere. They are therefore vulnerable to resistance to their activities or proposals for policy change from more powerful actors. CBCs frequently encounter either active or passive resistance from regulatory or land management agencies, environmental groups, landowners, or other resource users (Gray 1989; Margerum 2001; Curtis, Shindler, and Wright 2002; Lubell 2004). Passive resistance involves failure to support a CBC's efforts or failure to change detrimental behavior; this is particularly damaging when the resistant party is a large landowner or government decision maker. Active resistance may include the use of appeals and litigation to block collaboratively developed projects, or a partner's refusal to implement an agreement. Such resistance may be expressed behind the scenes and lead to private side deals with the agency, thus presenting a challenge to the collaborative ideal of openness and transparency (although some CBCs themselves engage in such maneuvering, sometimes even to the point of lobbying elected officials). Resistance to collaboratively designed projects is often expressed by nonparticipants who are unfamiliar with a CBC's goals and do not understand the process through which proposed actions were developed. In some cases, a negative history of conflict and consequent distrust among stakeholders fuels ongoing dissent and unwillingness to collaborate. Huntington and Sommarstrom (2000, 13) describe how avoiding confronting power imposes constraints, for example when the participants recruited for collaborative projects "frequently fail to include those individuals or corporations controlling activities on the most important . . . lands within a given watershed."

Lack of Authority or Legitimacy

Legitimacy or authority may be thought of as a license to operate; these terms are commonly used to refer to a government's right to hold and use power, based on the consent of the governed. CBCs may derive authority from the government by being more or less explicitly legitimated, sometimes through official mandate to undertake given responsibilities or through the participation of key decision makers. The degree of authority that a collaborative can invoke to achieve its objectives varies widely. In their study of fourteen watershed councils in the western United States, Huntington and Sommastrom (2000, 66, 39) found that half saw their role as "formal advisory" (clearly authorized in public documents), while at the other end of the spectrum five felt they had "no mandate to provide advice to anyone outside the council or council issues." Moreover, "none has any regulatory, enforcement or taxing authority." Because of their local nature, CBCs may find their influence does not extend to the resources they want to manage, as in the case of a CBC that created municipal bylaws and zoning regulations to address environmental management concerns, only to find them overridden by state and federal laws. Many CBCs voluntarily forming from a local base never obtain any sort of official imprimatur. In fact, a number of studies cite the absence of key stakeholders, in particular "decision makers" from government agencies, as a significant obstacle to the work of CBCs (Carr, Selin, and Schuett 1998; Huntington and Sommarstrom 2000; Belden Russonello and Stewart Research and Communications 2001, 36; Johnson et al. 2003; Lubell 2004).

Without official mandate or the less formal legitimization resulting from the government involvement or support, CBCs may lack the authority to implement projects. Furthermore, government units, mandated to represent the public at large, may not be empowered to accept a plan or policy developed by voluntary, self-appointed groups such as many CBCs. Groups that lack the involvement or support of key decision makers, especially government authorities and individuals or corporations that control important private lands, are most likely to encounter this obstacle.

Large-Scale Political-Economic Factors

Although CBCs may achieve success in addressing localized problems, they may have greater difficulty in confronting intractable large-scale issues such as the restructuring of regional economies (as with the shift in the West from natural resource– to service-based economies), population growth and movement, rapidly changing land-use and development patterns, depletion of the water supply, and overextraction of natural resources. These developments are shaped by larger economic trends—such as globalization, falling commodity prices and wages, trade deficits, national budget deficits, and privatization—and the national and international policies, politics, and power blocs that both drive and are driven by them. The local effects of these large-scale shifts can be devastating, particularly for rural communities. The resulting economic dislocations are among the motivating factors for community members to form and participate in CBCs. In different parts of the United States, the decline of the timber industry, ranching, and small-scale fisheries provides notable examples (Cestero 1999; Born and Genskow 2000; Sommarstrom and Huntington 2000).

The local impacts of regional socioeconomic trends can be obstacles to proposed solutions. For example, the effort to extract, process, and market the small-diameter wood products of forest restoration is impeded by the loss or lack of local industrial capacity, such as skilled loggers and processing equipment, as well as by preexisting barriers, such as the weakness of local markets and the long and expensive distances to larger markets. In some cases, CBCs may achieve success in addressing localized environmental problems but be forced to sidestep or ignore intractable issues such as urbanization, water supply, legal issues, and detrimental industrial forest practices (Born and Genskow 2000; Huntington and Sommarstrom 2000).

Strategies CBCs Use to Overcome Obstacles

When CBCs have overcome external institutional obstacles and have begun to reach some of their environmental goals, what strategies enabled them to do so? We have identified fourteen strategies that CBCs have used to overcome external institutional obstacles to achieving their environmental goals. The strategies can be grouped into four broader classes:

- Linking people effectively.
- Bringing in new resources.
- Transforming the ground rules.
- Staying focused and flexible.

Each of these strategies can be used to address any of the six external institutional obstacles identified above, although the applicability of any particular strategy will be case-specific. Each strategy is illustrated below with examples from our case studies and key informant interviews.

Linking People Effectively

Involving Influential and Diverse Stakeholders

Certainly, having influential stakeholders onboard as members of the collaborative helps CBCs overcome many obstacles, including resistance from powerful parties. In one case from our interviews, a collaborative included a member of a powerful national environmental group. When a local environmental group began to raise suspicions, the representative of the national group was able to make a phone call and use his credibility and clout to assure the local group that the collaborative's plans were environment-friendly.

To overcome lack of authority and legitimacy, it is especially important to get active support from government agency decision makers and elected officials. As a key informant from one of the agencies in question explained, implementation of reforms by an agency is more likely when someone from within is involved from the beginning, especially a high-level person with decision-making authority.

Diversity among participating stakeholders increases a CBC's ability to overcome external obstacles because it broadens the group's store of knowledge on matters both technical and pragmatic and increases the likelihood that someone in the group will know about additional sources of needed information. A diverse list of participants—particularly one that includes interest groups that are traditional rivals—lends considerable credibility to CBCs, which like to portray their efforts as integrating interests, not just representing a new interest group. That credibility can help attract funds and agency attention. As diversity increases, the total network of personal relationships of the collective expands, potentially including those with influence and the direct or indirect power to effect change.

A good example of the ability to overcome obstacles through the skillful inclusion of diverse stakeholders can be found in the collaborative resource management efforts in Wallowa County, Oregon. County leaders are committed to improving community well-being through a cooperative, inclusive atmosphere—not one of conflict as they have witnessed elsewhere. When the Nez Percé Tribe and the county commissioners led the salmon recovery plan efforts in the early 1990s, they learned the importance of reaching out to diverse interests and making them part of the process. As the timber industry faltered and harvest rates on Forest Service lands dropped in the mid-1990s, community leaders reached out broadly— to timber industry representatives, ranchers, agency personnel, tribal representatives, and environmentalists, among others—to seek solutions that all could agree on. They supported a new community-based nonprofit organization, Wallowa Resources, to help coordinate collaborative efforts and to develop and promote implementation of solutions to their natural resource issues. Because Wallowa Resources has taken great care to reach out to people in the county and to seek common ground from the start, resistance from powerful parties is not a major obstacle in the county. As they implemented projects such as river restoration, weed control, and fuels reduction in strategically chosen places and with people who could influence others, skeptics were slowly converted. Even a powerful environmental group that focuses on public lands preservation is among the team players. Wallowa Resources has not suffered from a lack of authority or legitimacy because it began at the behest of the county commissioners and continues with their full support. Moreover, the skillful founding director of Wallowa Resources was from a fourth-generation ranching family and had great personal credibility in the county and strong public stature beyond it.

Building Alliances and Networks

Many CBCs have discovered that joining forces with existing groups and individuals working on similar issues increases their power and effectiveness. Networks link collaborative group members to external parties and resources, connecting institutions across levels and scales, facilitating information flows and the identification of knowledge gaps, creating nodes of expertise, and mobilizing political support (Margerum 1999; Olsson, Folke, and Berkes 2004).

In the White Mountains Restoration case in Arizona, they call this phenomenon the "STP," the "same ten people." The same core group sits on the White Mountains stewardship contracting monitoring board, the multicounty Resource Advisory Committee, the Natural Resources Working Group (NRWG), and the Arizona Sustainable Forests Partnership. Many are also involved in statewide initiatives, such as the Governor's Healthy Forests Advisory Board and the Department of Commerce's Industries of the Future program. Groups in the White Mountains Restoration commonly credit each other for contributing to their collective success at implementing the largest long-term stewardship contract in the country. The NRWG played a key role in bringing environmental groups to the table and keeping them there through years of discussions of restoration goals and appropriate management and small demonstration projects in the Blue Ridge district. The Arizona Sustainable Forests Partnership brought the remnants of the local timber industry together and networked them to the point that local loggers and wood products manufacturers work closely together to coordinate wood supply and demand for particular types of wood. Increasingly, members of the NRWG and the Arizona Sustainable Forests Partnership have joined forces, to the extent that, according to one participant, now "we shake hands to work deals on resources or transportation."

Alliances and networks that link local groups at a national scale have also proved critical to the success of local collaborative efforts. A key informant related that the federal legislation about stewardship contracting her group had drafted was initially shot down because they lacked effective alliances with national-level interests:

> We were naive. We thought because local members of national groups agreed the national level would too. We had no contact with lobbyists and people like that who we now know are necessary . . . [but] once we surfaced [the draft legislation], other [groups] that we didn't know existed surfaced—we got to know them. [A national network] paid us to attend their annual meeting. I was invited to sit on the board of [another group]. We met many people. We hadn't known who our allies were. . . . Eventually, we got our input in to a pretty high level in the agency . . . now we have good working relationships at the regional and national level.

The next version of the legislation they proposed did pass.

Building Trust and Mutual Respect

Just as building trust internally among collaborative members is a hallmark of CBCs generally, many CBCs focus considerable effort on building trust within the local community and between the local community and others, such as federal agencies. A common strategy is to develop and maintain consistent outreach to nonparticipants, including critics, for example by keeping them on the mailing list, inviting them to make presentations to the group, taking them into the field to discuss management options, or involving them in monitoring. CBCs also often foster relationships with interest-group leaders and use those relationships to help win over skeptics. A common refrain is to "spend the time up-front," reaching out to skeptics, rather than risk "spending the time at the back end" when excluded groups or individuals challenge the CBC's efforts.

The Jobs and Biodiversity Coalition (JBC) in New Mexico regularly employs a multifaceted approach to defusing opposition to its forest restoration activities in the Gila National Forest. Before public input is solicited, for example as required by the National Environmental Policy Act, and before starting any activity in the forest, JBC members make a proactive effort to find out who might oppose their initiatives and invite that party to come to the table. If the skeptics decline to participate, JBC members try to elicit their concerns and figure out how to address them. Even if the resistant parties never come to group meetings, the JBC makes sure to keep them informed. The initial core group of the JBC included a district ranger, who ran interference for his group with the agency, and an environmentalist who enjoyed a high level of trust among his peers. Although local environmentalists may not trust the Forest Service and agency officials may not trust the environmental groups, both trust JBC, the intermediary, which is thereby able to overcome resistance to proposed projects.

Having Strong Leaders and Champions

In addition to influential and diverse participants, CBCs that successfully overcame external institutional obstacles tended to have strong, skilled group leaders who helped maintain the collaborative's focus and enthusiasm. For instance, a leader or neutral facilitator may act as a referee, tracking decisions and reminding the group of what has been said and done. Some successful CBCs practice shared leadership, in which different partners, both governmental and nongovernmental, take the lead at different times.

CBCs also can rely on influential champions who can influence major stakeholders outside the group. A champion may be just one person stepping forward, keeping in touch with major stakeholders, reassuring them about the collaboration, and letting them know what will be required of them. Opinion leaders can bring in and bring along whole categories of potential supporters who might not otherwise attend meetings or participate in projects.

In the White Mountains Restoration case in Arizona, several local champions who brought different interests to the table and kept them there also brought important contacts and resources to the overall effort. These individuals included agency leaders, local city and county elected officials, staff from the Cooperative Extension and the local Resource Conservation and Development Council, local forest-business owners, and local environmentalists. Local champions worked for years to build bridges and a working relationship among scientists, resource managers, and environmental groups in the region. As a result, local and regional environmentalists have been members of NRWG since its formation and ensure that environmental groups are comfortable accepting projects.

Bringing in New Resources

Expanding Knowledge Bases

A hallmark of many CBCs' process is mutual learning, in which the group invites and jointly examines information from a variety of sources and uses that information to inform its planning and decisions (see chapter 2). A key informant gave the following examples of CBCs gaining efficacy and options through expanding their knowledge base. One CBC learned how and when it could enter the National Environmental Policy Act process and influence decisions; it also researched the utility of local ordinances to address its environmental concerns. Another group addressed litigation (a court had found against their proposed action) by reeducating itself on options and finding some that fell outside the limitations imposed by the court's decision. Other examples of CBCs addressing obstacles by expanding their knowledge base include CBCs retrofitting old equipment to meet new resource conditions and forest restoration groups exploring new products and markets for materials from small-diameter timber formerly considered waste products.

In particular, many CBCs seek out the best available science on the issues they are addressing, a strategy that helps them overcome conflict and resistance from powerful parties. This knowledge also enables them to achieve better environmental outcomes (see chapter 2). For example, as a result of the participation of the Hoopa Tribe in the Trinity River restoration effort, the U.S. Fish and Wildlife Service introduced a new river-flow model that was better for reproducing salmon habitat than the one formerly used. That model was adopted and integrated into an adaptive assessment and monitoring program, and is now considered a model for dammed rivers in the West (Barinaga 1996).

Similarly, the Downeast Initiative in Maine is challenging the obstructive policies of regulatory agencies (the National Marine Fisheries Service and the New England Fisheries Council) by demonstrating that the policies are based on wrong and outdated science, namely, the use of single-species population models based on regional data to derive estimates for the whole range of that species (see chapter 2). The initiative aims to show scientifically that populations interact and display local distributions and variability. Thus, the use of policies developed at the regional scale creates barriers to ecosystem management. Moreover, these policies make it impossible for communities to have an effective role in protecting and managing local populations and spawning grounds. The solution is to rescale management. The Downeast Initiative seeks a policy alternative that would establish species-specific area management zones run by local management councils, within the larger framework of existing authorities and laws. Members employ a research-based strategy because, as one key informant averred, "Scientific capacity is what gives you the credibility to have a seat at the table. . . . Scientific capacity gives you the power . . . [it] gives the [government] the comfort-level to turn things over to local communities."

Expanding knowledge bases can change power relationships. When collaborative members learn the science that underlies environmental problems and proposed solutions, when they learn about the policy process, including where, when, and how they can influence difference, and when they learn the discourses that function in both arenas, then they have gained power.

Educating Agencies

CBCs also can gain power and overcome external obstacles by expanding the knowledge base of nonparticipant people and organizations, including government agencies. As noted above, collaborative members sometimes bring the latest science to the process. They may apply it in new ways of which agencies and others may not be aware. This benefits not only the collaborative but all involved in planning, decision making and implementation (often agency personnel), and the environment as well. Imperial and Hennessey (2000, 10) refer to collaboration itself as a strategy for "achieving environmental improvements," observing that "collaboration enhanced the management capacity of state and local institutions to solve environmental problems."

CBCs often work to build the capacity of resource management and regulatory agencies to engage in and support collaborative efforts as well. One important lesson that agencies have to be taught, a CBC participant in our study explained, is that collaboration does not preclude conflict; conflict is part of collaboration. Moore and Koontz (2003, 457) point out an indirect route to building agency capacity for collaboration, namely, through offering technical advice to decision makers and influencing their thinking, with the result that "away from the partnership, government officials' actions are altered because of new perspectives gained through partnership involvement."

Wallowa Resources participants frequently say that educating agencies—and reeducating when personnel are transferred—is one of their main tasks. They educate the agency not only about what is needed but also about what is possible, and what has already been done. They have, for example, helped the Forest Service understand stewardship contracting authorities and how they can be used locally to get projects done that benefit the forest and the community.

Obtaining Public Support

Another effective strategy that CBCs have used to increase their power is to court broad support among the public and elected officials. For example, CBCs sometimes educate the public or legislative bodies on environmental problems, their causes, and the solutions proposed by the collaborative, so that they will understand and be willing to modify their behavior and support policy changes. Some CBCs have been particularly strategic about educating elected officials, such as county commissioners and state legislatures, to seek their support. A related move involves linking the CBC's outreach to ongoing governmental or interest group efforts, such as land-use planning or economic development. The thrust of these approaches is to share information in such a way as to build common ground, forestall or manage conflict, and recruit supporters (Imperial and Hennessey 2000).

One example of a CBC that has effectively used this strategy is the Public Lands Partnership (PLP) in southeastern Colorado, which formed in 1992 to prepare the local community to participate effectively in a forthcoming forest plan revision and to preempt development of a local "wise use" group. The forest plan revision has been repeatedly delayed, but in the meantime, the PLP has helped initiate and foster important cross-jurisdictional land management projects, including the Uncomphagre Project, which involves habitat restoration treatments on thousands of acres using a habitat mosaic model that was jointly developed by four agencies. The PLP's primary strategy from the start has been education and information exchange—making sure people have the opportunity to make informed decisions. The group sponsors a well-attended evening discussion series on "hot topics" and hosts frequent field trips to new and proposed management project sites. PLP organizers say the education component is what keeps the community engaged in their efforts—the opportunity to learn about social and environmental issues of local concern in and of itself motivates participation. The education also provides a common basis of understanding, which allows people to work together on controversial and pressing issues.

Where the situation is not conflict-ridden, "obtaining public support" may simply mean cultivating good public relations. When a CBC has what one key informant referred to as "excellent P.R.," then local officials are eager to be seen as supporters and agency officials are inclined to attend field visits and promote it as a success story. The Elizabeth River Project, a nonprofit that leads collaborative efforts to restore a polluted industrial river in Virginia, is a case in point. A former director of the Environmental Protection Agency and a regional director have referred to the Elizabeth River Project as "a model." While this recognition and the local prestige of the project are no doubt predicated on its significant accomplishments, the organization also takes active measures to spread information about its cause, for example through recognition banquets, awards ceremonies, a user-friendly and informative website, educational materials, school programs, volunteer workdays, a logo, slogans, and mottos ("The goo must go," "Doin' right by the river"). Public and political support has translated into financial support for the Elizabeth River Project's work.

Contributing Funds and Human Resources

A sufficient and stable source of funding, adequate staffing, and access to information and expert support are all correlated with success. CBCs facilitate the pooling of resources from an array of public and private sources and have developed innovative ways to leverage and manage funds in order to achieve projects that no one partner could have funded alone. Nonprofit organizations, businesses, universities, and other institutional CBC members supply expertise and staff time that supplements, and at times substitutes for, the work of overextended agency personnel. CBCs also convene and coordinate volunteers from the community, some of whom are already expert and others who are happy to plant trees, do simple monitoring, or perform other activities that require a little training and a lot of enthusiasm.

The Elizabeth River Project was able to meet its financial needs in the face of a regional economic downturn by diversifying sources of income. Two of the more innovative funding sources include "River Stars" and a sediment remediation bank. "River Stars" is a program that provides incentives for corporations and others to undertake (and pay for) their own pollution cleanup and prevention, by assisting them and awarding them with a "river star." They are then committed to recruit and mentor another institution and are encouraged to publicize their achievements. By serving their own interests and following the "carrot," they advertise and expand the program—all by drawing on their own resources. The Elizabeth River Project also designed the first-ever sediment remediation bank, a facility along the lines of wetlands mitigation banks. If a new development or expansion is expected to disturb river-bottom sediment, the state Department of Environmental Quality and the Army Corps of Engineers can require developers to pay into the remediation bank as a condition for receiving permits. The Elizabeth River Project helped create an independent sister organization that holds and distribute funds for river cleanup projects. In addition, through its collaborative projects and via the agency of River Star organizations, the project has mustered thousands of volunteer hours in the service of restoring the river.

The Public Lands Partnership established a 501(c)(3), Unc/Com, to be its fiscal management agent. Unc/Com has proved an innovative tool for both pooling and leveraging funds. For example, when the PLP received a large grant from the Ford Foundation, it deposited that money in Unc/Com and used it to provide a match for various state and federal funds that would otherwise have been unavailable to the collaborative. The agencies have been able to "obligate" federal funds by depositing them in Unc/Com for future use, thereby avoiding the risk of unused funds being reallocated for emergency use (e.g., firefighting) or at the end of fiscal funding cycles. State and federal agencies have used the pooled resource source as further justification for ecosystem treatments across jurisdictional boundaries.

Transforming the Ground Rules
Seeking to Change Laws and Policies

One way to address obstacles to achieving environmental goals is to attack them head-on, as with the tactic of campaigning for reforms of policies or laws that obstruct the environmental work of collaboratives. CBCs can and have successfully lobbied for new legislation, from local zoning ordinances to national laws. In Trinity County, California, for example, local stakeholders succeeded several times in getting federal legislation passed that provided both restoration funding and collaborative oversight. A local county supervisor successfully pushed for the 1984 Trinity River Fish and Wildlife Management Act (PL 98-541), which funded restoration and monitoring activities, and formally established the Trinity River Task Force, which was composed of federal, state, local, and tribal government representatives and was later amended to include additional stakeholders. With urging from the Hoopa Tribe, whose reservation straddles the Trinity River, Congress passed the 1992 Central Valley Project Improvement Act (PL 102-575), which ordered and funded the completion of the Trinity River Flow

Evaluation Study and directed that its recommendations be implemented as long as the secretary of the interior and the Hoopa Valley Tribe both approve. As one key informant stated, the Trinity River "can become a national model of a restored river basin ecosystem below a federally-financed dam. It is the only river in the United States with such an opportunity because its recovery is written into law." It is written into law as a result of the efforts of local parties who insisted on a more collaborative approach.

CBCs have influenced specific provisions of new legislation and agency policies that affect not only their own locality but also communities nationwide. Our key informants identified a number of laws and policies that have been influenced by CBCs and which they find useful in their collaborative work. CBC leaders have helped to write language for stewardship contracting legislation that provides new contracting authorities useful for implementing multifaceted projects developed through collaboration. They have also helped to expand the community wildfire protection plan provisions in the Healthy Forests Restoration Act to allow projects developed through collaborative planning in rural communities. They worked to ensure that the restoration, utilization, and community assessment elements of the National Fire Plan had a collaborative framework. As part of a growing effort to institutionalize collaboration, CBC leaders have supported efforts to change job titles and performance measures to provide greater agency support for collaboration and to recognize and reward employees who collaborate

CBCs proactively identify and take advantage of existing laws and authorities. Once new regulations they lobbied for are in place, CBCs urge agencies to implement them, and often lead the way in showing them how it's done. At the local level, Born and Genskow (2000) have found that a particularly effective strategy used by watershed partnerships is to link their plans and activities to local governmental land-use planning authorities.

Instituting Accountability Mechanisms

CBCs have come up with creative ways to ensure that partners implement promised projects and decisions and thereafter provide some assurance that actions are having the desired result. One popular strategy is multiparty monitoring, which involves inviting those concerned about potential outcomes of an activity to help design a monitoring protocol to determine whether it is achieving its desired effect (see chapter 3). For example, the PLP's Burn Canyon Salvage restoration project withstood an appeal by an outside environmental group because of an extensive monitoring effort jointly developed by agencies and community members, including local environmental groups.

Whereas most collaboratives are not in a position to impose consequences for noncompliance or noncollaborative behavior, some have found
ways to provide positive incentives to encourage desired actions. Through
the River Star program mentioned earlier, the Elizabeth River Program
in Virginia has developed an innovative way to get resistant parties to collaborate, by providing incentives for industrial companies, government
agencies, and schools to contribute to pollution prevention and habitat restoration through the promise of being awarded a "star" in an annual public
ceremony. The three-level star is essentially an accountability mechanism.
The River Stars have to monitor their own progress and report to a peer
review panel. Another accountability mechanism is to use written agreements, which are morally, politically, and sometimes legally binding (Margerum 2001).

Mandating monitoring is one way of institutionalizing accountability. In
one of its early efforts, the Elizabeth River Project led a four-year collaborative process that generated a watershed action plan. The project effectively
changed state regulations when its watershed action plan was adopted in
its entirety by the state of Virginia. As a result, the state now mandates and
pays for part of the monitoring specified in the action plan.

Formalizing and Institutionalizing

Government agencies or officials, members of the public or interest groups,
all may question the standing and accountability of CBCs. Even agency
partners who wish to work with CBCs may have trouble justifying why
they should meet and come to accord with a self-appointed group of citizens. CBCs use formal agreements and legal recognition to increase their
legitimacy in the eyes of agencies, elected officials, funders, interest groups,
and the public. They may do this by employing or creating organizational
formality through mechanisms such as legislative charters, articles of in-
corporation, or nonprofit status. In other cases CBCs have set up working
agreements with agencies to carry out specific projects or types of work.
Such strategies serve to formalize and publicize a CBC's goals and rules of
operation, increasing the group's transparency, facilitating public accountability, and in some cases creating a mandate for the CBC to undertake
environmental improvement projects on public or private land. They may
also serve as models or guides to the fair process that CBC members desire
from other stakeholders.

Many CBCs are formalized through memoranda of understanding. Arizona's NRWG was formalized in a memorandum of understanding signed
by five eastern Arizona counties, the Arizona Game and Fish Department,
the U.S. Fish and Wildlife Service, the governor's office, supervisors of the

Apache-Sitgreaves, Tonto, and Coronado National Forests, and researchers from Northern Arizona University. This charter gives the group considerable legitimacy with stakeholders across the region, particularly government agencies and elected officials with significant control over resource management.

Staying Focused and Flexible

Staying Unstructured, ad hoc

Some collaboratives explicitly choose to remain informal in order to retain maximum flexibility and reinvent themselves as new people join and others drop out. Many wish to avoid being bogged down in endless meetings and procedural issues. Some feel they remain more accessible to community members, particularly volunteers (and the bureaucracy- or authority-phobic), when they do not define rules of membership or operation.

The Jobs and Biodiversity Coalition, a collaborative group that began as a loose association of formerly conflicting interests, has stayed unstructured and ad hoc and has resisted incorporating in any way or developing bylaws. Their attitude is, "Why change what's working?" While anyone is welcome to attend JBC meetings, they do not advertise them, because they believe traditional public meetings tend to bring out ideological stances and lead to more conflict, not progress. Their core membership—a group that can draw on years of personal experience to take what one informant called a "sophisticated approach" to working with the Forest Service—has remained consistent over time. By maintaining a loose, informal structure, JBC members say they are able to "stay focused on their goal—ecological restoration—without anyone else trying to take the group in a different direction."

When writing a charter for NRWG in eastern Arizona, "We kept it really simple," explains the group's coordinator. "We simply covered purpose and authority. The whole [charter] is [only] three pages long. [You can tell] it did not come from a university because it has a lot of brevity in it. The more complex you make the verbiage, the more complex it is to administer as you go along."

Flying under the Radar

Some CBCs avoid incurring resistance from outside groups and powerful interests by keeping a low profile and not advertising themselves. Instead of announcing that they intend to change resource management policies or practices, these groups focus their efforts on getting projects implemented and building support through informal communications. In parts where resource conflicts are very raw and where the appearance of any association between members of opposite camps could discredit all concerned, it may work best for a collaborative to keep its head down, get some practical and trust-building work done, and maintain a low profile.

One CBC participant described the path taken by the Ponderosa Pine Partnership in southwestern Colorado. This CBC was started by a small group of leaders getting agreements done on the ground, and it continues that way, gradually building up the number of acres of forest restored per year. It has avoided external obstacles by gaining neither national nor regional attention. It has not asked for any·special authority or more money after startup. It has not experienced conflict, has not "heard from environmentalists," and has more or less routinized its activities while managing to restore several thousand acres of forest.

The NRWG points to its explicit strategy of avoiding publicity as a reason for the success of the White Mountains Restoration effort. Looking at other collaborative efforts in the region, NRWG leaders see a correlation between opposition by powerful stakeholders, particularly environmental groups, and attention-getting tactics such as billing a CBC a "national model" or announcing plans for landscape-scale forest restoration. In contrast, the NRWG has worked unobtrusively to implement projects that all stakeholders agree should move forward. "We've kept everybody at the table, even [a litigious regional environmental group, because] we only work off what we have as common ground" and do not announce more grandiose plans.

Focusing on Projects; Using Demonstration Projects

Small or large, high profile or low, many groups have found that they achieve their environmental goals, build trust, and generate and maintain enthusiasm when they focus their efforts on on-the-ground projects. Particularly when a monitoring plan is in place and implemented, demonstration projects can allow skeptics to watch out for environmental damage and practitioners to experiment with how to achieve maximum beneficial effects under different circumstances.

The NRWG in Arizona's White Mountains selected the 17,000-acre Blue Ridge Ecosystem Analysis area on national forest land adjacent to town to demonstrate a variety of different forest restoration treatments. The group selected three distinct treatments: Forest Service silviculturalists designed the Forest Plan Treatment, forest ecologists at Northern Arizona University designed the Pre-settlement Restoration Treatment, and the Natural Processes Restoration Treatment followed guidelines proposed by representatives of the environmental community. A control area was also selected to aid comparison among the three treatments. Volunteers working with the Forest Service, the state Game and Fish Department, The Nature Conservancy, and the local Sierra Club chapter are monitoring all of the demonstration treatments. The demonstration plots serve a dual purpose: they illustrate the need for and beneficial results of forest restoration treatments for local residents, who often oppose forest thinning for aesthetic reasons, and they allow work to move forward despite conflict among key stakeholders—the agency, academic researchers, and the environmental community—each of which has strong opinions about the appropriate management needed to address forest health problems. By using demonstration plots and monitoring the results, the NRWG was able to implement projects while tangibly responding to critics' concerns about the potentially negative effects of forest restoration.

The JBC's mantra is, "Stay within the zone of agreement." That zone is found by focusing on an on-the-ground, in-the-forest, demonstration project. "Start with a project, not a grand plan, and leave aside other issues, about which you can agree to disagree." This way, even mutually antagonistic groups—environmentalists, the timber industry, and agency staff—can find common ground. As one member put it, "Once we got into the forest, it was astounding on how much we agreed on which trees should be cut. Immediately, our zone of agreement, and trust level, went up ten times!"

Implications for Practice: Recommendations for CBCs

This chapter has outlined fourteen different strategies CBCs have employed to tackle external institutional obstacles. The strategies are diverse, and their effectiveness in any given case will depend on a number of contextual factors. For example, the Downeast Initiative believes that attempting to educate fisheries agencies with entrenched views is ineffective. Armed with scientific and social welfare arguments, this group wants the existing system to be radically transformed and has chosen to transform the ground rules by attempting to change federal law. Furthermore, some of the strategies we have described are mutually exclusive. Flying under the radar, for example, may preclude self-advertising to obtain public support, and formalizing or institutionalizing may conflict with a desire to stay unstructured and ad hoc. Thus, the choice of strategy is clearly context dependent: a strategy that is effective in one case may go nowhere in another. Nonetheless, these fourteen strategies can be viewed as alternatives in a toolbox from which a CBC can select when confronted with external institutional obstacles.

We have classified the fourteen strategies into four overarching approaches to addressing obstacles of scale and power: (1) linking people effectively, (2) bringing in new resources, (3) transforming the ground rules, and (4) staying focused and flexible. The first set of strategies, linking people effectively, addresses challenges of scale. The second and third, bringing in new resources and transforming the ground rules, address power differentials. The fourth, staying focused and flexible, helps CBCs remain innovative and effective.

Addressing Scale

CBCs address challenges of scale by building linkages and networks that bridge multiple interests and reach from local to national spheres of influence. On closer examination of actual cases, it can sometimes be difficult to identify a single entity, "the collaborative," that is responsible for planning and taking action. Rather, what emerges is a process of collaboration in which individuals participate in multiple more and less formal associations with overlapping leadership and members (as in the "same ten people" phenomenon described above for the White Mountains Restoration project). In addition, over time, the forms collaboratives take evolve, with different forms best suited to taking on different challenges at different stages. For example, the Elizabeth River Project started out as "four people sitting around a table" and evolved into a nonprofit organization that fosters the formation of collaborative task forces to take on new local projects.

CBCs can help ward off resistance from powerful parties and address large-scale political and economic trends by building linkages to national organizations and policymakers. The local representatives of government agencies that sit on many CBCs can perform key bridging functions. Representatives can relate the perspectives of agencies and their constraints to the collaborative, and can also explain and advocate for the collaborative's proposals to their agency superiors.

Addressing Power Differentials

CBCs can address power differentials by transforming ground rules to gain legitimacy and create accountability, and by bringing to bear new resources, including new knowledge. CBCs can gain legitimacy and ensure accountability by instituting formal agreements, such as memoranda of understanding, charters, or legislative mandates. They also use informal mechanisms, such as multiparty monitoring and peer-reviewed incentive programs, to encourage compliance with environmentally friendly policies.

CBCs can shift the balance of power by changing the ground rules. They can do this by proposing and advocating new legislation and implementing regulations at any level of government. They can also do this by working with agency officials and teams from district to national levels to look at the ways in which bureaucratic procedures, staff training, and performance measures are posing obstacles for effective collaboration. In addition to the previously mentioned national policies they helped shape, the national impact of the work of collaboratives on ground rules may be seen in the Bush administration's Executive Order on Facilitation of Cooperative Conservation (White House, Office of the Press Secretary 2004) and the declaration by the former chief of the U.S. Forest Service that community-based stewardship is the future of federal forest management (Bosworth and Brown 2007).

Knowledge and money are both sources of power. To the extent that CBCs can contribute sources of funding and human resources to collaborative environmental management, they are more likely to influence its outcomes. To the extent that CBCs can contribute local knowledge, monitoring data, and "new science," they can participate more significantly in the adaptive management of the natural resources and environmental problems that concern them. CBCs also build support for their policies and projects by educating agencies, elected officials, and others who could either facilitate or block their implementation.

Innovation and Efficacy: Coming Up with Workable Solutions

Being proactive, flexible, and adaptive; solving problems; recognizing and acting on opportunities; thinking outside the box; finding new ways of doing business—these are the terms that informants used in describing what CBCs do best. These are not generally areas of strength for bureaucracies. Innovation, therefore, is something "localness" can contribute to the governmental responsibility to sustainable natural resource management and environmental protection on behalf of all citizens. CBCs come up with new solutions to previously intractable problems and help get projects implemented by focusing on projects within their "zone of agreement," avoiding overly bureaucratic structures and procedures, and not drawing unnecessary attention to themselves.

Implications for Policy: Recommendations for Government

CBCs can play key catalytic roles in creative problem solving and practical action to address certain environmental problems. They can propose alternatives to break gridlock and bring additional resources to the table to facilitate the planning and implementation of restoration activities. At the same time, the role of government agencies remains crucial in that collaboration. Government agents are key participants in collaborative processes owing to their authority, expertise, and resources. Government (for the most part federal government, when dealing with public lands) has a necessary role to play in funding collaboration and implementing collaborative agreements. Community-based collaboration cannot function outside the framework of national, state, and local law. If environmental laws are not enforced, then recalcitrant parties have no incentive to collaborate. Perhaps most important, collaboration cannot substitute for governmental responsibility in managing publicly owned national resources and regulating the environmental impacts of all parties in the public interest.

On the one hand, our research indicates that government poses among the most prevalent obstacles confronting CBCs, in the form of agency capacity and culture and obstructive laws and regulations. On the other, key informant and case study interviews repeatedly indicate that community members need strong government partners in crafting and implementing collaborative solutions, and that internal agency champions and ongoing support have been instrumental in achieving success. Budget and staffing cutbacks, however, have increasingly threatened the ability of agencies to play their part. For collaboration to yield fruitful outcomes, government resources must be devoted to providing agency staff the expertise, time, and support.

In sum, it is not so much the presence but the absence of government as an effective player that affects the ability of CBCs to achieve their environmental goals.

Implications for Research: Recommendations for Researchers

Our research indicates that CBCs can be innovative and catalytic forces for identifying and promoting actions to improve environmental health. They are limited, however, in their ability to address many of the most critical environmental problems, which are often associated with the external institutional obstacles we have identified. While it is of vital importance to understand how issues of scale and the distribution of power impede effective, equitable management of large-scale environmental problems, the research literature reviewed does not, in general, tackle these issues directly. This shortcoming may in part result from a failure to adequately explore power.

Applying different conceptions of power leads to different research questions, modes of analysis, policy implications, and practical recommendations. In one view, CBCs are composed of actors all subject to, but unequally positioned within, fields of power. That perspective prompts several questions. To what extent can members operate on a level playing field in assessing environmental problems, making management decisions, or implementing them? Might CBCs be able to subvert their lack of "disciplinary power" by exploring alternative courses of action that flow from other ways of knowing and valuing the environment, rather than settling on presumably value-neutral and science-based solutions (Foucault 1977)? If, by contrast, power is expressed as class domination or as control over access to resources, then researchers would look to see under what conditions collaboratives are able to shift control over access to resources to previously disadvantaged social groups. When do CBCs merely reproduce or mask the distribution of power and resources under the status quo? Can we see consequences of power and resource distribution in the form of changes in resource management? Research that further explores how issues of power and scale intersect with the scope and workings of CBCs would be a valuable addition to the literature.

Conclusions

CBCs draw many of their strengths from their localness. Among these strengths are local knowledge, a shared commitment to solving local environmental and economic problems, local multiplex relationships, and the capacity to innovate and respond flexibly and swiftly to incipient change. We set out to assess the capacity of CBCs to effect change in the face of supralocal challenges, namely, those that are externally imposed, or exceed the scale of collaboratives' influence, or are held in place by disproportionate power. To achieve this feat, CBCs must find a way to rise above the limits of their localness.

Burnout, frustration, and failure to achieve environmental goals in expected time frames are real in many CBCs and often result from conditions well beyond their initial sphere of influence. Yet our case studies provide reason for optimism that they can overcome the limits of scale and power to achieve their objectives and improve their environment. The seven cases we examined overcame significant power disparities and large-scale economic challenges. Almost all the CBCs we reviewed that successfully surmounted external challenges engaged in intensive networking and communication, displayed a willingness to learn and a capacity for negotiation, and were tenacious in reaching out to educate others, including opponents. Some CBCs combined strategies to navigate around obstacles by learning the details of laws and regulations, identifying zones of agreement, and finding ways they could work toward their goals without engendering op-position. Still others faced obstacles of power and scale head-on by building alliances with powerful entities, drafting and lobbying for policy changes, raising funds, and providing services to push through opposition. Signifi-cantly, by educating themselves and demanding to be heard, CBCs them-selves have become important players in scientific and policy arenas.

The contributions made by CBCs include not only innovating and imple-menting locally adapted solutions to environmental problems but also ac-tions that reverberate at higher scales: proposing new laws and regulations and improving existing ones; reforming agency bureaucracies; generating new data and knowledge; educating agency leaders and staff, politicians, and the public; providing incentives and tracking accountability; and build-ing supportive alliances, networks, and publics. Thus, the efforts of CBCs to overcome externally imposed barriers to environmental change may, over time, have a larger and wider impact than the relatively local environ-mental improvements they set out to achieve.

The fact of such successes, however, does not justify the retreat of the state. Collaboration cannot substitute for governmental responsibility in regulating environmental impacts and managing publicly owned national resources. With proper resources, training, and incentives, government agencies that have in the past stood in the way or simply stood aside can step up to become effective partners with CBCs in achieving environmen-tal goals for the public good.

References

Barinaga, M. 1996. "A Recipe for River Recovery?" *Science* 273 (5282): 1648–50.

Belden Russonello and Stewart Research and Communications. 2001. *Collaborative Pro-cess: Better Outcomes for All of Us: Communications Recommendations and Analysis of 54 Interviews with Decision Makers on Environmental Issues in the Western U.S.* Washing-ton, DC: Emily Hall Tremaine Foundation and Partners.

Born, S. M., and K. D. Genskow. 2000. "The Watershed Approach: An Empirical As-sessment of Innovation in Environmental Management." *In Learning from Innova-tions in Environmental Protection. Environment.gov* Research Papers, Report no. 00-12. Washington, DC: National Academy of Public Administration.

Bosworth, D., and H. Brown. 2007. "After the Timber Wars: Community-based Stew-ardship." *Journal of Forestry* 104 (July–August): 271–73.

Carr, D. S., S. W. Selin, and M. A. Schuett. 1998. "Managing Public Forests: Under-standing the Role of Collaborative Planning." *Environmental Management* 22 (5): 767–76.

Cestero, B. 1999. *Beyond the Hundredth Meeting: A Field Guide to Collaborative Conserva-tion on the West's Public Lands.* Tuscon, AZ: Sonoran Institute.

Coughlin, C. W., M. L. Hoben, D. W. Manskopf, and S. W. Quesada. 1999. *A Systematic*

Assessment of Collaborative Resource Management Partnerships. Ann Arbor: University of Michigan, School of Natural Resources and Environment.

Curtis, A., B. Shindler, and A. Wright. 2002. "Sustaining Local Watershed Initiatives: Lessons from Landcare and Watershed Councils." *Journal of the American Water Resources Association* 38 (5): 1207–16.

Dopplet, B., C. Shinn, and D. Johnson. 2002. "Review of USDA Forest Service Community-Based Watershed Restoration Partnerships." Report prepared for U.S. Department of Agriculture, Forest Service. September. Mark O. Hatfield School of Government. http://www.fs.fed.us/largewatershedprojects/DoppeltReport/index.html.

Foucault, M. 1977. *Discipline and Punish: The Birth of the Prison.* New York: Pantheon Books.

Gray, B. 1989. *Collaborating: Finding Common Ground for Multi-party Problems.* San Francisco, CA: Jossey-Bass.

Hays, S. P. 1959. *Conservation and the Gospel of Efficiency: The Progressive Conservation Movement, 1890–1920.* New York: Anthem.

Huntington, C. W., and S. Sommarstrom 2000. *An Evaluation of Selected Watershed Councils in the Pacific Northwest and Northern California.* Eugene, OR: Trout Unlimited and the Pacific Rivers Council.

Imperial, Mark T., and T. Hennessey. 2000. *Environmental Governance in Watersheds: The Importance of Collaboration to Institutional Performance. Learning from Innovations in Environmental Protection.* Research Paper no. 18. Washington, DC: National Academy of Public Administration. http://www.napawash.org/pc_economy_environment/epafile08.pdf.

Johnson, L. J., D. Zorn, et al. 2003. "Stakeholders' Views of Factors That Impact Successful Interagency Collaboration." *Exceptional Children* 69 (2): 195–209.

Kenney, D. S. 2000. *Arguing about Consensus: Examining the Case against Western Watershed Initiatives and Other Collaborative Groups Active in Natural Resources Management.* Boulder: University of Colorado School of Law, Natural Resources Law Center.

Kenney, D. S., S. T. McAllister, W. H. Caile, and J. S. Peckham. 2000. *The New Watershed Source Book: A Directory and Review of Watershed Initiatives in the Western United States.* Boulder: University of Colorado School of Law, Natural Resources Law Center. http://www.colorado.edu/law/centers/nrlc/publications/watershed.htm.

Koontz, T. M., T. A. Steelman, J. Carmin, K. Smith Korfmacher, C. Moseley, and C. W. Thomas. 2004. *Collaborative Environmental Management: What Role for Government?* Washington, DC: Resources for the Future Press.

Leach, W. D., and N. W. Pelkey. 2001. "Making Watershed Partnerships Work: A Review of the Empirical Literature." *Journal of Water Resources Planning and Management* 127 (6): 378–85.

Lubell, M. 2004. "Resolving Conflict and Building Cooperation in the National Estuary Program." *Environmental Management* 33 (5): 677–91.

Margerum, R. D. 1999. "Integrated Environmental Management: The Foundations for Successful Practice." *Environmental Management* 24 (2): 151–66.

———. 2001. "Organizational Commitment to Integrated and Collaborative Management: Matching Strategies to Constraints." *Environmental Management* 28 (4): 421–31.

McDermott, M. H., A. Moote, and C. Danks. 2006. "How Community-based Collaboratives Overcome External Institutional Barriers to Achieving Their Environmental Goals." *CBCRC Journal,* Winter. http://www.cbcrc.org/2005nationalconf/docs/McD_Moote_Danks.pdf.

Moore, E. A., and T. M. Koontz. 2003. "A Typology of Collaborative Watershed Groups: Citizen-based, Agency-based, and Mixed Partnerships." *Society and Natural Resources* 16:451–60.

Moote, A., and D. Becker, eds. 2003. *Exploring Barriers to Collaborative Forestry.* Flagstaff, AZ: Ecological Restoration Institute.

Olsson, P., C. Folke, and F. Berkes. 2004. "Adaptive Comanagement for Building Resilience in Social-ecological Systems." *Environmental Management* 34 (1): 75–90.

Sabatier, P. A., W. Focht, M. Lubell, Z. Trachtenberg, A. Vedlitz, and M. Matlock. 2005. *Swimming Upstream: Collaborative Approaches to Watershed Management.* Cambridge, MA: MIT Press.

Sabatier, P. A., J. Quinn, N. Pelkey, and W. Leach. 2002. *When Do Stakeholder Negotiations Work? A Multiple Lens Analysis of Watershed Restorations in California and Washington. Final Report to U.S. Environmental Protection Agency.* Washington, DC: EPA, National Center for Environmental Research.

Schuett, M. A., S. W. Selin, and D. S. Carr. 2001. "Making It Work: Keys to Successful Collaboration in Natural Resource Management." *Environmental Management* 27:587–93.

Takahashi, L. M. and G. Smutny. 2001. "Collaboration among Small, Community-based Organizations: Strategies and Challenges in Turbulent Environments." *Journal of Planning Education and Research* 21:141–53.

White House, Office of the Press Secretary. 2004. *Executive Order: Facilitation of Cooperative Conservation.* http://georgewbush-whitehouse.archives.gov/news/releases/2004/08/20040826-11.html.

Wondolleck, J. M., and S. L. Yaffee. 2000. *Making Collaboration Work: Lessons from Innovation in Natural Resource Management.* Washington, DC: Island Press.

5

Collaborative Governance
Integrating Institutions, Communities, and People

Gregg B. Walker and Susan L. Senecah

Angry as one may be at what heedless men have done and still do to a noble habitat, one cannot be pessimistic about the West. This is the native home of hope. When it fully learns that cooperation, not rugged individualism, is the quality of what most characterizes and preserves it, then it will have achieved itself and outlived its origins. Then it has a chance to create a society to match its scenery.

—Wallace Stegner, *The Sound of Mountain Water*

The cases introduced in previous chapters suggest the important role communities play in place-based collaborations concerned with natural resource management and environmental policy issues. From the Coos Watershed Association (highlighted in chapter 3) to the Malpai Borderlands Group in Arizona and New Mexico (featured in chapter 2) to the Elizabeth River Project in Virginia (described in chapter 4), these cases share a common and important attribute. Each is community-driven, led by local stakeholders as individuals and as members of local organizations (or local branches of national nonprofit organizations).

These community-based collaborative (CBC) success stories exemplify what Koontz and colleagues (2004) refer to as collaborations that are "citizen-driven" or "non-profit facilitated." Yet often looming over these CBC situations is an eight-hundred-pound gorilla, a government agency that holds significant decision authority on the matters that CBCs address. For example, members of the Northwest Colorado Stewardship (NWCOS) collaborative that Fernández-Giménez and Ballard feature in chapter 3 deal with issues and generate ideas about public lands managed by the U.S. Department of the Interior–Bureau of Land Management (BLM). As the authority for decisions on the Northwest Colorado federal lands it manages, the BLM determines the kinds of decisions made on the matters that concern NWCOS.

While many CBCs are community-driven or facilitated by nonprofit organizations, other CBC efforts rely substantially on the actions of a government agency. We have worked with many federal and state agencies over the past fifteen years, particularly on comprehensive planning projects. We have observed in our work with federal agencies that institutional structures play powerful roles in making or breaking collaborative processes and creating new governance frameworks in the natural resource management and environmental policy arenas. In addition to drawing on the literature, this chapter presents and analyzes a number of concepts and practices that we have learned and applied in our own work with institutions engaged in collaborative community efforts.

We initially address collaborative governance. Subsequently we discuss a number of critical elements of government institutions that must be recognized and attended to as institutions take more leadership to create collaborative governance. These elements include roles, leadership, and constraints for collaborative governance and community-based work.

Government institutions are often major players within CBC efforts. Government agencies are often the decision authority in natural resource management situations. They may also convene, lead, or sponsor CBC efforts. Finally, they may enact, support, or thwart whatever the CBC group recommends. Thus, to understand what CBCs can accomplish, it is critical to understand the roles that individuals and individuals within agencies play and the relationships of agencies to CBCs.

Collaborative Governance: The Context

Public officials, civic leaders, business leaders, nonprofit organizations, and the public are increasingly turning to collaborative processes to help them improve or find solutions to complex and potentially contentious issues across a wide range of natural resource and environmental concerns (Crocker et al. 1996; Weber 1998a, 1998b). These new governance networks will affect how decisions are made and implemented for the next twenty years (Bingham and O'Leary 2008). We and other researchers see the participatory revolution having an impact on institutions of all kinds, from local to global government agencies, nonprofit organizations, advocacy groups, business and industry, and citizen groups.

A 2005 White House conference promoting and directing collaborative approaches illustrates the appeal and legitimacy of community-based collaboration. In August 2005, 1,200 people met in St. Louis to participate in the White House Conference on Cooperative Conservation, directed by the Bush administration. The conference recognized the pivotal role that communities play in conserving natural resources and places. From this conference, in November 2005 the White House released a new set of federal environmental conflict resolution principles that reflected the key characteristics of CBCs and emphasized accountability and performance. This conference illustrated federal government endorsement and support for collaborative processes. It highlighted the opportunities, resources, and legitimacy of CBCs and raised issues to address (Office of Management and Budget and President's Council on Environmental Quality 2005).

These institutional and organizational issues can be difficult whether operating in municipal to global governance structures. The difficulties are inherent in decision-making contexts that fluctuate and are influenced by political forces. Further, many constraints or obstacles to community-based collaboration are embedded in the checks and balances of the U.S. democratic public policy process. The legislative branch makes laws, which the executive branch (agencies) creates rules and regulations to enact. When these laws and regulations reach communities for implementation, individuals or groups in the community may express their concerns through the judicial branch or appeal to legislators to change the law, appeal to their elected officials to change their decision, or try to amend the agency regulations. This dance may take many forms and last a long time as individuals and groups pursue their interests across local, state, and federal levels and across legislative-administrative and executive-judicial jurisdictions.

Therefore, as inspiring as the formal calls for more collaborative processes are, they do not automatically transform institutions. Changing government institutions is difficult, even if all the actors know how to engage in collaborative processes. Furthermore, that transformation has to emerge out of the contentious, suspicious, frustrating, expensive, distrustful legacies that have driven stakeholders to create CBCs in the first place. Thus, the White House Conference project, like so many other reports about and critiques of traditional public involvement and decision-making processes, produced a compilation of hundreds of successful and inspiring cases, but also a long list of needs and directions to support multiparty collaborative processes.

This context draws attention to an important distinction that Koontz and colleagues make in their insightful book, *Collaborative Environmental Management: What Role for Government?* (2004). Koontz and colleagues emphasize that in order to understand natural resources and environmental policy collaborations, it is first necessary to understand the roles of government, in all forms and at all levels. They begin their discussion of government roles by drawing an important distinction that provides a focus for this chapter: government as institution and government as actor. Koontz and colleagues explain that "governmental institutions are the structures, processes, rules, and norms of the administrative state." "Governmental actors," they note, "are the flesh-and-blood employees, elected officials, and other people in government who take action within the context of institutions." They observe that "governmental actors and institutions, together or separately, constitute governmental roles in a particular collaborative effort" (ibid., 22).

In this chapter, we draw on a number of useful reviews, research reports, and case compilations. These are referenced at the end of the chapter. In particular, as part of the 2005 White House Conference on Cooperative Conservation, conference planners assembled illustrations of community collaboration. The work, *Faces and Places of Cooperative Conservation: Profiles in Citizen Stewardship* (Hess and Michaels 2005), highlights more than eight hundred cases from across the United States. We recommend this compilation for examples of collaborative governance.

Collaborative Governance

Writing in the *Christian Science Monitor,* former governors Geringer of Wyoming and Kitzhaber of Oregon advocate for "collaborative governance" as a way to elevate civil discourse in the United States. They explain that collaborative governance means "getting everyone—every agency, citizen, community—with a stake in a particular issue to come together to talk about what ought to be done" (Geringer and Kitzhaber 2004, 1). They note that "collaborative governance takes as its starting point that truly working together creates better solutions that more people can live with" (ibid.).

Governors Geringer and Kitzhaber acknowledge that collaborative governance is not easy and requires committed leadership. To rebuild the trust that leaders need in order to be effective, we must step out of the hearing rooms and into schools, universities, libraries, and even the town square. This collaborative governance requires leaders to do certain things:

- Identify and raise issues that can be resolved only through people working together.
- Create an opportunity and place for people to come together and address issues.
- Use clear, commonsense language to talk about possible solutions without predetermining the outcome.
- Conduct public negotiations that integrate contending interests.

- Create agreements about what we're willing to do and under what conditions, and then take action. (ibid., 2)

Governance is fundamentally about the exercise of power in making decisions in the public sphere (Blaney 2003). Collaborative governance emphasizes shared power and joint decision making. As Blaney explains, collaborative governance "crosses jurisdictional boundaries and builds its agenda and actions through consensus." It "includes all involved parties, as equals, in the decision making process." He adds that "the essential condition of collaborative governance is the creation and maintenance of trust" (1). According to the Policy Consensus Initiative and the National Policy Consensus Center (PCI/NPCC), governance "is the process by which public ends and means are identified, agreed upon, and pursued." In contrast, government "relates to the specific jurisdiction in which authority is exercised." Governance, the PCI/NPCC notes, "is a broader term and encompasses both formal and informal systems of relationships and networks for decision making and problem solving" (PCI/NPCC 2009).

Collaborative governance requires three elements: (1) a sponsor to initiate and provide support, such as an agency, foundation, civic organization, or public-private coalition; (2) a convener or leader with the power to bring diverse parties together to work on common problems, such as elected state or local officials and civic leaders in education, religion, business, and cultural affairs; and (3) a neutral forum, that is, an impartial organization or venue that provides for good process management (Carlson 2008; PCI/NPCC 2009). In the environmental policy arena, collaborative governance creates a "civic square" in which discourse, science, place, and space are featured (Walker 2009).

Some scholars have advocated for "adaptive governance," a concept related somewhat to collaborative governance (Brunner et al. 2005; Scholz and Stiftel 2005b). Drawing on work in adaptive management, Scholz and Stiftel explain that adaptive governance "involves the evolution of new governance institutions capable of generating long-term, sustainable policy solutions to wicked problems through coordinated efforts involving previously independent systems of users, knowledge, authorities, and organized interests" (2005b, 5).

Scholz and Stiftel (2005a, 2005b) present five challenges to adaptive governance: (1) representation (who should be involved; include all affected interests), (2) decision process design (ways for authorities and stakeholders to reach sound agreements; methods for reaching consensus), (3) scientific learning (policymakers need methods for developing and using knowledge effectively; adaptive management; research and monitoring program),

(4) public learning (translate science into public understanding; methods for resource users and relevant publics to generate common understanding as basis for consensus; convince all parties to support and comply with agreements), and (5) problem responsiveness (decisions that achieve natural resource management goals, including sustainability, equity, and efficiency; improvement over the status quo).

On its surface, Scholz and Stiftel's view of adaptive governance retains some features of conventional natural resource management, such as giving scientific and technical knowledge privileged status and emphasizing the need to convince parties that a particular decision is best. Still, adaptive governance does share with collaborative governance the importance of involving stakeholders meaningfully in the decision development process. As Brunner and colleagues (2005) note, "adaptive governance relies on open decision-making processes recognizing multiple interests, community-based initiatives, and an integrative science in addition to traditional science" (see also Brunner et al. 2002).

Does collaborative (or adaptive) governance in community-based collaborations start with government, with community, or with both? The work of Koontz and colleagues (2004) indicates that government agencies or communities can be initiators. Regardless of the roots of CBC efforts, institutions of various forms play important roles.

Recognizing and Adapting Institutional and Individual Roles

Perhaps surprisingly, there are very few comprehensive discussions of agency or institutional roles in the natural resources management and environmental policy arenas. The many case study accounts of community-based ecosystem management that have been published (for examples, see Wondolleck and Yaffee 2000; Weber 2003; Hess and Michaels 2005) provide insights into institutional and individual roles, but not systematic evaluations.

Still, some scholarship discusses roles in collaborative processes. Representative of the group dynamics literature, Straus (2002) highlights the roles of leader, group member, facilitator, and recorder. He asserts that "when the roles in small-group problem solving are explicit and differentiated, collaboration is likely to be more effective" (115). Focusing on policy decision making, Koontz and colleagues (2004) address the roles of government in collaborative environmental management. They identify three: government as follower, encourager, and leader. They note that these roles can be enacted by institutions as well as by the actors who represent those institutions. In a related essay, Moore and Koontz (2003) emphasize the global role of partner. Based on their examination of sixty-four watershed groups in Ohio, Moore and Koontz propose three distinct partnership types: citizen-based, agency-based, and mixed. Although not an explicit topic in his work, Fischer (2000) explores the role of expert and differentiates professional expertise, technical expertise, specialized citizen expertise, and local knowledge expertise. More recently, the Red Lodge Clearinghouse (2005) has presented a discussion of key roles in a public lands planning process.

Wondolleck and Ryan (1999) offer the most comprehensive discussion of agency roles. They examine sixty-five cases of federal-level natural resource management and environmental regulation collaborations. Wondolleck and Ryan note that these cases reflect a shift in the way in which agencies made decisions: from conventional administrative actions to multi-stakeholder collaboration. As they have explored this change, Wondolleck and Ryan (1999, 118) ask:

> But how should agency participants in collaborative negotiation processes juggle the reality that they are the ultimate decision-making authority with the consensus-seeking premise of the collaborative interaction? After decades of being cast in a comfortable role—where expectations were clear, procedures were well-defined, and decisions were sufficiently cloaked in the mantle of agency expertise and professional judgment—the tide has now turned upon these decision makers. What additional "hats" are now needed in their procedural wardrobe in order to be effective in a collaborative context that dramatically differs from their role and context of old?

As a result of their review of cases, Wondolleck and Ryan propose three significant roles that agency participants enact in natural resource management collaborations. "The experiences of agency participants in these different settings suggest a new conception of agency behavior and administrative roles in an era of collaborative decision making," they write, "one merging the distinct yet essential roles of *leader, partner* and *stakeholder*" (121, emphasis theirs).

Wondolleck and Ryan's conceptual framework does not explicitly include the roles of advocate, technical expert/information provider, or facilitator. They explain that

> agency representatives who participated in a peripheral manner (for example, serving solely in an oversight capacity or providing only technical data and expertise) were far less effective in guiding the process to a

mutually acceptable and implementable agreement. Furthermore, and contrary to conventional wisdom, the *facilitator* hat was not found to be an appropriate piece of the agency representative's wardrobe and, when worn, was often at significant cost. (121)

Regarding the role of leader, Wondolleck and Ryan explain that "the leadership of the agency participant is fundamentally different" from the leadership other parties may provide "and more central to the process because of their distinct decision-making authority" (121). In agency- or institution-initiated cases (Koontz et al. 2004), Wondolleck and Ryan claim that "the agency is the party that provides the opportunity for negotiations to occur in a meaningful manner; moreover, the agency's presence and authority gives legitimacy to the collaborative process" (121).

In the sixty-five cases reviewed, Wondolleck and Ryan note that "leadership was either provided, or clearly needed, in three different realms: first, leadership about *the process;* second, leadership about *the issues under discussion;* and, finally, leadership about *the decisions* to be made" (121, emphasis theirs). Process leadership includes convening the collaborative effort and setting a positive atmosphere for collaboration, issues leadership emphasizes setting the agenda and framing the discussion, and decision leadership draws attention to decision authority and implementation.

The role of partner, Wondolleck and Ryan note, is difficult for agencies to enact. "Being a partner was a uniquely challenging role for agency participants in the collaborative processes studied," they write, "as it was the role that was least consistent with traditional agency procedures" (124). The role of partner, they surmise, stresses sharing a problem, interest, or opportunity in common with others, and a willingness to work with others to solve that problem or share a vision is needed. Partners are open-minded and flexible in approach, willing to listen, able to teach and be taught, and respectful of other perspectives (123–24; see also Ryan 2001).

Wondolleck and Ryan (1999, 127) differentiate the third role they identify, stakeholder, from the partner role:

In contrast to partners who acknowledge the "we" dimension of the relationship, a stakeholder recognizes the "me" component of the problem and solution. Effective stakeholders are clear about their own interests, how these interests are similar to or different from those of the other stakeholders, and who within the organization can effectively articulate these interests and persuasively advocate on their behalf. Moreover, stakeholders understand their priorities within these interests and where tradeoffs might acceptably be made. Stakeholders are prepared, ready with persuasive information, data and other resources that can help educate and influence others so that their own interests will be acted upon.

As stakeholders, agency participants in a collaborative process communicate the interests of their organization. "To be effective stakeholders," Wondolleck and Ryan report, "agency participants must be clear about their range of interests and positions before entering the negotiations" (127). Enacting the stakeholder role is most effective when it includes "firm flexibility" (Pruitt 1983), that is, firmness about objectives and flexibility about the means to achieve those objectives (Wondolleck and Ryan 1999, 127). Wondolleck and Ryan caution that enactment of the stakeholder role can be perceived negatively by other parties in the collaborative effort. Transparency in the stakeholder role is therefore essential.

This last observation speaks to something we have noticed in CBC projects: the role a party wants to assume may not be a role other parties will accept. In other words, roles are enacted, roles are perceived, and roles are negotiated.

Based on their review of the public policy decision-making literature (including case studies) and fieldwork, Daniels and Walker (2001, 181–82) have identified a variety of roles that parties may enact in a CBC process. Each role that a party enacts in a given natural resources management or environmental policy situation will influence that party's way of assessing and understanding the situation. Common roles include the following:

Participant: This party has an interest in the situation but no strong positions. A participant wants to be involved in the situation but is not a primary voice for a particular point of view or outcome.

Advocate: This party holds a strong position on one or more of the major issues. An advocate is generally a primary stakeholder who is prepared to support a specific policy decision.

Representative: This party participates in or advocates on behalf of a group or organization. The representative may or may not have decision authority from the party that she or he represents.

Decision maker: This party has the authority to make and implement a decision. The decision maker establishes decision parameters and decision space.

Information provider: This party provides data or information pertaining to issues in the conflict situation. The information provider may see himself or herself as a "technical expert" or important source of local knowledge.

Initiator: This party identifies the need for a process. The initiator may then become a convener or sponsor or seek parties to fulfill these roles.

Sponsor: This party provides public support for the process. A sponsor may simply lend its name to the process or may also provide resources (money, a site, supplies, speaker, etc.).

Convener: This party brings parties together and provides a venue. The convener may also participate in the process design.

Designer: This party designs decision-related processes appropriate for the conflict situation at hand.

Facilitator: This party guides the process in an impartial manner. The facilitator may be internal to the situation (e.g., a member of an involved organization) or may be external (e.g., a consultant).

Evaluator: This party evaluates whatever processes may be employed for working through the conflict situation.

Both Wondolleck and Ryan's and Daniels and Walker's role categories apply to the individual or actor in an ecosystem management situation. In contrast, the roles of follower, encourager, and leader identified by Koontz and colleagues are assigned principally to government institutions. Taken together, the work of Wondolleck and Ryan, Koontz and colleagues, and Walker and Daniels suggests a community-based collaboration roles typology. The typology associates roles with institutions, communities, and individuals or actors. Although one could argue that all roles apply to institutions, communities, and individuals, we have indicated in this chapter where we think these roles primarily apply. The role categories are not mutually exclusive but can be defined distinctly.

When one considers this or some other conceptualization of roles in community-based ecosystem management, four points stand out. First, roles can be viewed as "macro" or "micro." A macro-role is one that is enacted broadly, generally by an institution, across a set of similar collaborative efforts or across the entire scope of a collaborative group or project. A microrole is one displayed most often by an individual actor, community, or institution specific to a project, a community group, or place, such as local officials functioning as part of a watershed group (Webler et al. 2003).

For example, the BLM's Cooperative Conservation Initiative features both macro- and micro-roles. The initiative "was a new initiative in President Bush's 2003 budget request to Congress to remove barriers to citizen participation in the stewardship of our natural resources and to help people take conservation into their own hands by undertaking projects at the local level. Projects must seek to achieve the actual restoration of natural resources and/or the establishment or expansion of habitat for wildlife. Funding must be matched through new cash, materials, or in-kind service" (www.blm.gov). Through this program, the BLM plays the macro-roles of funder and sponsor. BLM staff, as actors on behalf of the institution, may be information providers, representatives, and decision makers.

Roles are understood in different ways in a decision-making or conflict resolution situation. Institutions, communities, and actors may desire to play a particular role, only to discover that other parties do not accept that role and expect a different one. Roles are constructed and enacted, but their acceptance depends on the expectations and perceptions of others. For example, a member of a government agency may offer to serve as facilitator of a community-based collaboration. Depending on how that institution is perceived in the community, that person may or may not be viewed as fair and impartial, attributes that are essential to a facilitator's credibility and effectiveness. Similarly, a university scientist may seek the role of information provider, but some stakeholder might have questions about the appropriateness of that role. Consequently, stakeholders in a collaborative effort may want to conduct preliminary (and periodic) role assessments of their own roles and the roles of fellow stakeholders. A preliminary role assessment could be conducted using the framework outlined here.

Finally, roles are social constructions, and as such can be negotiated. The social construction view regards interaction as a process to create shared meaning and understanding (Daniels and Walker 2001). In terms of roles, parties assign meanings and related role labels to the verbal and nonverbal actions of others. They engage in verbal and nonverbal behavior consistent with the role they want to enact, hoping that others will accept them in that role.

The meanings assigned to behaviors observed draw on one's knowledge and experience. When enacted role and perceived role differ, parties can negotiate meanings and interpretations of the roles desired or expected. Roles are not enacted in isolation; actions occur within relationships, groups, and communities. Our communication is directed at others or affects others and is interpreted by others. Through communication interaction about roles (perhaps as part of a commitment to collaboration compact), parties can learn from one another as they coordinate their meanings and interpretations of roles. In doing so, they can negotiate the roles they desire and expect in order to gain legitimacy and voice (Senecah 2004).

Fostering and Building Internal and External Institutional Capacity for Collaboration

Government institutions often seek to achieve measurable objectives to address technical, scientific, economic, ecological, or even political outcomes. For example, local to national governmental institutions are typically bound to hierarchical, command-and-control management styles. Citizen-based institutions are typically looser, but as a result may be characterized by fractious leadership struggles or a weak decision-making structure. As the regulated community, business and industry groups are typically most interested in a decision's impact on their profitability and subsequent stock value. Nonprofit organizations place their highest priority on attracting and maintaining membership and funding to sustain their mission. Institutions involved in CBCs represent a range of objectives, but also a range of cultures and management styles, many of which are not role models for collaborative behavior. Not every process calling itself collaborative is what Booher (2004) labels authentic.

Command-and-control and coercive styles of management applied to collaborative processes may produce what Booher (2004) calls counterfeit processes. Saxton (2005) denotes these as false participation, marked by leadership that unwittingly engages in a top-down hierarchical approach when managing staff and thus brings that style to "collaborative" processes, and expects staff to do the same.

As "pracademics," we not only study collaborative processes, we design and guide them. On a recent project we met with three members of an agency planning team who asked us to conduct a collaborative learning project as part of an agency planning effort. We were impressed with the three staff members' commitment to working collaboratively and innovatively with stakeholders and communities. The three planners interacted well and exhibited mutual respect, indicative of shared leadership.

Although the three planners may have been leading the project of which we were a part, they reported to the head of the local agency office. As part of this project, we met periodically with this local agency senior administrator, the three staff members' supervisor. He told us about his experience with collaboration at other agency locations. The administrator explained that much of what we were teaching in a staff training program he had heard before and many of the activities we featured in community workshops he had experienced before. He pointed out that he was a champion of collaboration and supported our collaborative learning project with his agency.

While this administrator talked positively about collaboration (and we believe was sincere and well-intended in doing so), his actions communicated something else. Both his style and his behavior communicated command and control to staff as well as to the involved citizens. It stymied some staff members' ability to take risks and engage authentically. For several key citizens, it clouded their full investment in the potential of the process.

Certainly, no one in a supervisory position escapes criticism, nor is leadership an easy role to enact. Still, effective leadership is essential to a successful collaborative effort. Chrislip and Larson (1994) call such a leadership approach "collaborative leadership." They explain that "the role of leadership in collaboration is to engage others by designing constructive processes for working together, convene appropriate stakeholders, and facilitate and sustain their interaction" (127). Chrislip and Larson differentiate collaborative leadership from tactical (or heroic) leadership and positional (or hierarchical) leadership. They clarify that collaborative leadership is a "different kind of leadership" through which leaders

> promote and safeguard the collaborative process rather than take unilateral, decisive action. The power of position is of little help in this world of peers, nor are the traditional hierarchical, political, and confrontational models of leadership. Those who lead collaborative efforts—transforming, facilitative, "servant" leaders—rely on both a new vision of leadership and new skills and behaviors to help communities and organizations realize their visions, solve problems, and get results. (127)

Heikkila and Gerlak (2005, 583) label these government leaders "policy entrepreneurs" who can provide "a vital spark" for collaborative processes. These sparks may be current or former legislative actors at the state or federal level, state governors, or agency administrators.

In the natural resource management and environmental policy arenas, the power of position may be an asset, and there may be times when collaborative leaders engage in constructive confrontation (Burgess and Burgess 1996). Leaders representing government agencies, for example, participate in collaborative planning and projects while retaining legal decision authority. Furthermore, collaborative leadership can be provided by an organization's representatives (e.g., an agency or NGO employee) or by citizens in a community (e.g., a retired person serving as a watershed council chair).

Reporting on a decade of case study research, Wondolleck and Yaffee remark that in their cases, "project leaders, community leaders, agency field staff, landowners, and elected officials all played a leadership role in various projects and often kept projects alive despite a lack of resources, political support, or agency direction." These people were change agents, fostering trust and motivating stakeholder involvement and support. They played such roles as "cheerleader-energizer, diplomat, process facilitator, leader, convenor, catalyst, and promoter" (Wondolleck and Yaffee 2000, 178). Such efforts characterized civic leadership as a form of collaborative leadership (Chrislip 2002).

Consistent with Wondolleck and Yaffee's observations, McKinney and Harmon stress that managing natural resources in the twenty-first century "requires a new style of leadership" (2004, 248). "The new 'collaborative' model of leadership," they assert, "emphasizes dialogue and building relationships" (249). McKinney and Harmon point to the creation of the Montana Natural Resources Leadership Institute to illustrate the importance of creating mechanisms for building collaborative leadership capacity. This is also one of the goals of the Natural Resources Leadership Institute (North Carolina State University), the Natural Resources Leadership Academy (Washington State University), and the Virginia Natural Resources Leadership Institute (University of Virginia). All of these leadership efforts focus on capacity building, addressing situations in which leadership may be an important yet unacknowledged role (Wondolleck and Ryan 1999).

Although McKinney and Harmon, Chrislip and Larson, and Wondolleck and Yaffee emphasize collaborative leadership, other leadership theories and approaches abound. Browsing through a bookstore reveals books on leadership by coaches, CEOs, and consultants. Scholars have been studying leadership for decades, developing enduring theories such as situational leadership, transformational leadership, participatory leadership, and autocratic leadership (for reviews, see Hackman and Johnson 2003; Northouse 2004; Yukl 2005; www.changingminds.org).

Taking into account the nature of natural resource management and environmental policy decision situations; the diverse literature on leadership, conflict resolution, and decision making; and our experience working with community-oriented collaborative projects, we propose three leadership approaches that seem most germane to community-based collaboration: (1) leadership as command and control, (2) leadership as administration, and (3) leadership as collaboration. These are not mutually exclusive leadership approaches, but they differ fundamentally in terms of what they emphasize. Generally one leadership approach is not superior to all others; rather, each is best suited for particular organizations and tasks.

Working through natural resource and environmental conflict situations and making good decisions can be thought of as making progress—on the substance of the situation, on procedural aspects of the situation, and on relationship factors (e.g., face, power, trust) relevant to the situation (Daniels and Walker, 2001; Walker and Daniels 2005, unpublished findings). As the subsequent discussion illustrates, the three leadership approaches we present address the three dimensions of progress differently.

Command-and-Control Leadership

"Command and control is by far the most common change leadership style," Anderson and Anderson write, noting that "most of today's leaders were mentored themselves by command and control managers, and the culture of most organizations is still based on command and control norms" (2002). This leadership approach, as its name suggests, emphasizes centralized authority. Command-and-control leaders are clearly identifiable (often by title or position) in the hierarchical structure of an organization. They value the chain of command and going through conventional communication and decision-making channels. Command-and-control leaders are the people "in charge" and see themselves as decisive.

Command-and-control leaders focus on substance and to some extent on procedure, but very little on the relationship factors of a planning or decision situation. They want to get the job done, to accomplish the identified goal. Command-and-control leadership relies on unilateral decision making and embraces the assumption that "shaping policy is an important prerogative of status and power" (Yankelovich 1999, 171).

Command-and-control leadership embraces clear, explicit rules and division of labor. Efficiency is valued and power is centralized. As noted in our earlier discussion of command and control, communication is intentional, structured, and constrained. The leader also controls the manner in which others participate in making and implementing decisions.

Command-and-control leadership corresponds well to a military metaphor. "The generals develop the strategy, the officers translate that strategy into action, and the soldiers implement the actions on the ground" (Malloy 2002). Situations that benefit from command-and-control leadership include crisis situations (e.g., an incident commander and fighting fires), military and national security situations (e.g., responding to terrorism threats), law enforcement situations (e.g., criminal activity), and crowd control situations (e.g., public demonstrations, music concerts). Many command-and-control behaviors, though, work against effective collaboration and the development of a learning community (Frydman, Wilson, and Wyer 2000).

Administrative Leadership

Some leaders control and command, others administer. Administrative leadership is another approach evident in natural resource management situations. Also known as bureaucratic leadership, this leadership style is often associated with public organizations (Terry 2003, cited in Graham 2006).

Administrative leaders focus on procedure as well as on substance, and, like command-and-control leaders, minimize the importance of relationship factors in a decision situation. They emphasize measurable outcomes and effectiveness, value decisions guided by data, and establish and support formal rules for work tasks and for decision procedures. Job responsibilities and division of labor are clear. They value hierarchy and order and pay attention to detail. "Micromanagement" may be characteristic of administrative leaders. They may want tasks done "by the book."

The metaphor of a machine represents administrative leadership well. Every part has a purpose; every part is essential; every part is replaceable. Situations in which administrative leadership may be visible include the management of large organization (e.g., multinational corporations, government agencies, universities), the criminal justice system (e.g., civil and criminal courts), the regulatory system (e.g., Internal Revenue Service, a state fish and wildlife agency), and the political arena (e.g., fundraising, campaigns, legislative decision making).

Collaborative Leadership

Collaborative leaders seek progress on all aspects of a conflict or decision situation. They pay attention to relationship, substance, and procedure factors, with the greatest emphasis often placed on relationship elements. Collaborative leaders identify what skills, capacities, and resources are present in the organization or community and its people. They also assess capacity-building needs and develop strategies to address them. Collaborative leaders are "internally focused" (sensitive to issues and concerns within the organization or community), but not to the exclusion of external attention.

The practice of public management is increasingly collaborative. "Public managers who work collaboratively find themselves not solely as unitary leaders of unitary organizations," O'Leary and colleagues write. "Instead, they often find themselves facilitating and operating in multi-organizational networked arrangements to solve problems that cannot be solved, or solved easily, by single organizations" (O'Leary et al. 2009, 1; see also Bingham and O'Leary 2008).

Retired corporate executive and consultant Iva Wilson identifies three organizational or institutional conditions that foster collaborative leadership: (1) individual and organizational learning, as well as stewardship of and support for the learning process by leaders; (2) a set of values to guide the company in building a vision, developing strategy, and designing tactics; and (3) a model for distributing power (Malloy 2002).

In natural resource collaborations, distributing power means sharing power. Power rests less with the individual actor or organization and more with the collective. All parties have the opportunity to influence the directions taken and decisions made. As such, leadership in a collaborative effort is less of a hierarchy and more of a distributed, shared network (Senge et al. 2005, 186). Leadership is shared among members of the collaborative group. It emerges within the group; the group moves forward without having to wait for a single person to become the leader (Senge et al. 2005).

According to the Turning Point project on collaboration in the health care arena, collaborative leadership features six central elements: (1) assessing the environment for collaboration: understanding the context for change before acting; (2) creating clarity, imparting vision, and mobilizing: defining shared values and engaging people in positive action; (3) building trust: creating safe places for developing a shared purpose and action; (4) sharing power and influence: developing the synergy of people, organizations, and communities to accomplish goals; (5) developing people: committing to the development of people as a key asset through mentoring and coaching; and (6) self-reflection and personal continuous quality improvement: understanding one's own leadership and engaging others. Drawing on the work of Chrislip and Larson (1994), the Turning Point project identifies conflict management, communication competence, perspective-taking, and adaptability as essential skills areas (Turning Point 2006).

Collaborative leadership is represented well by the metaphor of improvisational jazz. All players in the jazz ensemble are important and interdependent. Their music comes from working together, from building on one another, different players at particular times performing as "soloists" supported by other members of the group. Situations that are both complex and controversial (Walker, Daniels, and Cheng 2005) benefit from collaborative leadership. In the natural resource management and environmental policy arenas, the list of complex and controversial situations is substantial. Examples include toxic waste cleanup, forest planning, species recovery, urban growth policies, and local sustainable agriculture, to name just a few (see Wondolleck and Yaffee 2000, 2001, for a compelling set of examples).

Internally, administrators can support more collaborative agency cultures by supporting capacity-building training for agency staff. Laninga's (2005) study of BLM managers indicates that collaboration is more likely in situations where agency managers exhibit transformational leadership (another term for collaborative leadership). Externally, because institutional leaders are often in a position to provide the initial social capital for CBC parties unfamiliar with collaborative processes (Heikkila and Gerlak 2005), they can sponsor training in partnership with other institutions. Concerning

this role, Lubell (2004, 353) notes that "the interaction between local government representatives and grassroots stakeholders is the crucible in
which social capital is formed. Local government officials are the bearers
of policy promises, who communicate expectations about political agreements." They can partner with institutions of higher learning where scholars and "pracademics" are generating curricula for public administration,
public policy, political science, environmental studies, planning, and communication studies, and where research into theory and best practices is
ready for application (Booher 2004).

Institutional leaders can structure everyday practices to be more participatory. In particular, they can build recommendations for and demonstrations of collaborative skills into management performance incentives, and
attach rewarding mechanisms to more collaborative staff performance (see
essays in Bingham and O'Leary 2008; see O'Leary and Bingham 2003 for
examples).

Beyond Leadership to Other Essential Roles: Convener, Sponsor, Funder

There are many roles that contribute to good, implementable decisions in
community-based collaborations. In addition to leadership, the information provider, advocate, and facilitator are important participants in the
constructive dialogue and deliberation about a community group's concerns and projects. These roles are typically undertaken by individuals
rather than by institutions.

In contrast, institutions take on the roles of convener, sponsor, and
funder. While individuals and communities can convene and sponsor, rarely
do they provide all the funds needed for a collaborative effort. Governmental and nongovernmental institutions may have resources (both money and
staff) dedicated to CBC work on natural resource issues.

Government Programs

Many federal and state government natural resource management and environmental policy agencies offer programs that encourage and support
community-based collaboration. We feature a limited set here and encourage readers to consult the websites of relevant federal and state agencies.

The U.S. Department of Agriculture–Forest Service offers a variety of
programs that provide resources for collaboration. Sturtevant and colleagues (2005) provide an accessible list of resources of the Forest Service
related to fire management. They explain (2005, 40) that the

Forest Service wild land fire and fuels management staff can draw on several policies to facilitate and support collaboration. These policy resources come and go with different initiatives and programs, so agency staff members need to monitor what resources are currently available. State and Private Forestry's Collaborative Forestry staff of the Forest Service has long collaborated with communities through its Economic Action Programs, Urban and Community Forestry Program, and Landowner Assistance Programs. Their ability to collaborate with local communities has expanded with an influx of funds from President Clinton's National Fire Plan that started in 2000. National forest line officers and staff too have access to a number of relatively new tools for collaboration, including new authorities under the Healthy Forests Restoration Act, the Wyden Amendment, the County Payments Act, stewardship contracting, and other new programs. In addition, the agency has many mechanisms by which it can partner with tribal, State, and local governments, private businesses, nonprofit organizations, and individuals. Many of the new authorities, as well as innovative new uses for existing authorities, were developed in collaborative processes.

The Environmental Protection Agency (EPA) features programs that encourage collaboration. For example, the National Estuary Program (NEP) offers support for implementing a community-based watershed approach. The program emphasizes federal, state, and local organizations working together to address coastal watershed management challenges. NEP projects focus on the watershed, use science to inform decision making, emphasize collaborative problem solving, and involve the public (www.epa.gov). The EPA considers this program a success because it establishes governance structures according to watershed boundaries rather than political jurisdictions; the NEPs define their management areas and management committees according to watershed boundaries and the ecosystems within them. Additionally, the NEPs employ science to develop and implement a management plan and foster collaborative decision making. According to the EPA's website, "The NEPs invest a considerable amount of time to facilitate consensus on complex environmental issues. They develop mechanisms such as charters, bylaws, or memoranda of agreement to provide a framework for resolving conflicts." They also inform and involve "stakeholders to sustain commitment."

The EPA provides a number of pilot programs that endorse community-based collaboration. These include Urban Rivers Restoration Pilots, Environmental Justice Pilots, RCRA Targeted Site Efforts, Brownfields

Showcase Communities, and Re-evaluating Superfund Cleanups (the "Tear Down the Wall" Initiative).

The Natural Resource Conservation Service's Resource Conservation and Development (RC&D) program "helps people care for and protect their natural resources, and improve local economies and living standards." It pulls "together people, communities, various units of government, and grassroots organizations—uniting in shared purpose and pooling resources and skills to get work done. RC&D projects and activities are determined by the area's problems and needs" (www.nrcs.gov). Earlier in the 2000s the NRCS launched the Cooperative Conservation Partnership Initiative (CCPI). This is "a voluntary program established to foster conservation partnerships that focus technical and financial resources on conservation priorities in watersheds and airsheds of special significance. Under CCPI, funds are awarded to State and local governments and agencies; Indian tribes; and non-governmental organizations that have a history of working with agricultural producers" (www.nrcs.gov).

Other federal agencies that address natural resource management and environmental policy issues support collaboration through various programs. For example, the U.S. Army Corps of Engineers' program on regional sediment management calls for collaboration with multiple stakeholders. The BLM's Cooperative Conservation Initiative, highlighted earlier, strives to remove barriers to citizen participation, encourage stewardship, and support conservation projects at the local level.

State government programs also support community-based collaboration. For example, the Oregon Water Enhancement Board allocates state funds to watershed councils. The Ohio Environmental Protection Agency provides a similar program to assist watershed groups. In California, the CALFED program, which manages much of California's water system, has embraced a new, collaborative governance model.

Foundations and Corporations

CBC efforts may find support from private foundations and for-profit companies. Established CBCs such as the Catron County Citizens Group (New Mexico), the Malpai Borderlands Partnership (Arizona), and the Kaskaskia Watershed Association (Illinois) receive some of their funding from foundations. In St. Paul, Minnesota, both 3M (Minnesota Mining and Manufacturing) and Wells Fargo Bank provided resources to restore the Phalen Corridor.

Beyond Barriers: Critical Elements for Institutional and Individual Change

CBC governance on environmental and natural resource management issues operates in the face of potential barriers and constraints. At the 2005 CBCRC (Community-Based Collaborative Research Consortium) National Conference, Tilt (2005) highlighted a number of barriers to collaboration, including external forces (e.g., the "Washington Office"), parties with insufficient knowledge, skills, and abilities to address the situation, and agency culture. At that same conference, Danks, McDermott, and Moote reported the results of their research on institutional barriers to community-based collaboration. Based on a literature review, interviews, and case studies, Danks and colleagues identified six barriers: (1) agency capacity and culture, (2) obstructive laws and policies, (3) lack of financial and human resources, (4) resistance from powerful parties, (5) lack of legitimacy or mandate, and (6) local or regional economic distress (Danks, McDermott, and Moote 2005; see also McDermott, Moote, and Danks 2005). In a study featuring twenty-eight interviews of planners, Lachapelle and colleagues identify five barriers to collaborative planning: inadequate goal definition, lack of trust, procedural obligations, inflexibility, and institutional design (2003, 480). Also drawing on interviews, Bardati (2005) notes a variety of potential impediments to community conservation efforts, such as ill-defined goals, limited community cohesiveness, inadequate communication, and historical antecedents. In a place-based study, Wing and colleagues (1996) address racism as a barrier to community-based collaboration to address environmental justice concerns.

These scholars and others (e.g., Wondolleck and Yaffee 2000; Hoffman et al. 2002; Koontz et al. 2004) provide important discussions of the obstacles stakeholders—communities, agencies, organizations—need to address and overcome to achieve community-based conservation goals. Meaningful, enduring CBC efforts require more: change at both the institutional and individual level.

Insulating Institutions from Political and Administrative Changes

New administrations bring policy priorities with them (Meadowcroft 2004). When a new president, governor, or even local official takes the reins of office, collaborative processes run the risk of being shelved or never initiated. Every agency can tell stories of planning efforts, collaborative processes, and training programs that were halted or modified when administrations changed, even if the new administration was of the same political party (Rossi 2001). When the political party that holds the presidency or congressional majority changes, complex regulatory initiatives can get undermined. A three-way tension among a president, career agency executives, and a decentralized and assertive Congress can also amplify ideological differences and significantly affect collaborative processes that represent enormous investment of stakeholder resources and good will (Dobel 1995). Dobel (1995) describes how even the divisions in such a government situation can generate levels of conflict that impact managerial power and consequently, for CBCs, the capacity for innovation and interagency coalition building. The ability to take advantage of strong executive support or strong interest-group or congressional support may be hampered and create challenging counterpressure.

When elected administrations change at the federal and state levels, new political appointments to top agency administrative posts follow, rippling through the management of regional and district offices. Another impact of a divided government is the intensive screening endured by these appointees, who may be uncomfortable with or even hostile to the laws and agencies they are charged to administer (Dobel 1995).

Even at the local level, members on the zoning board of appeals are often appointed by the current elected official. This election cycle turnover for political appointees is rapid and often repeats itself during the term of any administration. Many CBCs may span one or more administrations. Sustaining the durability òf administrative commitment to a particular collaborative process is a critical component of CBC motivation and effectiveness.

According to Dobel (1995), to counter such intrusions and impacts on collaborative processes, agencies must try to protect collaborative efforts by building their internal capacity to work competently with CBCs. The agencies need to demonstrate capacity and commitment, build an agency culture that internalizes this capacity and commitment, and construct coalitions that support collaboration.

Creating Mechanisms for State and Federal Agency Adaptation and Flexibility

For accountability measures and equity considerations, federal regulations often apply across the country, yet a modification might better serve the context and opportunities of unique local situations (Fiorino 2004). Without the ability to be more flexible and adaptive, rigid federal regulatory structures will increasingly be incongruent with the problem-solving approach of CBCs.

Regulatory agencies and their programs were established before the current recognition of best management through an ecological or sustainability systems perspective. The result is a suite of disjointed agencies (Allwell 2003; Heikkila and Gerlak 2005), each with responsibility for overseeing a part of the system, often overlapping in jurisdiction but bound to different laws and regulations for achieving their mandate. Agencies need supporting mechanisms to integrate their activities or "these prescriptive regulations may hinder the consideration of more innovative proposals" (Rossi 2001, 1015).

Many state and federal agency staff will disclose that they are overextended and under-resourced. As budgets are squeezed, more energy is often relentlessly spent justifying and protecting budgets, programs, and staff resources. To make a compelling case to their central agency office and decision makers for maintaining or increasing their budgets, a regional or district unit may build support among its own local or regional constituencies to advocate for its budget requests, or at least not criticize the unit. This might put the local agency office in a potential double-bind with enforcement and making decisions that may be counter to powerful local concerns. Certainly, agency staff members have pondered this dilemma. Because of this, regional or district offices may jealously guard their territories, and agencies may guard against other agencies whose mandates overlap theirs. Not surprisingly, agency staff in regional and district offices often form stronger alliances with legislators and interest groups than do agency heads.

Nevertheless, for collaborative processes to be most fruitful, agencies must create opportunities to establish what Brown and Linden (2001) call a culture of "barrier busting" in multiple areas. Allwell (2003) describes such innovations by state departments of transportation to engage other agencies to achieve streamlining multiple permit processes.

Another example is Service First (Brown and Linden 2001), a joint agency approach between the BLM and the U.S. Forest Service in southern Colorado and central Oregon. Service First was invented out of budget belt-tightening in the early 1990s and formalized in the mid-1990s. It originated in the recognition of dual management responsibilities for a wide range of land values and uses and was driven by regional constituencies for improvements in multiple service delivery mechanisms. The staffers initially addressed issues of safety and public information that carried low institutional collaboration costs and high public and agency benefits.

Initially, staff members worked under the radar to swap staff time. This evolved into power exchanging, information and resource sharing, dual position designations, and integration of resources. Eventually, the idea was taken to then BLM acting director Michael Dombeck and USFS chief Jack Ward Thomas. In 1996, the impressed chief administrators announced a new national Trading Post initiative to encourage collaboration, cut costs, and improve service to its customers.

According to Brown and Linden (2001), allegiance to and identification with staff agencies remained strong, and the laws and policies that governed them did not change. Local agency as well as top administrative support has been strong. Although the program originated in the Clinton administration, during the subsequent Bush administration the Service First Initiative remained a priority. Early indications are that the Service First program will continue during President Obama's tenure.

Moving In and Out of the Collaborative Process

Sustained collaborative governance practices need to account for actor and institutional movement. Key personnel—leaders and representatives—may change during the life of a collaborative project. They may move in and out of a collaborative process as a result of institutional requirements, professional growth, personal preferences, or staffing changes.

For example, a new military commander of a U.S. Army Corps of Engineers district office is assigned approximately every two years. Board members and staff of nonprofits often change. Two years into a collaborative process we facilitated, very few of the management agency's key administrators and planning team members remained, the others having obtained promotions or moved to other districts or left the agency. Even at the local level, new town board members, mayors, and town supervisors are elected. Citizens move on or become fatigued. One can expect that in the ongoing and enduring processes that characterize CBCs, parties will change, involvement will ebb and flow, and valuable process history and relationship values may be vulnerable. To address this, and to maintain the integrity of the collaborative effort in the community and agency memories, process histories need to be accessible not only for incoming process participants but also for community members in general and the media. One CBC used a regularly updated PowerPoint presentation that ran at the beginning of each public meeting and was available in CD and paper versions. Another took advantage of two members' talent for scrapbooking. Others created orientation booklets. Still others arranged for mentoring opportunities.

Mindfully Attending to Trust

Throughout the case literature on community-based collaboration, trust stands out as a critical factor. After a process is completed and deemed successful or not, the element most commonly pointed to is the presence or absence of trust, often expressed as stakeholders claiming they had no voice in the process or decision. The challenge posed is the development and maintenance of trust, but this is an abstract term, easy to know it when you see it but difficult to deliberately plan for with any confidence of effect. Senecah (2004) offers a process design and diagnostic tool to increase the chances that trust will be supported. A collaborative process that builds and maintains trust needs to be based on relationship building, monitoring, and adjusting. Then the thorny, uncertain, and potentially contentious content issues can be tackled with safety, openness, and effectiveness. Such a process must be characterized by the three critical process elements that form what she calls the trinity of voice.

The trinity of voice consists of three interdependent markers of access, civic standing, and influence. If any one is missing or severely out of balance with the other two, tensions will develop, effectiveness will be obstructed, energies will be invested in elbowing into the process to claim or force the missing elements, and conflict will escalate. Any process that builds productive, trusting relationships must include a conscious effort to account for providing voice in terms of access, civic standing, and influence.

Access. Access refers to having access to information and a process that offers opportunity and safety, as well as the potential for being heard. Without meaningful access, public policy decision making can become contentious and escalate into pervasive animosity among stakeholders. Their interactions may become hostile, driven by distrust, frustrations, skepticism, and entrenched perspectives about their own and other stakeholders' positions and motivations. Access of voice must put people into a place where real opportunity exists for their ideas and opinions to achieve civic standing. Access does not guarantee standing, but flawed access can prevent it. Agencies traditionally measure adequate access as the minimum required by law, including participation via written public comment or a public hearing. If no comments are submitted or if few people attend the public meeting or open house, does that mean that the public is in agreement or that the access was flawed?

Two critical aspects of access must be present and mindfully accounted for. The first consists of the practical logistics that support the participation of anyone who desires to contribute. The second is a format that will support honoring participants' contributions and achieving shared objectives. Using a "one size fits all" format as a cookie-cutter template for all situations is not effective, as evidenced by the role that public hearings play as the flash points of conflict.

However, access alone does not constitute the generative trust that supports collaborative processes. Access offers entrance to a process appropriate for that unique context and holds the potential for participants' ideas and concerns to be accommodated and respected. It provides an opportunity and format for civic standing, but to build trust, the process in place must be a process in action. Access and standing are mutually dependent in the generation of trust.

Standing. Standing is closely connected to access. It is an articulated demonstration of stakeholders being "heard," an assurance that their contributions are valued and considered. How does a process support standing? A guiding principle from *Getting to Yes,* a classic in dispute resolution (Fisher, Ury, and Patton 1991), emphasizes looking beyond positions to interests. Senecah (2004) suggests we go one step deeper by striving to understand what fears are driving the interests. What most people in high-stakes decisions (high stakes to them) fear is that they and their experiences and knowledge are not taken seriously, do not count; that they lack civic standing. When frustrated or fearful to the breaking point, good people denied access or standing will create ways to claim their voice that lead to escalation and more distrust. Nevertheless, as good as having access and standing feel, they do not constitute trust, and although they are essential, they will do more harm than good unless they lead to influence.

Influence. Without access to process and civic standing, contentiousness becomes the tool with which to claim influence. Influence does not necessarily mean that every stakeholder gets what she or he wants, although this kind of influence may certainly occur. Nor does it mean that agencies can abdicate their authority over a decision. They cannot. Influence dictates that stakeholders' meaningful participation in a process is legitimized in ways that lead to opportunities for gaining understanding, contributing knowledge, and influencing outcomes before a project is completed or a decision is made. A way that some describe this is that decision space is created, and with it, criteria are set for what constitutes a defensible decision.

Although stakeholders may not have the ultimate authority to make or carry out a particular technical decision, they can influence priorities, alternative strategies, or even whether a proposal proceeds. Through asserting meaningful influence, stakeholders contribute better or more creative ideas and gain greater confidence in the results. They see evidence that their work made a difference.

The trinity of voice—access, standing, and influence—offers a template not only to account for the specifics of success or failure of individual cases but also to use in the design of collaborative processes. It can serve as a useful analytical frame for examining stakeholders' procedural preferences (Walker, Senecah, and Daniels 2006). Explicitly hitting on all the cylinders of the trinity of voice is useful in designing a process, and can also be used to diagnose and treat troubled processes or escalated disputes. As a template, it can be fitted to a case's unique context and resources. If any of the elements of voice—access, standing, or influence—is out of balance or missing, the process and relationship factors of any public involvement process will likely suffer, and content issues will dominate and overwhelm, leaving relationships essential for implementation damaged. Trust will be stymied and parties will become weary, angry, frustrated, suspicious, or resigned but resentful.

An ill-conceived process is often worse than no process at all, whether the issue involves two people or five thousand. An effective, vital, deliberative democracy depends on the continual weaving and reweaving of a fabric of trust among stakeholders in collaborative processes. The trinity of voice helps us do this.

Recognizing the Value of Nonregulatory Incentives

The public administration literature has long described the dynamic among the branches and levels of democratic government in the United States, and this dynamic is especially active in heavily regulated environmental issues. The dance among the parties may take many forms and last a long time as it moves among local-state-federal levels and across legislative-administrative and executive-judicial jurisdictions. Many parties that enter a CBC have likely experienced the impacts of this dance from diverse perspectives and roles. In its wake may be suspicion, distrust, and antagonisms. Other such nonregulatory tools may be impending deadlines for funding opportunities, administrative policy priorities, public pressure, election cycles, public image, legal deadlines, or finances. As the Chesapeake Bay Foundation (2006) declares, a lawsuit "is not a tool of last resort but rather a way to bring about change." For example, legal action was the catalyst for Florida governor Lawton Chiles to agree to launch a comprehensive ecosystem restoration and protection plan for southern Florida, a successful collaborative process for restoring and sustainably managing the Everglades (Heikkila and Gerlak 2005). Such legal mechanisms often trigger the production of important links to information and data.

Recommendations for Action and Inquiry

This and earlier chapters have emphasized action: what CBC organizations and efforts need to do to foster meaningful change and enduring stewardship. This chapter and the previous chapter have emphasized obstacles to overcome and actions to do so. For example, in this chapter we have encouraged parties in a CBC project to examine the roles they and others may play and how those roles affect progress and desired outcomes. Here we propose some areas for further investigation. The practice of collaborative governance generally and CBC work specifically provides a range of opportunities for evaluating processes, products, and best practices. We have organized our ideas under the themes of clarity and capacity.

Clarity

Lines of inquiry into clarity focus on identifying the goals that institutions seek to satisfy by entering into CBCs. These goals are both external and internal. As we have found in our experience, the institutional foci often concentrate on the external processes and relationships between the institution and external parties. This is a critical juncture and productive research site, to be sure. That most research addresses processes at this area stands as testament to the usefulness of and interest in this kind of research. After all, agencies are under tremendous political pressure to make things happen and achieve objectives, and stakeholders want to engage in processes that have enough of a payback to make their investment of time and good faith worthwhile. Other chapters in this book provide keen insight into guiding these important lines of inquiry.

In addition to this kind of inquiry, CBCs would also greatly benefit from research that looks at the internal dynamics of institutions and the impacts these have on CBCs. Internal dynamics are multifaceted, and through our work we have observed that how agencies operate day to day is often critical to how the external processes unfold.

For example, in what ways and to what degree do organizations' internal capacity to operate collaboratively affect their ability to interact effectively in a CBC? We are reminded of agencies or research centers that were internally characterized by embracing risk-taking, encouraging collaborative teamwork, a strong collaborative leadership or an enduring culture of collaboration that survived leadership shifts, and identifiable internal structural mechanisms for collaboratively addressing tensions and deliberating on complex decisions. On the other hand, we have also experienced organizations that were internally characterized by dysfunction and noncollaborative patterns of interaction and beliefs. Questions about the internal dynamics of institutions involved in a CBC worth asking include the following: (1) Which internal practices are most influential in supporting or undermining the effectiveness of agencies' roles in CBCs? and (2) What roles contribute to the overall satisfaction of participants in CBCs?

We have noted concerns about the turnover rate of agency staff over the life span of a multiyear CBC. This could be an important issue to examine. For example, what is the impact of changing personnel and stakeholder presentation on both process and outcome variables? What tools and mechanisms are most appropriate for agencies' maintaining consistency of understanding, support, and skills amid personnel changes?

Another line of research on institutional clarity addresses identifying and understanding the dynamics of the internal goals of bureaucratic institutions as well as the aspirations of individuals within them. For example, how do individuals with aspirations for collaborative interaction with external stakeholders reconcile or get around an agency culture at odds with these aspirations? What internal mechanisms can build in collaborative accountability even when a leader engages in a CBC without a commitment to or ability to be collaborative?

Capacity

We cluster the other major lines of inquiry under the theme of capacity. This area deals with the actual skills, climate, and culture for institutions to interact productively as part of CBCs and internally, within their own organizations.

Concerning capacity, institutions are bureaucratic creatures, built deliberately to evolve slowly to maintain consistency throughout political, administrative, and economic changes. Many have tight, top-down levels of management and control. Often their mission defines their practices. For example, some have military cultures or regulatory missions that make them superb technical problem solvers or objective achievers but poor relationship builders. They may think linearly, have ultimate faith in biotechnical data, and be uncomfortable with uncertainty or integrating local knowledge. For example, the director of a state coastal management program emphatically declared at a meeting of a CBC that the best thing about managing with an ecosystem-based approach was, "Now, you'll have to go by the science, and that's that!" Finally, they may operate on zero-sum power assumptions and have little comfort or experience with shared power. Consequently, at a macrolevel an investigator could examine the ways in which institutes enact power to encourage or discourage community-based collaboration.

At a microlevel, research could analyze the discourse of CBCs and how that discourse frames perceptions of power, incentives, and integrative decision making (Fischer 2003; Rydin 2003; Simmons 2007).

At the same time, even as they may function slowly, institutions have a parallel obligation to carry out a current administration's policies and preferences in a timely manner, and these can shift with each administration and budget cycle. The people who work in and lead these institutions may be somewhat skeptical or timid about going beyond their comfort zone, and this has implications for the effectiveness of their participation in CBCs. Still, enduring institutions are arguably reflexive and capable of embracing innovative change (Arts and Goverde 2006).

Methodologically rigorous case studies, interviews, and surveys can help organizations identify strengths and needs at both macro- and microlevels. At the macrolevel, agencies and community organizations can determine institutional needs (e.g., resources) and actions to address them. At the microlevel, institutions can examine collaborative leadership and skills essential to enduring collaborative work. Research can construct and evaluate effective mechanisms or approaches for building higher collaborative skills and leadership, as well as the confidence and comfort in applying them to their participation in CBCs.

Conclusions

Regardless of a CBC's process achievements, its effectiveness will be measured on indicators of accountability and outcomes. By viewing CBCs as experiments in collaborative governance, procedural success will be considered alongside the stewardship and sustainability products CBCs generate. Evidence of effective process work and environmental outcomes provides justification for agencies and organizations to endorse, support, and participate actively in community-based collaboration and conflict resolution efforts (see Emerson et al. 2009). As organizations do so, they create opportunities for their key actors, personnel whose participation is essential in a multi-stakeholder effort.

Still, even in a climate of collaborative governance, CBCs run the risk of being bureaucratically co-opted and therefore misunderstood, misapplied, or held to impossible quantitative accountability (Toker 2005). They need to regularly take stock of both process and outcome variables, and construct safeguards to maintain their commitment to collaboration.

Government agencies and nonprofit organizations are most often the conveners of CBC efforts, and their resources are critical to successful results. Even so, the appeal of collaborative engagement may be outstripping the political and institutional capacity of agencies and organizations to keep up. Yet a growing pool of innovative processes stands as testament that not only can government institutions face and change the realities of their cultures and other critical elements traditionally viewed as barriers, they must. Although perhaps daunting, these challenges cannot be ignored.

The critical elements and tasks we have raised in this chapter emerge from our understanding of the dynamic and complex nature of natural resource systems and the controversial and complex policy choices that communities and governments face. Communities and governments working together at the local level can demonstrate effective collaborative governance and provide stakeholders with meaningful voice. Our critical elements draw attention to issues to which we hope community activists and agency staff will attend. With a commitment to work through the difficult and challenging natural resource management situations agencies and communities face, CBCs' efforts can be productive and sustainable. Institutions can act in ways that foster rather than discourage collaborative governance. Many community efforts thrive through collaborative governance; institutions can, through their people, contribute leadership and share influence. Institutions, communities, and people can work together to maximize their integrative potential and develop and implement sound decisions.

References

Allwell, C. C. 2003. "Reviews on the Fast Track: A Step-by-Step Guide to Practices That States Employ to Streamline the Environmental Review Process." *Public Roads* 67 (1): 49–54.

Anderson, D., and L. A. Anderson. 2002. "How Command and Control as a Leadership Change Style Causes Transformational Change Efforts to Fail." *Change Resources Newsletter,* Being First, June. http://www.beingfirst.com/changeresources/articles/200206/.

Arts, B., and H. Goverde. 2006. "The Governance Capacity of (New) Policy Arrangements: A Reflexive Approach." In *Institutional Dynamics in Environmental Governance,* ed. B. Arts and P. Leroy, 69–92. Dordrecht: Springer-Verlag.

Bardati, D. R. 2005. "An Innovative Community-based Collaborative Promoting Conservation in an Energy Utility Corridor." *Journal of Community-Based Collaboratives Research,* October. http://www.cbcrc.org/php-bin/news/showArticle.php?id=54.

Bingham, L. B., and R. O'Leary, eds. 2008. *Big Ideas in Collaborative Public Management.* Armonk, NY: Sharpe.

Bingham, L. B., R. O'Leary, and T. Nabatchi. 2005. "Legal Frameworks for the New Governance: Processes for Citizen Participation in the Work of Government." *National Civic Review* 94 (1): 54–64.

Blaney, J. 2003. "Collaborative Governance for River Basin Management." Paper presented at the 2003 Georgia Basin/Puget Sound Research Conference. http://www.psat.wa.gov/Publications/03_proceedings/start.htm.

Booher, D. E. 2004. "Collaborative Governance Practices and Democracy." *National Civic Review* 93 (4): 32–47.

Brown, H., and R. Linden. 2001. "Daring to Be Citizen Centered: The Forest Service and Bureau of Land Management Are Working Together to Better Serve Their

Common Customers—A Breakthrough in Collaborative Governance." *Public Manager* 30 (4): 49–53.

Brunner, R. D., C. H. Colburn, C. M. Cromley, R. A. Klein, and E. A. Olson, eds. 2002. *Finding Common Ground: Governance and Natural Resources in the American West.* New Haven, CT: Yale University Press.

Brunner, R. D., T. A. Steelman, L. Coe-Juell, C. M. Cromley, C. M. Edwards, and D. W. Tucker. 2005. *Adaptive Governance: Integrating Science, Policy, and Decision-making.* New York: Columbia University Press.

Burgess, H., and G. Burgess. 1996. "Constructive Confrontation: A Transformative Approach to Intractable Conflicts." *Mediation Quarterly* 13:305–22.

Carlson, C. 2008. *A Practical Guide to Collaborative Governance.* Portland, OR: Policy Consensus Initiative/National Policy Consensus Center.

Chesapeake Bay Foundation. 2006. "Building Blocks for Emerging Environmental Non-profit Organizations: Lessons from the Chesapeake Bay Foundation." www .cbf.org (accessed January 15, 2006).

Chrislip, D. D. 2002. *The Collaborative Leadership Fieldbook: A Guide for Citizens and Civic Leaders.* San Francisco, CA: Jossey-Bass.

Chrislip, D. D., and C. E. Larson. 1994. *Collaborative Leadership: How Citizens and Civic Leaders Can Make a Difference.* San Francisco, CA: Jossey-Bass.

Crocker, J., M. DuPraw, J. Kunde, and W. Potapchuk. 1996. *Negotiated Approaches to Environmental Decision Making in Communities: An Exploration of Lessons Learned.* Study sponsored by National Civic League, National Institute for Dispute Resolution, and the Coalition to Improve Management in State and Local Government. Washington, DC: Program For Community Problem Solving.

Daniels, S. E., and G. B. Walker. 2001. *Working through Environmental Conflict: The Collaborative Learning Approach.* Westport, CT: Praeger.

Danks, C., M. H. McDermott, and A. Moote. 2005. "Overcoming Institutional Barriers to Achieving Environmental Goals." Paper presented at the Fifth National CBCRC Conference, Sedona, AZ, November 17–19.

Dobel, J. P. 1995. "Managerial Leadership in Divided Times: William Ruckelshaus and the Paradoxes of Independence." *Administration & Society* 26 (4): 488–515.

Emerson, K., P. J. Orr, D. L. Keyes, and K. M. McKnight. 2009. "Environmental Conflict Resolution: Evaluating Performance Outcomes and Contributing Factors." *Conflict Resolution Quarterly* 27 (1): 27–64.

Fiorino, D. J. 2004. "Flexibility." In *Environmental Governance Reconsidered: Challenge, Choices, and Opportunities,* ed. R. F. Durant, D. J. Fiorino, and R. O'Leary, 393–426. Cambridge, MA: MIT Press.

Fischer, F. 2000. *Citizens, Experts, and the Environment: The Politics of Local Knowledge.* Durham, NC: Duke University Press.

———. 2003. *Reframing Public Policy: Discursive Politics and Deliberative Practices.* New York: Oxford University Press.

Fisher, R., W. Ury, and D. Patton. 1991. *Getting to Yes: Negotiating Agreement without Giving In,* 2nd ed. New York: Basic Books.

Frydman, B., I. Wilson, and J. Wyer. 2000. *The Power of Collaborative Leadership: Lessons for the Learning Organization.* Woburn, MA: Butterworth-Heinemann.

Geringer, J. E., and J. A. Kitzhaber. 2004. "Gridlock Impossible at 'Kitchen Table.'" *Christian Science Monitor,* December 23. www.csmonitor.com/2004/1223/p09s01-coop.html.

Graham, A. 2006. "Leadership in Public Sector Organizations: Theoretical Perspectives." Lecture, Queen University, Kingston, ON. post.queensu.ca/~grahama/MPA809C/8Leadership06.ppt.

Hackman, M. Z., and C. E. Johnson. 2003. *Leadership: A Communication Perspective.* Chicago: Waveland Press.

Heikkila, T., and A. K. Gerlak. 2005. "The Formation of Large-scale Collaborative Resource Management Institutions: Clarifying the Roles of Stakeholders, Science, and Institutions." *Policy Studies Journal* 33 (44): 583–613.

Hess, K., and G. Michaels, eds. 2005 (August). *Faces and Places of Cooperative Conservation: Profiles in Citizen Stewardship.* St. Louis, MO: White House Conference on Cooperative Conservation.

Hoffman, A. J., H. C. Riley, J. G. Trost, and M. H. Bazerman. 2002. "Cognitive and Institutional Barriers to New Forms of Cooperation on Environmental Protection: Insights from Project xl and Habitat Conservation Plans." *American Behavioral Scientist* 45 (5): 820–45.

Koontz, T. M., T. A. Steelman, J. Carmin, K. Smith Korfmacher, C. Moseley, and C. W. Thomas. 2004. *Collaborative Environmental Management: What Role for Government?* Washington, DC: Resources for the Future Press.

Lachapelle, P. R., S. F. McCool, and M. E. Patterson. 2003. "Barriers to Effective Natural Resource Planning in a 'Messy' World." *Society and Natural Resources* 16:473–90.

Laninga, T. J. 2005. "Planning for Public Lands: Examining Why Collaborative Approaches Are Adopted by the BLM." Paper presented at the Fifth National CBCRC Conference, Sedona, AZ, November 17–19.

Lubell, M. 2004. "Collaborative Watershed Management: A View from the Grassroots." *Policy Studies Journal* 32 (3): 341–61.

Malloy, J. 2002. "From Command-and-Control to Collaborative Leadership: An Interview with Iva Wilson." Pegasus Communications. http://www.pegasuscom.com/levpoints/wilsonint.html#cont.

McDermott, M. H., M. A. Moote, and C. Danks. 2005. "How Community-based Collaboratives Overcome External Institutional Barriers to Achieving Their Environmental Goals. Final Report to the Community-Based Collaboratives Research Consortium, University of Virginia, Charlottesville." www.cbcrc.org.

McKinney, M., and W. Harmon. 2004. *The Western Confluence: A Guide to Governing Natural Resources.* Washington, DC: Island Press.

Meadowcroft, J. 2004. "Deliberative Democracy." In *Environmental Governance Reconsidered: Challenge, Choices, and Opportunities,* ed. R. F. Durant, D. J. Fiorino, and R. O'Leary, 181–217. Cambridge, MA: MIT Press.

Moore, E. A., and T. M. Koontz. 2003. "A Typology of Collaborative Watershed Groups: Citizen-based, Agency-based, and Mixed Partnerships." *Society & Natural Resources* 16:451–60.

Northouse, P. G. 2004. *Leadership: Theory and practice,* 3rd. ed. Thousand Oaks, CA: Sage.

Office of Management and Budget and President's Council on Environmental Quality. 2005. "Memorandum on Environmental Conflict Resolution." Washington, DC: Executive Office of the President, November 28. http://www.ecr.gov/pdf/OMB_CEQ_Joint_Statement.pdf.

O'Leary, R., and L. B. Bingham. 2003. *The Promise and Performance of Environmental Conflict Resolution*. Washington, DC: Resources for the Future Press.

O'Leary, R., B. Gazley, B. McGuire, and L. B. Bingham. 2009. "Public Managers in Collaboration." In *The Collaborative Public Manager: New Ideas for the Twenty-first Century*, ed. R. O'Leary and L. B. Bingham, 1–12. Washington, DC: Georgetown University Press.

PCI/NPCC. 2009. "What Is Collaborative Governance?" Policy Consensus Initiative/National Policy Consensus Center, Portland, OR. http://www.policyconsensus.org/publicsolutions/ps_2.html.

Pruitt, D. 1983. "Integrative Agreements." In *Negotiating in Organizations*, ed. M. Bazerman and R. Lewicki. Beverly Hills, CA: Sage.

Red Lodge Clearinghouse. 2005. "Process Essentials: New Planning Roles." www.redlodgeclearinghouse.org/legislation/nationalforestmanagement.

Rossi, J. 2001. "Bargaining in the Shadow of Administrative Procedure: The Public Interest in Rulemaking Settlement." *Duke Law Journal* 51 (3): 1015–59.

Ryan, C. M. 2001. "Leadership in Collaborative Policy-making: An Analysis of Agency Roles in Regulatory Negotiations." *Policy Sciences* 34:221–45.

Rydin, Y. 2003. *Conflict, Consensus, and Rationality in Environmental Planning: An Institutional Discourse Approach*. New York: Oxford University Press.

Saxton, G. D. 2005. "The Participatory Revolution in Nonprofit Management." *Public Manager* 34 (1): 34–40.

Scholz, J., and B. Stiftel. 2005a. "Adaptive Governance and Water Conflicts." Paper presented at the Midwest Political Science Association Conference, Chicago, April 8. www.csus.edu/ccp/cdn/conferences.

———, eds. 2005b. *Adaptive Governance and Water Conflict: New Institutions for Collaborative Planning*. Washington, DC: Resources for the Future Press.

Senecah, S. L. 2004. "The Trinity of Voice: The Role of Practical Theory in Planning and Evaluating the Effectiveness of Environmental Participatory Processes." In *Communication and Public Participation in Environmental Decision Making*, ed. S. P. Depoe, J. W. Delicath, and M.-F. Aelpi Elsenbeer, 13–33. Albany: State University of New York Press.

Senge, P., C. O. Scharmer, J. Jaworski, and B. S. Flowers. 2005. *Presence: Exploring Profound Change in People, Organizations and Society*. London: Nicholas Brealey Publishing.

Simmons, W. M. 2007. *Participation and Power: Civic discourse in Environmental Policy Decisions*. Albany: State University of New York Press.

Stegner, W. 1969. *The Sound of Mountain Water*. New York: Doubleday.

Straus, D. 2002. *How to Make Collaboration Work*. San Francisco, CA: Berrett-Koehler.

Sturtevant, V., M. A. Moote, P. Jakes, and A. S. Cheng. 2005. *Social Science to Improve Fuels Management: A Synthesis of Research on Collaboration*. General Technical Report NC-257. St. Paul, MN: U.S. Department of Agriculture, Forest Service, North Central Research Station.

Terry, L. D. 2003. *Leadership of Public Bureaucracies.* Armonk, NY: Sharpe.

Tilt, W. 2005. "Getting Federal Land Management Agencies to the Collaborative Table: Barriers and Remedies." Paper prepared for the Collaborative Action Team and distributed at the Fifth CBCRC National Conference, Sedona, AZ, November 17–19.

Toker, C. W. 2005. "The Deliberative Ideal and Co-optation in the Georgia Ports Authority's Stakeholder Evaluation Group." In *The Environmental Communication Yearbook,* vol. 2, ed. S. L. Senecah, 19–48. Mahway, NJ: Lawrence Erlbaum.

Turning Point. 2006. "Leadership Development National Excellence Collaborative." http://www.collaborativeleadership.org/index.html.

Walker, G. B. 2009. "Constructing the Civic Square: Dimensions of Public Participation in Environmental Policy Conflict and Decision Situations." Paper presented at the Western States Communication Association Conference, Mesa, AZ, February.

Walker, G. B., and S. E. Daniels. 2005. "Assessing the Promise and Potential for Collaboration: The Progress Triangle Framework." In *Finding Our Way(s) in Environmental Communication: Proceedings of the Seventh Biennial Conference on Communication and the Environment,* ed. G. B. Walker and W. J. Kinsella, 188–201. Corvallis: Oregon State University, Department of Speech Communication.

Walker, G. B., S. E. Daniels, and A. S. Cheng. 2005. "Facilitating Dialogue and Deliberation in Environmental Conflict: The Use of Groups in Collaborative Learning." In *Facilitating Group Communication in Context: Innovations and Applications with Natural Groups,* ed. L. R. Frey. Creskill, NJ: Hampton Press.

Walker, G. B., S. L. Senecah, and S. E. Daniels. 2006. "From the Forest to the River: Citizens' Views of Stakeholder Engagement." *Human Ecology Review* 13 (2): 193–202.

Weber, E. P. 1998a. "Successful Collaboration: Negotiating Effective Regulations." *Environment* 40 (9): 10–22.

———. 1998b. *Pluralism by the Rules.* Washington, DC: Georgetown University Press.

———. 2003. *Bringing Society Back In.* Cambridge, MA: MIT Press.

Webler, T., S. Tuler, I. Shockey, P. Stern, and R. Beattie. 2003. "Participation by Local Governmental Officials in Watershed Management Planning." *Society and Natural Resources* 16:105–21.

Wing, S., G. Grant, M. Green, and C. Stewart. 1996. "Community-based Collaboration for Environmental Justice: South-east Halifax Environmental Reawakening." *Environment and Urbanization* 8 (2): 129–40.

Wondolleck, J. M., and C. M. Ryan. 1999. "What Hat Do I Wear Now? An Examination of Agency Roles in Collaborative Processes." *Negotiation Journal* 15 (2): 117–33.

Wondolleck, J. M., and S. L. Yaffee. 2000. *Making Collaboration Work: Lessons from Innovation in Natural Resource Management.* Washington, DC: Island Press.

———. 2001. *Sustaining the Success of Collaborative Partnerships: Revisiting the "Building Bridges" Cases.* Report no. 95-0728. U.S. Department of Agriculture, Forest Service, Pacific Northwest Research Station.

Yankelovich, D. 1999. *The Magic of Dialogue: Transforming Conflict into Cooperation.* New York: Touchstone.

Yukl, G. A. 2005. *Leadership in Organizations,* 6th ed. Montclair, NJ: Prentice Hall.

6

Building a Theory of Collaboration

William D. Leach

This chapter develops a simple theoretical framework to synthesize many of the recurring themes of the preceding four chapters. The purpose of the framework is to help structure our knowledge about community-based collaboratives (CBCs) and to help explain why, in study after study, scholars find that certain factors play critical roles in shaping CBC outcomes. Coming on the heels of the previous chapters, many of the ideas presented here should be familiar by now. What I try to accomplish is to organize the most well-documented and theoretically supported insights on a scaffolding that makes it easier to recall and think through the implications of each lesson learned. By summarizing recent theoretical and empirical research, this chapter seeks to review many of the essential building blocks of successful CBCs, and to trace the roots of their influence back to a small number of fundamental insights into human behavior, culture, psychology, and cognition.

Theory is essential for guiding empirical research and placing its findings in the context of previous studies. Without theory, we cannot demonstrate how a study contributes to the accumulation of knowledge in a particular field.

However, many stakeholders and professional facilitators view theory with apprehension. Too much of the theoretical literature that academics produce seems to be written for other academics, with little concern for practical applications. Even one connotation of the word—an approximate antonym for "reality"—discourages its acceptance among results-oriented stakeholders: "That idea might work in theory, but not on the ground."

Still, stakeholders and facilitators usually invoke an often unspoken sort of working theory whenever they make decisions about how to design a collaborative process. Chris Argyris and Donald Schon (1974) coined the phrase "theories of action" to describe the type of reasoning that forms "the conceptual basis on which we act and choose between particular courses of action" (Macfarlane and Mayer 2005a, 15, 2005b, 261). When facilitators explain why they recommend a specific approach in a particular situation, either they are applying a mental model of an ideal situation type, or they are making assumptions about causes and effects, or they are making other assumptions about the fundamental nature of the stakeholders and the circumstances they face. Theory is what allows us to respond effectively and efficiently to new circumstances by relating them to what has worked in similar situations encountered previously.

Thus, theory is at once essential and elusive. By anchoring this chapter in a rudimentary theoretical framework, I hope to provide a useful structure for organizing the huge quantity of information that makes up the current state-of-the-art knowledge of how CBCs function. Although each conclusion presented in the chapter is well documented, we still have much to learn about the dynamics of collaboration for environmental change. Scholars may wish to approach the framework as a road map for deriving hypotheses to test in future research.

To organize the material, I have devised a convention called a theoroid. Each theoroid consists of a single postulate about human nature and one broadly stated implication about how stakeholders should act or how they should structure CBCs for optimum effectiveness. The premise of this practical approach to building a theory of collaboration is that people—scholars and stakeholders alike—generally do not carry around entire social science theories in their heads. However, they do regularly remember and employ subsets of theories, something like the theoroids introduced here.

For example, if you ask professional facilitators to explain how they handled a specific situation, their answer will often include a basic assumption about human behavior plus a practical implication of this assumption.

Researcher: Why did you decide to stop the discussion when Jim told the joke about the governor? Doesn't a little humor lighten the mood and get everyone to relax?

Facilitator: Jim told a joke that poked fun at our governor, who's a Democrat. We have a ground rule that says humor is welcome, but never at the expense of another person. The joke probably offended some of the Democrats in the room. I admit, the joke *was* funny, but if I hadn't noted the ground rule violation, they might have questioned my impartiality and lost trust in me.

This facilitator has identified a basic assumption or postulate (people will not trust the facilitator if they do not believe she is impartial) and its practical implication (ground rules must be enforced scrupulously and equally so for all parties). I contend that this simple pairing of postulates and implications—that is, theoroids—is essentially how people use theory in their daily lives and professional practice.

By asserting that most of the essential building blocks of successful CBCs can be traced to merely ten theoroids, I am offering an admittedly simplified and reductionist theory of collaboration. I hope that the result is an instructive and user-friendly structure for organizing what we know about how people behave in CBCs, and to what effect. The ten theoroids are organized into three sections, as detailed below.

The first section, "The Essence of Collaboration," describes and illustrates three theoroids about human societies and cognition that influence how people learn, innovate, and negotiate in groups. As discussed in chapters 2 and 3, stakeholders often begin a collaborative process by striving to achieve greater understanding of local environmental problems and how those problems affect various interest groups. Stakeholders then typically try to harness their newfound knowledge to collectively create better ways of living and working in the local community. Ultimately, the power of CBCs lies in their ability to invent new policies, projects, or practices that address the fundamental interests of all parties.

The second section, "The Legitimacy of Collaboration," illustrates four theoroids about core human values that influence how people judge whether a process is fair. Procedural fairness is important, first, because it is essential for sustaining a collaborative process, second, because it promotes compliance with the rules and decisions of the groups, and third, because people value fairness as an end in itself.

The third section, "The Economics of Collaboration," illustrates three theoroids about how people evaluate whether a process is worthwhile. Sustaining a CBC takes time, money, and personal energy. Every stakeholder has other issues competing for attention, and the option of stepping away from the table is an ever-present threat to the sustainability of the collaborative process. Economics is a body of scientific theory about human behavior that provides important insights into how people decide whether to collaborate, especially in situations where the costs of collaboration are clear and immediate but the benefits are often deferred and uncertain.

To introduce each theoroid, I begin with a general discussion about the basic postulate, frequently drawing concepts and evidence from a wider swath of the social sciences than appears elsewhere in the book. I then narrow the focus to what works for CBCs, with conclusions drawn primarily from empirical studies of community-based collaboration.

The Essence of Collaboration: How People Learn, Innovate, and Negotiate in Groups

For complex environmental issues that play out at the local scale, the interests of multiple segments of society are often interdependent. No one group or individual is likely to possess sufficient knowledge or power to address a given socioenvironmental problem to his or her satisfaction. Theoroid 1 establishes why collaboration is often essential for resolving such issues and identifies basic conditions for effective collaboration. Theoroids 2 and 3 each present a major cognitive obstacle to effective collaboration, followed by a general approach to overcome the obstacle.

Theoroid 1

Postulate: Each person's welfare depends on the values, knowledge, and resources of others.

Implication: CBCs are most effective when they address environmental problems systemically by involving representatives of every group with a stake in the outcome.

This postulate about the interdependence of people's fates is a simple and perhaps incontrovertible statement. Its simplicity might tempt us to dismiss it as a truism, but simple truths are not without value. This particular truth is a sensible place to begin organizing our knowledge of CBCs because bringing people together to solve interrelated environmental and social problems is the most fundamental function CBCs serve. In the United States, CBCs are frequently born out of political stalemate and mutual dissatisfaction with the status quo. By coming together, participants are recognizing that their destinies are interdependent and that no one individual or group has sufficient knowledge or power to resolve issues by working alone.

American CBCs are partly a response to the limitations of the expert-centered approach to natural resource management that dominated the landscape during the first two-thirds of the twentieth century. As public concern over the environmental consequences of public works projects grew during the 1960s, new statutes emerged to create opportunities for citizens to participate in government policymaking (Koontz et al. 2004; Sabatier, Weible, and Ficker 2005).

The importance of a holistic perspective marked by inclusive and representative participation is an almost universally cited finding in research on CBCs. Indeed, it can be called a defining CBC characteristic. The rationale is twofold. The first reason is to ensure that all relevant perspectives are brought to bear on a problem so that participants can collectively invent novel policy solutions that effectively address the values and interests of each segment of society. No one person can possibly anticipate every important consequence of a proposed action. Most solutions to problems create new problems of their own. By getting the whole system in the room at the outset, stakeholders are more likely to consider the issues from all points of view and less likely to pursue policies with unintended consequences (Schuett, Selin, and Carr 2001). The participants must collectively possess the right combination of knowledge and expertise necessary to address complex environmental problems.

The second factor that inextricably ties together stakeholders' fates is the fact that all stakeholders have a variety of resources that they can either contribute to the success of the process, or withhold if dissatisfied, or use offensively to undermine the work of the CBC. Some of the more conspicuous types of resources are financial and regulatory powers, and various forms of physical capital (including ownership of land, water rights, mineral rights, or grazing permits). Other stakeholders may have the ear of key legislators or the ability to sway public opinion, engage the media, or mobilize citizen activists—leading to changes in law or budgetary priorities. Others have the ability to seek judicial review and enforcement of existing laws and regulations. Stakeholders who remain outside a CBC, whether involuntarily or by choice, can raise roadblocks down the line by withholding necessary political support or by challenging the CBC's policies through other venues. A whole-system approach is needed to cultivate support for the policy among all parties whose cooperation will be required during implementation. Broad participation coupled with a search for common ground should result in proposals that are viable politically as well as technically.

What Works

A systems approach to environmental management, including diverse and representative stakeholder participation, is thought to be essential (Daniels and Walker 1996). Involving influential stakeholders is also the first strategy identified in chapter 4 for overcoming external obstacles to community-based collaboration. This reasoning features prominently not only in the CBC literature but also in scholarship on advocacy coalitions (Weible 2005), adaptive management (Gunderson and Holling 2002; Norton 2002), risk assessment (National Research Council 1996), complex adaptive systems (Innes and Booher 1999a; Dietz, Ostrom, and Stern 2003), and postnormal science (Ravetz 1999).

1. *Inclusive membership rules.* An open invitation to join a CBC is often all that it takes to bring stakeholders to the table—especially once a critical mass has coalesced and begun to meet regularly. Most organized interest groups are eager to be present whenever rival interests are talking to government agencies about public policy. One must assume that unless someone shows up to advocate on your behalf, the CBC might make decisions that affect you adversely. As the saying goes, "If you're not at the table, you're on the menu."

An inclusive CBC—meaning one that places few formal restrictions on participation—is also likely to enjoy greater legitimacy in the eyes of stakeholders (see chapter 4). Restricting participation to a select group of stakeholders often raises doubts about who was excluded and why. For example, Ashford and Rest's (1999, VII-7) study of collaborative management of toxic waste sites concluded that restricted participation "can easily reproduce and reinforce the existing power imbalances in the community." At least one study suggests that restricted participation can have practical disadvantages as well: stakeholders in twenty-six environmental CBCs in Oregon were more likely to give their collaborative low marks on overall effectiveness and timeliness when the CBC restricted participation (Dakins, Long, and Hart 2005).

2. *Taking affirmative steps to achieve skilled, representative participation.* Inclusive participation rules do not guarantee that every societal faction will be represented, or that all participants will have adequate skill and authority to represent their constituents effectively. CBCs can employ several measures to improve representation.

One aspect of representativeness is whether each faction has an advocate at the table. Achieving this goal may entail holding meetings at a convenient time and place to involve more local citizens or small landowners (Smith, McDonough, and Mang 1999; Tuler and Webler 1999). In CBCs with a large geographic scope, travel distances can vary widely from one stakeholder to the next, making representation harder to achieve. Another tension is that some stakeholders inevitably prefer to conduct CBC business during normal work hours, whereas others can only participate evenings or weekends. Some well-financed CBCs offer child care or stipends to encourage participation by stakeholders with modest incomes.

Occasionally, a relevant sector of society will be unengaged in the policy process (e.g., homeless people who camp in areas potentially affected by open space policies). To incorporate their perspectives, existing members of the CBC may need to go to great lengths to find an appropriate advocate for the affected community and to educate that individual on the issues being discussed.

One way to efficiently achieve both inclusivity and representativeness is to ask the stakeholders to assemble themselves into caucuses (e.g., industry, environment, local government). Each caucus then nominates a representative to participate in the collaborative process. This approach allows all interested individuals to participate in designing the process even if they do not ultimately participate in the CBC itself.

Another important facet of representation is the participants' competence and skill (Webler 1995). Pertinent capabilities range from technical knowledge to fluency in acronyms to confidence in public speaking. In a study of national forest planning in Oregon, Shindler and Neburka (1997) recommend handpicking participants who are knowledgeable about the issues. They also find value in ground rules that restrict participation to individuals who can commit to a year's worth of meetings and exclude new members from joining established groups to avoid the delay of bringing them up to speed.

A third facet of representation is the extent to which participants are able to accurately reflect the views of the people or organizations they represent (see chapter 4). In particular, it is helpful if participants are decision makers with sufficient authority to commit their organizations to a particular course of action (Selin and Myers 1995; Yaffee, Wondolleck, and Lippman 1997). Ideally, more than one individual is present to represent larger organizations, where the perspectives of top administrators often differ from those of their subordinates, who will play the most direct role in implementing any new agreements or policies. As Potapchuk and Crocker (1999, 534) explain:

> Common wisdom is to seek the most senior persons to ensure that the representatives can make commitments on behalf of their organizations. Indeed, this rule of thumb has become the norm in public policy consensus building. However, some observers have begun to challenge this approach to representation. Westley (1995) in an analysis of multiple environmental policy-making processes, argues that "many middle- and lower-level managers are deliberately excluded from the rich face-to-face discussions that forge the backdrop, the meanings, and the frames for policy discussions." He goes on to note that this exclusionary practice limits overall organizational learning, blocks innovation, and fails to address implementation.

Perfect representation is often difficult to achieve. One major study of seventy-six West Coast watershed partnerships found that nearly a third of stakeholders disagreed or strongly disagreed that their partnership "represents the interests of most people in the local community" (Leach 2006a, 106). Moreover, 54 percent agreed or strongly agreed with the statement, "Some critical interests are *not* effectively represented."

3. *Periodically reassessing representation.* The representativeness of a CBC's participants changes over time. As the scope of the CBC's work expands or as participants discover new implications of the projects they are pursuing, new participants may have to be brought in to reflect this enlarged scope. Furthermore, the participants themselves are also dynamic, as are the organizations and constituencies they represent. For example, individuals and organizations can shift priorities as they learn and adapt to new information and circumstances. For both practical and philosophical reasons, it is helpful if constituents and their representatives evolve roughly in step. Frequently, however, CBC participants evolve faster because of their personal involvement in the collaborative process and their exposure to diverse points of view. Reassessing and rebuilding the alignment between a participant's interests and those of his or her constituents is particularly important when the CBC is on the verge of making major decisions. By and large, it is the constituent organizations and individuals who will be called on to implement most of the provisions of a CBC agreement, not the negotiators themselves (Scholz and Stiftel 2005, 8–9).

To ensure that negotiators don't get too far ahead of the people they represent, many facilitators insist that the parties regularly confer with their constituents to inform them about developments occurring at the negotiating table and to ascertain what types of concessions or commitments they might be willing to support. Planning scholar John Forester (2005, 154), citing Bruce Stiftel (2001), describes this challenge as one of "working effectively at 'two tables,' one that we can call 'at home,' at which they try to resolve the ambiguous and internally contested formulation of their own interests, and another 'in public,' at which they as representatives seek to articulate, defend, and promote their interests in the face of potential adversaries." Both types of negotiations must proceed in concert.

As negotiations approach their culmination, Susskind and Cruikshank (2006, 187) recommend a deliberate "check-off process" in which each representative takes a near-final version of the agreement back to his or her constituents to ask for their consent.

Theoroid 2

Postulate: No two people interpret new information in precisely the same way because individuals' differing experiences and beliefs lead them to view the world differently.

Implication: CBCs are most effective when stakeholders first focus on developing a common understanding of the problems they seek to address.

Perhaps it is no coincidence that the blossoming of the environmental collaboration movement in the mid-1980s came shortly after several major social movements in the United States had crested, particularly the women's movement, the civil rights movement, the postmodern movement in popular culture, and the postpositivist movement in the philosophy of science. After achieving a less segregated workforce through the political struggles of the 1960s and 1970s, the major accomplishments of the women's movement and the civil rights movement in the 1980s were less about changing the law and more about learning to coexist in a new, diversifying society. Concurrently, a different type of social integration was happening in the "New West," as the land became more crowded and environmental regulations enacted during the prior two decades stoked long-smoldering conflicts over how to accommodate incompatible land uses. People whose lives rarely would have crossed a decade earlier were now interacting regularly.

At the same time that American society was becoming more integrated and diverse, the postpositivist and postmodern movements were changing the way ordinary people thought about science, literature, arts, and popular culture. Postmodernism emphasizes the notion that different cultures hold different worldviews, and it questions the existence of absolute truths. Postpositivism similarly posits that reality is socially constructed, and it questions the ability of humans to perceive the world objectively.

Landmark developments in the postpositivist movement include Karl Popper's (1959) falsification doctrine, which holds that scientific propositions can never be conclusively proved true—and, in the strictest formulation, can never be proved false—because the observations on which all scientific inferences are based can always be challenged (Brown 1977). Festinger's (1957) experimental work in psychology led to the concept of cognitive dissonance, which holds that people readily adopt false beliefs when doing so helps them reconcile two conflicting pieces of evidence they otherwise believe to be true. In 1962, Thomas Kuhn published *The Structure of Scientific Revolutions,* in which he coined the phrase "paradigm shift" and helped change popular perceptions of scientific authority by arguing that scientists (like everyone else) tenaciously cling to their current beliefs in the face of contradicting evidence. In 1979, experimental research by Lord, Ross, and Lepper (1979) found that the tenacity of existing beliefs and biased assimilation of new information is not limited to scientists. When citizens with strong positions on a particular political issue are presented with ambiguous evidence, people on both sides of the debate tend to interpret the new data as support for their prior conclusions. Ambiguous evidence causes policy positions to polarize further, not converge.

In the mid-1980s Paul Sabatier and Hank Jenkins-Smith worked out the implications of cognitive dissonance and biased assimilation for what they termed "policy subsystems," the networks of public officials, advocacy groups, and other stakeholders seeking to influence public policy on a particular topic. Because individuals who differ on core beliefs see the world through different lenses and often interpret a given piece of evidence in different ways, they reasoned, people who reach opposite conclusions on factual issues tend to question each other's motives or intelligence. Even on policy topics where the scientific evidence is relatively clear, stakeholders who lack a common set of perceptual filters will tend to view their adversaries as backward, ignorant, or malevolent. Distrust and polarization are exacerbated when the relevant data are ambiguous.

The basic problem CBCs face is that they often bring together people with strikingly different cultural backgrounds, life experiences, beliefs, and values. As Walker and Senecah review in chapter 5, people with different backgrounds learn in different ways (Adler and Birkhoff 2002). For example, Curtin in chapter 2 describes how even seemingly minor philosophical differences, such as those that separate scientists trained in different disciplines, can impede communication and learning.

At the same time, many of the environmental issues that CBCs struggle with are complicated by spotty data documenting local trends in environmental and social parameters. This ambiguity in the scientific record fuels biased assimilation, theory tenacity, and distrust. Even when CBCs are fortunate enough to have relatively good information to work with, that is not enough. To achieve trust and a common base of knowledge for collaborative decision making, the stakeholders must come to agree on the facts, and their relevance for policy.

Arguably, one of the primary functions CBCs serve is to help stakeholders cope with the barriers to trust and communication that stem from the socially constructed nature of people's perceptions of the physical word. Perhaps it is no accident that virtually all of the academic researchers who were drawn to the collaboration phenomenon at its inception in the mid-1980s were trained with heavy doses of postpositivist philosophy. Very few positivist-leaning, quantitative researchers discovered the movement until it was well underway a decade later.

What Works

To facilitate learning, innovation, and negotiation among stakeholders with diverse cultural backgrounds, CBCs need to help stakeholders develop a common base of knowledge and assumptions, a process that Innes and Boo-her (2010) call social learning. Several studies (and chapter 4) support the value of dedicating the early stages of collaboration to the sole purpose of education (Daniels and Walker 1996; Huntington and Sommarstrom 2000). During such an educational phase, CBC participants or outside guests are invited to make presentations to the group to educate each another about the issues and their respective stakes in the outcomes. A dedicated educational phase can lay the groundwork for later brainstorming and negotiation, and might stretch on for months or years before negotiations begin.

Another approach to learning and innovation with considerable empirical support is frequently termed "joint fact-finding" (Karl, Susskind, and Wallace 2007). Joint fact-finding involves stakeholders with differing interpretations of the scientific evidence working together to develop common assumptions, commission new studies or analyses, and define remaining areas of disagreement or uncertainty (Ozawa 1991; Lee 1993; Ehrmann and Stinson 1999; Lenard and Finlayson 2004). Joint fact-finding techniques can help stakeholders critically examine their own assumptions and explain the reasoning behind their stated positions (National Research Council 1996). Achieving agreement on empirical issues enhances trust by demonstrating that the other stakeholders are reasonable people who can be convinced by sound evidence (Leach and Sabatier 2005b).

Joint fact-finding often requires considerable scientific expertise, either among the members of the CBC itself or by paid or pro bono consultants from industry or academia. Access to scientific information and expertise is noted as a key to successful CBC outcomes in a number of studies (e.g., Margerum 1999a, 1999b). Yaffee, Wondolleck, and Lippman (1997) emphasize the need for access to appropriate technology for communications and decision support—from the Internet to GIS. Survey data from studies of estuary- and watershed-based CBCs indicate that the level of scientific expertise available to a partnership correlates with the level of consensus, cooperation, newly generated human capital, and perceived effects on environmental and social outcomes (Lubell, Leach, and Sabatier 2009).

Building consensus on disputed scientific issues is frequently aided by the services of a neutral facilitator who pressures scientific experts on each side to justify their claims before their peers by using accepted standards of data quality and inference (Zafonte and Sabatier 1998). When the policy arena includes both scientists and stakeholders without technical backgrounds, the literature points to the importance of a mediator who can skillfully translate technical jargon into plain, accessible language and can coach scientists to focus on policy-relevant aspects of their research (McCreary 1999).

Finally, building consensus around the science is easier when stakehold-ers share an ethos of mutual respect for each other's ways of knowing, including, for example, local knowledge or indigenous knowledge along-side scientific knowledge (Adler and Birkhoff 2002). Dryzek and Niemeyer (2003) refer to this ethos as "epistemic metaconsensus"—consensus that others' epistemologies, or ways of knowing, are valid, even if different from one's own.

Theoroid 3

Postulate: People's beliefs and values lie along a spectrum from fundamental to instrumental, and people often confuse their fundamental interests with their instrumental positions.

Implication: CBCs are most effective when stakeholders seek to invent novel policy positions that satisfy each other's fundamental interests.

The notion that people's beliefs, values, or motivations are arranged on a continuum has a substantial history in the social sciences, going back at least to Abraham Maslow's (1943) hierarchy of needs. For CBCs, one of the most useful distinctions is the interest versus position dichotomy de-scribed by Roger Fisher and William Ury in their landmark book, *Getting to Yes* (1981). Interests are the fundamental values or conditions that we wish to achieve for ourselves or for society, such as environmental quality, eco-nomic security, justice, or happiness. Positions are the policies we pursue in the belief that obtaining them will help realize our fundamental interests.

Fisher and Ury convey a number of important insights about the rela-tionship between interests and positions. First, a given interest can usually be satisfied through a number of different means. Second, people often lose sight of the difference between their interests and positions, and come to view their positions as nonnegotiable ends in themselves. As a result, often they either take a hard bargaining stance and refuse to yield any ground on their positions, or take a softer stance and do give ground but later regret having compromised.

The tendency to confuse positions and interests probably lies in the cognitive habit that economist Herbert Simon (1957) termed "satisficing." Simon hypothesized that when choosing among options or searching for solutions to problems, people often stop searching as soon as they find one that works *well enough*. Rather than find the best solution, they accept the first satisfactory solution they find. Having looked for and found only one solution, it is easy for people, over time, to come to believe it is the only solution possible. Having made this cognitive error, one logically equates one's positions with the interests they were designed to achieve. Because many political struggles stretch on for many months, years, or decades, there is ample time for stakeholders to confuse their interests and positions. The longer a position is held, the more difficult it becomes to revisit the assumptions on which it was originally based.

Consequently, negotiators often focus on positions rather than interests. Position-based bargaining assumes a zero-sum game in which one party's gain is another's loss. Under this model of negotiation, parties may try to gain advantage over their counterparts through subterfuge, psychological manipulation, or other unethical tactics. Because neither party is focusing on fundamental interests, fundamental interests are rarely satisfied. Instead, each party ends up conceding one or more policy positions to achieve a compromise agreement, and everyone walks away from the negotiation dissatisfied.

To overcome the pitfalls of position-based bargaining requires a change in perspective. Rather than searching for the first position that satisfies one's *own* interest, stakeholders must adopt a Tocquevillian (1840) notion of enlightened self-interest and search for a position that will satisfy not only their own fundamental interests but also those of all other parties. This naturally takes more work and more time, and requires a certain level of mutual trust among the parties. It requires the parties to honestly reveal sufficient information about their own core interests to allow the other parties to work toward policy proposals that might satisfy them. Exposing oneself in this way requires faith in others to negotiate honestly and without malice. Interest-based negotiation also requires the parties to recognize that although they might not share the same underlying interests as the other parties, each party's interests are still legitimate and worthy of being satisfied. Although this type of negotiation is costly and somewhat risky, the reward is the potential for creating innovative policy solutions that were not apparent previously (Dukes and Firehock 2001).

What Works

Interest-based negotiation in CBCs requires stakeholders to (1) know what their own interests are (which is not always as simple as it seems), (2) learn about the other parties' interests, and (3) invent new positions that satisfy the interests of every party. The theoretical and empirical literature on CBCs and consensus building suggest that a number of meeting management techniques described below facilitate these three tasks.

Fisher and Ury (1981) identify the two basic approaches to learning about the interests of other parties, which, simply enough, entail either asking other parties to describe their interests or trying to anticipate their interests by "putting yourself in their shoes." One of the advantages of CBCs is that they place much greater emphasis on informal dialogue among the stakeholders relative to other types of public policy forums, such as public hearings. Public hearings are relatively antagonistic in that the lead agency advocates for and defends a proposal while citizens testify for or against it. They are characterized by one-way communication, from the lead agency to the public and from the public to the agency. There is some evidence that the informal nature of many CBCs helps stakeholders speak more openly and naturally, whereas the classic parliamentary procedures, such as Robert's Rules of Order, reinforce antagonistic tendencies and impede open dialogue (Susskind and Cruikshank 2006).

One way to put oneself in the shoes of other stakeholders is through formal role-playing games or simulations. Planning scholars Judith Innes and David Booher (1999b) liken the entire consensus-building process to a role-playing exercise in which participants come to better understand other players' interests as well as their own. Reflecting on a role-playing exercise conducted during an international summit on disaster preparedness, Barrett et al. (2003) find that "simulation is not only an opportunity for the participants to explore creative options toward resolution of the real-life situation [but also to] build relationships and understandings that may help to achieve workable solutions."

Inventing creative solutions is the final critical component. One of the comparative advantages of CBCs is they provide a relatively informal, nonconfrontational environment in which participants are permitted to brainstorm, offering up unusual or partially formed ideas for discussion. By contrast, classic parliamentary procedures such as Robert's Rules of Order (which set strict rules for proposing, discussing, and voting on new ideas) are thought to squander the productive energy that stakeholders bring to issues they care about (Susskind and Cruikshank 2006).

Facilitators often encourage participants to characterize their initial ideas as "trial balloons" intended for group discussion and analysis rather than as "proposals." Proposals are ideas that the proponent is expected to support and defend, whereas trial balloons invite further creative reflection. A period of nonjudgmental brainstorming allows ideas to evolve gradually before being scrutinized. Brainstorming is in keeping with the motto, variously attributed to Aristotle or Confucius, "It is the mark of an educated mind to be able to entertain a thought without accepting it." Innes and Booher (1999b) liken collaboration to the French concept of bricolage, the piecing together of diverse materials in novel and unexpected ways, often without a clear vision of the end product. CBCs can work in a similar fashion by piecing together diverse sets of skills, knowledge, and perspectives

to create original ideas addressing stubborn social and environmental problems. Complexity theorists argue that an organization's ability to innovate
and adapt depends on the freedom it affords its members to entertain new
ideas and to question established assumptions, a process known as double-
loop learning (Argyris 1993; Innes and Booher 2004; Rose-Anderssen et al.
2005; Stiftel and Scholz 2005).

The Legitimacy of Collaboration: How People Decide Whether the Process Is Fair

A number of human tendencies influence how people judge whether a
process is fair and legitimate. Procedural fairness is important because it is
essential for sustaining a collaborative process, because it promotes compliance with the rules and decisions of the groups, and because fairness is
itself an important goal that stakeholders strive to achieve.

Theoroid 4

Postulate: People value a fair process nearly as much as a favorable outcome.
Implication: CBCs should devote time and effort to establishing, maintaining, and
*   assessing procedural fairness.*

By most accounts, the primary reason stakeholders participate in CBCs is
to promote whatever private and social interests they care about, be they
economic, social, or environmental. When reflecting on the success of a
CBC, most stakeholders rightly and understandably focus on whether it
has made measurable progress toward achieving substantive goals. Nonetheless, theory and research suggest that unless stakeholders also pay close
attention to their perceptions of the fairness and legitimacy of the collaborative process, they risk failing to sustain the process through the day-to-day
and year-to-year struggles of deliberation, negotiation, and implementation.

A diverse academic literature spanning more than thirty years has shown
that, in addition to being an important goal in itself, the fairness of a decision-making process can pay off in terms of substantive outcomes (Thibaut
and Walker 1975). Evidence can be found both outside and within CBCs.
For example, in a review of procedural justice theory applied to natural
resource decision making, Lawrence, Daniels, and Stankey (1997) conclude
that perceptions of procedural fairness result in "greater acceptance of, and
higher levels of compliance with, decisions (Tyler 1987; Gibson 1989)." Research led by social psychologists Tom Tyler and Steven Blader shows that

cooperation in groups and deference to decision makers tend to correlate with the perceived legitimacy of the decision-making process (Tyler and Blader 2000; Tyler and Huo 2002). A large study of estuary-based collaboratives found that stakeholders' perceptions of procedural fairness correlate with three measures of CBC outcomes, including the levels of consensus, cooperation, and perceived effectiveness (Lubell, Leach, and Sabatier 2009). In another large study focusing on West Coast watershed partnerships, Leach and Sabatier (2005a) found that procedural fairness correlates highly with the levels of interpersonal trust among stakeholders and with the amount of new human and social capital generated within the partnership.

Remarkably, research suggests that people often value a fair decision-making process nearly as much as they value a favorable decision (Hibbing and Theiss-Morse 2001). According to a review by Tyler and Blader (2003), this assertion received impressive support in early experimental studies, which showed that people object when the outcomes of a process seem too favorable to some while unfairly disadvantaging others. "This finding suggested that people will give up resources and accept less when they believe doing so is fair" (Tyler and Blader 2003, 350). Summarizing research on workplace compensation by Greenberg (1987), Katz (2000) writes that employees "tolerated a distribution of rewards that they felt was unfair so long as the process of determining the distribution seemed fair." Lawrence, Daniels, and Stankey (1997, 586) conclude that "regardless of outcomes, failure of procedures to comport with societal norms of fairness will result in disaffection. Fair procedures can be expected to increase participant satisfaction, compliance with laws, and opinions of decision makers."

For example, participants will rely on their perceptions of procedural fairness when deciding whether the issues on the table are ripe for decision making. Were opposing opinions equally scrutinized? Were any important data or expert opinions either censored or accepted without debate? Judgments about the fairness and legitimacy of the process will again loom large during the implementation phase as stakeholders decide whether the collective decisions of the CBC are legitimate and worthy of being honored.

What Works

The diverse literature on procedural justice has roots in psychology, sociology, political science, and even evolutionary biology. These distinct lineages tend to emphasize different factors necessary for establishing and maintaining perceptions of procedural justice, some of which are highlighted below in theoroids 5, 6, and 7.

Theoroid 5

Postulate: People primarily define fairness as equal treatment of all parties.
Implication: CBCs should have impartial facilitators and clear process rules, faith-
  fully implemented to give all parties equal opportunity to speak, vote, or veto.

In his January 10, 2005, State of the State speech, Oregon governor Ted
Kulongoski summed up the frustration stakeholders feel when they believe
a collaborative process is stacked in favor of one party over another: "Make
no mistake: I believe in a strong state-federal partnership. The federal government owns more than half of Oregon's forestlands. We have to work
together; but as equals—not as landlord and tenant. After two years of
dealing with the federal government on environmental issues that are critical to Oregon's future, I've learned an important lesson: On our side of the
table 'partnership' means what the dictionary says it means. On their side
of the table it means consultation—and then doing whatever they want."
    In the book *Collaborative Environmental Management: What Role for Govern-*
ment? Tomas Koontz and five co-authors (2004) effectively seek to discover
whether Governor Kulongoski's vision of collaboration among equals is
workable in practice, particularly in the context of CBCs. Specifically, the
book asks "whether government could be an equal partner while often
being the party accountable for the decisions reached and the outcomes
achieved" (viii). The authors eventually conclude that the legitimacy of a
CBC hinges on its ability to achieve "equal power and influence for governmental and nongovernmental actors alike" (175–76).
    Equality-based theories of procedural fairness that call for an equitable
distribution of power among the stakeholders are intuitively appealing,
but probably should not be interpreted literally. As Koontz and colleagues
clearly demonstrate, each individual stakeholder brings different personal
skills to the table, and each wields different types of political and legal
power. In particular, each individual is unique and unequal with respect to
speaking skills, the number of constituents he or she represents, and the
power to disrupt the CBC's work by withholding consent or walking away
from the table altogether. Through six case studies, the book catalogues the
many critical roles that government officials play—roles that often could
not be fulfilled by other types of stakeholders. The authors conclude that
the utility of any collaborative endeavor stems from the complementarity
of the participants' differences (41).
    Rather than pinning a definition of procedural fairness on a strict notion
of equal power, stakeholders can focus on creating a process that treats
each participant equally.

What Works

The key to achieving equal treatment of all parties is transparency, meaning clear procedural rules faithfully implemented with the assistance of an impartial facilitator, if necessary. Procedural equality should extend both to voice—meaning the opportunities stakeholders have to express their views—and to decision-making authority—meaning the right to participate in formal votes or to raise objections during a consensus-building effort.

Another area where transparency is crucial is each participant's intention to comply with group decisions. In CBCs that focus on providing advice to a lead decision-making agency, it is particularly important that the agency be transparent about its intentions. Agencies that signal their willingness to implement any agreements resulting from the process give stakeholders greater incentive to collaborate and negotiate in good faith. Agencies that merely promise to consider public comments offer stakeholders few assurances that their concerns will actually be addressed. Cheng and Mattor (2006, 558) argue that agencies must "clarify exactly how and where stakeholder input will be incorporated into planning decisions." Based on a study of participants and nonparticipants in a National Forest planning process, they recommend convening "preplanning 'policy education' workshops for key stakeholders and the general public to define which resource management decisions are open for influence by the collaborative process and which issues are constrained by existing authorities" (558).

Attentive implementation of all procedural ground rules is an essential facet of procedural equality. Some of the clearest evidence comes from a study of workplace cooperation, which found that employees evaluate procedural justice in terms of the fairness of the firm's formal decision-making procedures and the consistency with which it carries them out (Tyler and Blader 2000; Blader and Tyler 2003).

Although ground rules are important, they can be overdone. Some studies suggest that flexible or informal process rules can work well, especially if the group is small and participants already know one another well. For example, Selin and Chavez (1994) describe the benefits of informal protocols and a "homey atmosphere," which may account for the negative correlation that Selin and Myers (1995) found to exist between participants' assessment of the group's effectiveness and the perceived adequacy of its structure. The trade-off between clarity and informality of a process should be adjusted to meet the needs of each particular group.

Theoroid 6

Postulate: People are highly sensitive to cues about their social status in groups.
Implication: CBC participants will view the process favorably if they are treated
  with civility and respect, and if their participation materially influences the
  outcomes of the process.

To one extent or another, we all are conscious of how others perceive us. Evolutionary theorists reason that our preoccupation with social status stems from the reproductive advantages it confers in terms of greater access to food, shelter, and mates. As Hibbing and Theiss-Morse (2007, 4) argue, natural selection has produced a species of

> highly social animals who care deeply about the judgments of those around them. They want to feel they have contributed to the group and that others in the group value (and respond to) their input. Research from psychology and across the social sciences stresses people's desire to be a valued part of a social unit. . . . One of the outgrowths of humans' social nature is a powerful desire for validation, for assurance regarding worth and place within the group. People are neurotic about this. They want to know that others in the group, particularly powerful group members, view them and their needs with respect since losing a place within the group could be dangerous—or at least this was the case in humans' evolutionary past.

Regardless of how we arrived at this condition, evidence suggests that our social status matters to us and influences how we perceive the groups we join. Specifically, this theoroid predicts that individuals' perception of the value of a collaborative group will correlate with their perceived status in the group.

One indicator of high social status is evidence that one's participation has had a material influence on decisions. In experimental research, Hibbing and Theiss-Morse (2007) found that people's perceptions of the fairness of a decision (as well as their satisfaction and compliance with that decision) are improved when they believe they have successfully persuaded the decision maker to revise a preliminary decision in a favorable direction.

Another indicator of high social status is evidence that others in the group treat you with civility and respect. In the watershed partnerships study discussed previously, for example, we found that stakeholders' perceptions of the civility and respectfulness of the deliberations was the single strongest correlate with perceptions that "the process treats all parties fairly" ($r = 0.65$, n $= 1,425$).

Mutual respect and attention to cultural differences may be the dominant indicator of sound working relationship in CBCs involving Native American tribes (Reza 2003). For example, Sherman (2004, 3–4) describes how the Western concepts of forgiveness and apology have no counterpart in Native American cultures. "A mediator who doesn't understand this may try to get two Native parties to shake hands and apologize to each other. Such a solution may not ultimately work because the parties may be forced to look each other in the eyes and touch flesh, which is unacceptable behavior in many Native cultures." Differences in culture and communication styles and the ignorance of many non-natives about these differences may inhibit the development of productive stakeholder relationships (Jostad, McAvoy, and McDonald 1996; Lane and Hausam 2003), resulting in a loss of confidence in the process itself.

What Works

Boosting stakeholders' perceptions of their social standing within a CBC can be achieved through the two key indicators that people use to gauge their social standing: (1) their influence on group decisions and (2) the civility and respect with which other members address them.

Influence is difficult to manage but can be addressed both in terms of the personal influence of individual stakeholders and in terms of the collective influence of the CBC as a whole. To ensure that each stakeholder has an opportunity to influence the group to the maximum extent possible, given her or his available skills and resources, it is helpful for facilitators to work with disadvantaged stakeholders to help them develop a clear picture of the basis for their negotiating power within the CBC, including their BATNA, or "best alternative to a negotiated agreement." Many stakeholders approach a new CBC without fully contemplating the various types of power and influence they might be able to wield.

At the collective level, every stakeholder is likely to come away disaffected if the goal of the CBC has been to provide policy recommendations to official decision-making bodies and if those decision makers appear to ignore the CBC's advice. As noted in the context of other theoroids, the relationship between the CBC and external decision makers should be transparent, and ideally the CBC should work closely with the decision-making authority at every step to build mutual support for draft recommendations.

The other major indicator of social standing is civility and respect. To a surprising extent, it may be possible to legislate civility by adopting and enforcing ground rules defining the expected norms of interpersonal behavior. For example, many CBCs prohibit stakeholders from interrupting each other or questioning each other's motives or character. Civility and respect can also be cultivated by creating opportunities for informal social interaction outside regular meetings, such as during shared meals or field trips to demonstration projects (Schuett, Selin, and Carr 2001).

Finally, several factors can raise the stakes of social status without directly influencing perceptions of status (Hibbing and Theiss-Morse 2007). One is voice. To have one's views solicited and then ignored sends a direct message of low status. In Hibbing and Theiss-Morse's laboratory experiments, voice increases satisfaction and perceived legitimacy when it appears to have had a positive influence on decision makers but reduces satisfaction and perceived legitimacy when decision makers appear to have ignored the subject's advice. In summary, these preliminary findings suggest that stakeholders should be granted the *opportunity* to speak and participate but should not necessarily be pressured to state opinions, especially if it is unlikely that their participation will affect outcomes. These findings are consistent with Senecah's (2004) concept of the trinity of voice and the idea that having access and standing "will do more harm than good unless they lead to influence" (see chapter 5).

Another factor that raises the stakes is group size. In small groups, it is easier for each member to identify whose input was received and whose was dismissed. A third is the prestige of the group. People care most about their status in groups that they regard highly (Tyler and Blader 2003). Stakeholders should remember that perceptions of social status will be even more important as the size of the group diminishes and the prestige of a group swells. Finally, stakeholders should pay attention to cultural differences, which can cause people to inadvertently send signals of disrespect.

Theoroid 7

Postulate: People desire the right to self-determination.

Implication: CBC participants will judge the process to be fair if they participate in convening the process and designing the ground rules that govern deliberation and decision making.

The premise of this theoroid is that people, by nature, seek dominion over the rules that govern them. A decision-making process is viewed as fair only to the extent that the people subject to the decisions have played a role in convening the process and drafting the constitutional rules that define the decision-making process (Born and Genskow 2000).

What Works

The conveners of a CBC can create a broad sense of self-determination by involving all stakeholders in designing and managing the process. Stakeholders should ideally be involved as early as possible, and should have a significant role in drafting the ground rules, bylaws, or other constitutional rules governing the deliberations and decision making. The concept of ownership has become a prominent theme in the literature on natural resource planning, and several studies have linked ownership of a plan to greater chances for political support and implementation (Wondolleck and Yaffee 2000; McCool and Guthrie 2001; Van Riper 2003; Lachapelle and McCool 2005).

Distributed ownership may seem threatening to convening agencies if they fear it would mean losing control or abdicating their management authority. According to Potapchuck and Crocker (1999, 537),

> All too often, institutions and governmental entities . . . believe it is their right to dictate how the work of the group should proceed. The implicit message that other stakeholders often take away is that their views about participation do not count. Furthermore, these stakeholders often perceive that the process belongs to the initiator or convener, not to them. Addressing questions of ownership can be critical to developing a solid commitment that will lead to implementation. . . . Remember, ownership of the process leads to ownership of the results.

Facilitators can foster a sense of responsibility for the process by spreading managerial tasks broadly or by rotating them among all of the participants. Concerns about ownership are one reason why professional facilitators and mediators often strive to remain behind the scenes, not appearing prominently on group literature or in press accounts, and avoiding routine managerial tasks such as maintaining group mailing lists. "It's their process, not mine" is a common refrain.

The Economics of Collaboration: How People Decide Whether the Process Is Worthwhile

Most people associate the word "economics" with concepts such as profit, inflation, or unemployment rates. However, as a social science, economics is concerned with much broader issues. Economics is actually a theory about human behavior, focusing mainly on how people behave when they cannot have everything they want and must make trade-offs among two or more options. The following discussion singles out three economic postulates about aspects of human behavior that are particularly relevant to CBCs.

Theoroid 8

Postulate: People are motivated by both private and collective costs and benefits of collaboration.

Implication: CBCs should provide participants a range of financial, institutional, and social incentives and should appeal to their personal sense of community and mission.

How do people decide whether collaborating with others is worthwhile? A major advance in modern understanding of the personal calculus of collaboration came in 1965 when Mancur Olson published *The Logic of Collective Action: Public Goods and the Theory of Groups* (Olson 1971). According to one account, the historic significance of Olson's contribution is that it shifted attention away from the goals and resources of the group as a whole and toward those of the individual participants: "The reigning political theories of [Olson's] day granted groups an almost primordial status. Some appealed to a natural human instinct for herding; others ascribed the formation of groups that are rooted in kinship to the process of modernization. Olson offered a radically different account of the logical basis of organized collective action" (Wikipedia 2010). Instead of thinking of groups as organic, self-sustaining entities, Olson argued that groups are made of autonomous individuals who evaluate their participation in the group by focusing on whether or not their participation furthers their personal interests.

Olson's approach is grounded in the model of individual behavior that forms the basis of all economic theory, which assumes people are rational and self-interested, meaning they attempt to further their own welfare to the maximum extent possible given their available resources and information. Such a rational actor would decide whether to participate in a group according to the rule, "I will participate only if the benefits that I receive outweigh the costs I incur by my participation.

In relatively large groups, any one individual's contribution to the total group output is likely to be quite modest. Therefore, any one individual could shirk her or his responsibilities to the group (such as attending meetings or paying dues) without significantly affecting the group's success. In very large groups, any one individual's contribution is almost negligible. Rational actors would question why they should contribute to the group if their participation makes very little difference.

The problem of sustaining collective action is exacerbated if individuals are able to enjoy the fruits of the group's effort without contributing. For example, employees covered by a labor agreement negotiated by a union might be entitled to work under the terms of the agreement regardless of whether they have actively participated in the union. Under such circumstances, employees have a strong incentive to "free ride" on the efforts of labor union activists without getting involved themselves.

Olson sought to solve the riddle of how organizations such as labor unions persist if contributing to such groups is irrational. Of course, if everyone acts rationally and fails to contribute, then the collective goods provided by the group will fail to materialize, and all may find themselves worse off than if everyone had contributed. Knowing this, a person might continue contributing to the group in the hope that others will follow his example and resist the temptation to defect. "He might; or he might not . . . the result is indeterminate" (Olson 1971, 43). According to this logic, the viability of large groups is tenuous at best.

Olson argued that groups can maintain themselves only by offering every member personal incentives of greater value than the personal costs of participation. The incentives can be positive (as in membership benefits) or negative (as in labor regulations that force employees to pay union dues even if they refuse to join the union). They can be economic (such as taxes and subsidies) or social (such as peer pressure and public recognition). Furthermore, the incentives must be private (Olson used the term "selective"), meaning they are available only to members, and not to potential free riders. For example, the Automobile Association of America pursues one of its primary objectives, lobbying legislatures on behalf of the auto industry, by enticing dues-paying members with selective incentives such as maps, a travel magazine, and emergency roadside assistance.

The free-rider problem that most groups face is a subset of a larger category of problems known as social dilemmas. Social dilemmas are an ever-present challenge for CBCs addressing environmental issues. They occur when individuals acting purely in their own best interest would generate outcomes that leave everyone worse off than they would have been had everyone opted to cooperate.

Most CBCs address two types of social dilemmas: (1) the provision of public goods and (2) the tragedy of the commons. Public goods are resources that, by nature, are accessible to everyone regardless of how much or how little each person contributes to bringing them about, such as air quality or public highways. Without selective incentives, economic theory predicts that society will supply too few public goods because people will not contribute to their provision voluntarily. The tragedy of the commons refers to the depletion of natural resources when access is open to everyone, so that everyone has an incentive to consume as much as possible as quickly as possible before the resource is exhausted. It would not be unreasonable to say that the purpose of all CBCs is to help communities learn, innovate, and work together to resolve social dilemmas.

Although the assumption of rational self-interest helps us understand people's behavior in groups facing social dilemmas, it does not tell the whole story. Drawing on advances in game theory in the 1950s, Olson recognized that the ultimate outcome of any specific social dilemma hinges on the sum of each individual's strategic decisions and judgments about how other members of the group will react. Individuals may cooperate in the hope that others will follow suit, or they may defect assuming that others will also defect to gain a short-term advantage.

This leaves plenty of room for other pararational factors to wield significant influence over individual behavior. For example, the latest research on social dilemmas pays close attention to the role of culture, such as norms governing socially acceptable behavior (Dietz, Ostrom, and Stern 2003). Other authors highlight the importance of spiritual or psychological factors (Cheng, Kruger, and Daniels 2003). The bottom line is that, as countless empirical studies have shown, the assumption of rational self-interest is often useful but insufficient to explain people's behavior and decisions (Green and Shapiro 1994), particularly decisions involving public policy (Tedin 1994).

What Works

Economic models of group behavior suggest that sustained collaboration is more feasible when the personal costs of collaboration are low and the prospects for personal and collective benefits are high. In one recent study consistent with such an economic approach, Irvin and Stansbury (2004) found that despite "heroic efforts" to convene a citizens working group to manage the Papillion Creek watershed in Omaha, Nebraska, members of the public refused to participate. In this case, the main problem seems to have been insufficient prospects for personal or collective benefits. As Irvin and Stansbury write, "Omaha appears to require a crisis—or at least a defined policy issue—to motivate participants, as well as a decision-making structure that grants authority to citizens" (61). In another study examining collaborative planning for a western Colorado national forest, the collective benefits were apparent to those who chose not to participate despite their expectation that the collaborative process would "genuinely confer shared decision-making power to stakeholders. . . . In the calculus of costs and benefits, the perceived value of the collaborative process does not translate to a personal benefit to these stakeholders" (Cheng and Mattor 2006, 558).

Although some of the factors that influence personal costs and benefits are relatively fixed and difficult to mitigate (such as the geographic scope of the issues being addressed), stakeholders can exert some control over other factors by employing selective incentives. Selective incentives may be financial, institutional, or social.

Financial incentives are the most obvious type. A survey of empirical research on collaborative watershed management found that funding is the single most frequently cited key to success (Leach and Pelkey 2001). For stakeholders employed by government agencies, success requires funding earmarked to support consistent staff attendance (Frentz et al. 2000) and ultimately project implementation (U.S. Forest Service 2000). Convening agencies can improve the likelihood of success by funding various startup costs such as retaining skilled facilitators or conducting situation assessments or public outreach (Wondolleck and Yaffee 1994). Local residents whose livelihoods are tied to the land will often have a direct financial stake in the outcomes of the process, and thus have a personal incentive to get involved.

Several studies conclude that sustained collaboration requires institutional incentives such as "the willingness of leaders to evaluate staff . . . using measures appropriate to collaborative activities" (Wondolleck and Yaffee 1997, 9). Similarly, staff workloads must be adjusted to accommodate the time demands of collaborative management. Otherwise, the benefits of collaboration that accrue to the organization as a whole may place an unsustainable burden on employees (Manring 1998).

Social and educational benefits can provide a powerful selective incentive for participants, and can come in the form of new professional networks, technical training, or mutual camaraderie. Within participating organizations, "Even simple things like recognition and praise provide a positive context and impetus" to sustain an individual's commitment to the collaborative endeavor (Wondolleck and Yaffee 1997, 10).

Although attention to the private costs and benefits of collaboration is essential, it is rarely sufficient. The benefits of collaboration are too diffuse in space and time, and the costs too concentrated on a relatively small number of participating stakeholders—all of which often adds up to a free-rider situation too severe to overcome through selective incentives. One of the most recurring conclusions from empirical research is the importance of having participants who display "an undeniable passion and commitment to the collaborative process" (Weber and Khademian 2008, 343). Being invested in the outcomes of the CBC in an emotional way can sustain participation well after one's financial stake is no longer sufficient to justify continued involvement. An individual's personal commitment can take many forms, including the following:

1. *A spiritual conviction to pursue peace building or community service.* For example, mediators of environmental conflicts have described the professional guidance they find in religious texts such as the Bible (Bourne 2005) and Qur'an (Abu-Nimer 2005).

2. *A profound sense of place, community, or bioregional identity* (Kusel et al. 1996; McGinnis 1998; Cheng, Kruger, and Daniels 2003). In a study comparing two largely successful watershed councils and a third council that disbanded after reaching an impasse with statistical analysis of survey data suggests that the third case failed because it was a top-down effort led by government agencies: "The lack of a sense of community may be the single most important barrier to successful long-term watershed planning" (McGinnis, Woolley, and Gamman 1999, 9).

3. *A sense of duty to uphold fundamental values.* Such values might include social equality, civil rights, environment justice, biodiversity, economic efficiency, free enterprise, or property rights. One of the most relevant studies on this topic concluded that local governmental officials decide whether to participate in watershed management collaboratives "based on three general considerations: They feel they can help make a positive difference; they see working on the problem as consistent with their environmental ethic; and it is in their community's interest that they participate in the process" (Webler et al. 2003, 105).

If intangible incentives and motives are critical, can anything be done to cultivate them? A number of empirical studies have tendered recommendations. For example, Schuett, Selin, and Carr (2001) suggest creating opportunities for social interaction among participants outside regular meetings. Wondolleck and Yaffee (1994, 1997) argue that a well-defined geographic scope helps foster a sense of community and constructive social norms. Leach and Sabatier (2005a, 499) prescribe "empathy-building exercises, such as field trips to the local businesses or environmental sites affected by the partnership's actions."

Theoroid 9

Postulate: People have positive discount rates, meaning they devalue the future costs and benefits of collaboration.

Implication: CBCs are most effective when the participants have long-term perspectives or face relatively urgent problems.

One of the most fundamental and verifiable tenets of economic theory is that people discount future costs and benefits. Given the choice between receiving a valuable resource now or later, people usually choose now. Moreover, people almost always choose to incur costs later rather than sooner. Individual discount rates can be quantified by observing markets for money, where people are willing to pay interest in the future for the privilege of borrowing money to spend today.

Personal interest rates vary from one person to the next but tend to range between 1 percent and 30 percent per year (Warner and Pleeter 2001, 33). It is well established that discount rates tend to vary with a number of demographic characteristics. For example, in one convincing field experiment conducted in Denmark, low discount rates (i.e., long-term perspectives) were associated with people who owned homes, had high incomes, had high professional skills and high levels of formal education, and were middle-aged but not retired (Harrison, Lau, and Williams 2002).

What Works

Discount rates have two main implications for CBCs. The first is to accentuate the salutary effect of stakeholders who have relatively long-term perspectives. The length of an individual's time horizon is shaped partly by personal circumstances, such as homeownership and length of residency, which create a stronger sense of place and commitment to the local natural environment (Woolley, McGinnis, and Keller 2002). Institutional incentives also play a role. The National Marine Fisheries Service might take a long-term view because the Endangered Species Act charges the agency with maintaining viable fish populations in perpetuity. A state forestry agency may take a short-term view if elected officials evaluate the agency mainly in terms of its success in meeting annual targets for timber harvest. Farmers who own their own farm may have a greater incentive to conserve the land's productivity from one generation to the next compared to tenant farmers. Corporate leaders are often compelled to take a short-term view because they are accountable to stockowners, who want to realize a strong return on their investment quarter by quarter. If feasible, CBCs can attempt to select for participants with lower discount rates. The more the stakeholders' personal and institutional incentives promote a long-term view, the greater the prospects for CBC success.

The second main implication of discount rates is the importance of boosting near-term benefits while mitigating near-term costs. For example, chapter 4 illustrates the value of achieving modest successes early in the process. Even relatively simple or uncontroversial projects, such as hosting a public education event, give stakeholders a tangible accomplishment they can point to (Wondolleck and Yaffee 1997). The importance of small, early successes is one reason why Sacramento-based mediator Lisa Beutler always insists that groups begin by drafting a list of procedural ground rules: "It becomes their first agreement." Small agreements prove to the stakeholders that they are capable of working together, and allow them to practice the skills and habits of consensus building that they will need to tackle weightier issues.

Another potentially viable strategy for dealing with the effects of discounting is to reduce the short-term costs of collaboration whenever feasible. One way to do this is by carefully choosing which issues to work on first (U.S. Forest Service 2000). Occasionally, intractable problems become easier to resolve over time as changes in electoral politics, socioeconomic trends, or funding mechanisms open new windows of opportunity. For example, in the debate over whether to remove the reservoir in Yosemite National Park and restore the flooded Hetch-Hetchy Valley, civil engineering professor Jay Lund suggests that the value of this project will become clearer with time as California's growing population boosts demand for wilderness recreation, while improvements in water-use efficiency and off-stream storage capacity mitigate the state's demand for additional water supply. As long as an intractable problem is not getting worse over time, deferring the costs of addressing it can improve the discounted benefit-cost ratio of the CBC's full portfolio of current projects.

Studies also suggest that it helps if weightier issues take the form of a pending crisis (Rieke and Kenney 1997) rather than a long-term chronic problem, many years in the making and requiring many years to resolve. Motivating stakeholders to work on problems is difficult if the fruits of their labor will not be realized until far into the future. Because many of the problems that CBCs need to address are of the chronic variety, it helps to have an institutional trigger, such as the threat of new legislation or regulation, to create a sense of urgency (Rieke and Kenney 1997; McGinnis, Woolley, and Gamman 1999).

At first blush, another seemingly viable strategy is to overpower the effects of discounting by increasing the prospects for large long-term benefits. Sadly, winning the race to a positive benefit-cost ratio is difficult to do by boosting long-term benefits. Even large long-term benefits, once discounted, can have nearly negligible present value if they occur far into the future.

Theoroid 10

Postulate: People are generally risk averse (meaning they fear potential losses more than they welcome potential gains), and are wary of opportunities with uncertain outcomes.

Implication: CBCs are most effective when the participants trust each other to negotiate in good faith and honor their commitments.

A long line of research in economics and social psychology demonstrates that most people are risk averse much of the time, meaning they weigh losses more heavily than gains, and therefore frequently avoid taking chances unless the odds are strongly in their favor. Risk aversion plays a protective function by discouraging reckless behavior, but it can also harm social welfare by suppressing innovation (Yaffee 1994). Fear of failure can prevent people from trying new things such as cooperating with long-time adversaries for mutual gain.

CBCs tend to be marked by uncertainty at every turn, and particularly when it comes time to commit to a proposed course of action tentatively worked out among the stakeholders. Part of the uncertainty regarding such agreements lies in our ever-incomplete understanding of complex environmental systems, where we can rarely be certain about how our actions will influence key social and ecological parameters (see chapter 3). However, this theoroid focuses on the uncertainty that stems from doubts about whether other members of a CBC will negotiate in good faith and uphold their commitments. Ultimately, CBCs consist of people learning, negotiating, and working together—tasks that are difficult to pull off without sound personal relationships rooted in mutual trust.

The importance of trust is intuitive, and is also supported by empirical research of CBCs and related processes (Dietz, Ostrom, and Stern 2003). For example, survey data suggest that interpersonal trust precedes policy agreements and is not simply a side effect of successful conflict resolution (Leach and Sabatier 2005a). Interpersonal trust is also one of the more frequently cited keys to success in the literatures on collaborative watershed management (Leach and Pelkey 2001) and forest planning (Leach 2006b)

What Works

Assuming the success of a CBC often rests on the level of trust and respect among stakeholders, can anything be done to promote these qualities? As Frank Dukes (2004, 198) suggests in his review of research on environmental conflict resolution, "Anecdotal evidence from many cases can be found describing powerful relationship changes" and changes in individual empowerment and capacity. However, Dukes notes, most of these "have been single case studies that relied on disputants' reported perceptions (Birkhoff 2002)." Peter Adler and Juliana Birkhoff (2002) (with assistance from some seventy advisers) have summarized much of the conventional wisdom regarding ways to foster sound working relationships through twenty "tools, tips and trust building strategies."

One of the most detailed empirical analyses of the determinants of interpersonal trust in CBCs comes from the study of watershed partnerships in California and Washington, based on approximately 250 interviews and 1,625 survey respondents in seventy-six partnerships (Leach and Sabatier 2005b). The most important predictors of trust in these partnerships included a small and stable number of participants, perceptions of procedural fairness, generalized social trust (meaning some individuals appeared to have a higher predisposition for trust than others), clear decision rules, congruence on policy-related beliefs among the stakeholders, and an absence of devil-shift (an exaggerated belief that one's opponents wield more power than one's allies). Some of these variables are difficult for facilitators or stakeholders to influence directly. However, others can be addressed structurally (e.g., clear decision rules) or through practices such as education and joint fact-finding, which may help stakeholders approach greater accuracy and consensus on their perceptions of scientific issues, policy proposals, and the distribution of power among the parties.

Another condition shown to be conducive to trust in this study is a "hurting stalemate" in which all parties believe they have few viable options outside the CBC for pursuing their interests. Many stakeholders spend considerable amounts of time shopping for alternative venues (such as sympathetic agencies, legislatures, journalists, or courts) where they might have a competitive advantage. Stakeholders know that parties pleased with the status quo have little incentive to negotiate, and that parties may break their commitments if a more attractive option comes along in the future. Although the American political system generally provides multiple venues of appeal to dissatisfied stakeholders, agreements are more likely to be reached and implemented when alternative venues are relatively few in number and unappealing. Interpersonal trust (and the prospects for successful collaboration overall) is enhanced when all parties have arrived at an unsatisfactory policy stalemate, and when higher authorities signal their willingness to respect any consensus decision that emerges from the CBC.

Recommendations for Researchers

Although researchers have made significant strides in uncovering the keys to successful collaboration, we know somewhat less about what collaboration is capable of achieving in comparison to alternative approaches. Put another way, we know much about *how* to collaborate but less about *when* to collaborate. The great variety of CBCs and the diversity of challenges they confront preclude making blanket claims about collaboration being "better" or "worse" across the board (Dukes 2005). But we ought to be able to identify the types of outcomes that CBCs are comparatively effective at achieving and the types of situations in which collaboration is likely to outperform other approaches (Leach 2006c). Ideally, researchers could supply stakeholders with concrete guidance about when to pursue a collaborative strategy and when some alternative approach would likely serve their interests better.

To date, professional mediators have made more progress in producing such guidance than have researchers. One example is the list of eleven "Conditions Needed to Sustain a Collaborative Process" developed by mediators at the Center for Collaborative Policy (2006).

Practitioners' knowledge about when to collaborate is based primarily on their experience of trial and error. Over the course of a career, a professional mediator can look for conditions that are common among failed collaboratives and absent from relatively successful ones. While such observations are exceedingly useful, they lack certain advantages of carefully designed scientific studies. For example, independent researchers may have the ability to deliberately select cases and measure variables in ways that control for confounding factors that could lead the practitioner to make inaccurate inferences about cause and effect. Researchers may also be able to use sophisticated analytical tools—formal statistical models, simulation models—to determine why some collaborations succeeded while others failed. Whereas our knowledge about *how* to collaborate is reinforced by a robust combination of practitioner experience, empirical research, and theory, our knowledge about *when* to collaborate is primarily grounded in experience alone. To make further contributions to this topic, researchers will need to develop a second generation of studies that employ more nuanced theory and stronger research designs that include comparative aspects and long-term data collection.

Comparative and Longitudinal Research Designs

To develop further knowledge about when and how to collaborate, we need to devise studies that compare at least one collaborative process and one alternative, and that use the same criteria to evaluate each process. Studies of this sort fall into a family of designs called quasi-experiments, meaning they compare two cases (or two groups of cases) sampled so that they are as comparable as possible on all dimensions except in regard to the intensity of collaboration (the main explanatory variable) and the measures of outcomes. Comparability of this sort allows the researcher to rule out competing explanations for the observed differences in outcomes.

To date, researchers have attempted very few comparative studies measuring the outcomes of actual CBCs against the outcomes of other types of environmental planning or management. Some noteworthy research has been done on collaborative planning that is not particularly community-based, such as the National Estuary Program (Schneider et al. 2003; Lubell 2004a, 2004b) and federal agencies' experiments with regulatory negotiation (Coglianese 1997, 2001; Langbein and Kerwin 2000; Langbein 2002, 2005). Another notable comparative study examined a range of collaborative and less collaborative approaches to public participation in environmental planning (Beierle and Cayford 2002). Mostly these studies confirm that collaborative approaches yield greater levels of learning, social capital, and participant satisfaction. The hypotheses that collaboration reduces litigation or generates better environmental conditions have been either unsupported or inconclusive in these studies. We need new research to either replicate or disprove these findings in the context of local CBCs.

In addition to comparative research designs, we need to advance other aspects of research methods. All things equal, knowledge of CBCs is likely to accumulate faster by pursuing large, detailed, long-term studies (Koontz and Thomas 2006). In an assessment of the field, Emerson and colleagues (2004, 222, 229) proclaim, "We need to do a much better job validating the claims made for [environmental conflict resolution], and this can be done only through the collection of considerably larger data sets and the application of more powerful, multivariable analyses . . . [and] longer-term, longitudinal analysis." Large samples of cases are preferable to smaller samples, both because the results are more likely to generalize beyond the cases examined and because larger samples allow the quantitative researcher to build more complete models for each performance measure.

However, the quest for large samples should not eclipse efforts to collect sufficiently detailed information about each case. Detailed data are necessary to increase the validity of each concept being measured, to ensure that every important variable is included in the analysis, and to allow the quantitative researcher to examine interrelationships among multiple variables.

One potentially important class of variables omitted from the theoretical framework is the local environment in which a CBC operates (e.g., hydrologic and ecological parameters, social demographics, economic diversification, land ownership patterns). In an effort to ground each theoroid in assumptions about human behavior or cognition, I have intentionally relegated contextual variables to a secondary position in the framework, discussing them only with regard to how they interact with each postulate about human nature. To the extent that context matters, it might deserve a more prominent treatment, such as that provided in chapters 4 and 5. Contextual variables could be featured more explicitly in future empirical and theoretical research.

Finally, future studies should include a series of observations over time so that knowledge of the order in which events occurred can bolster the investigator's inferences about cause and effect. To date, very few studies of CBCs have collected repeated measurements on the same variables over time. Ideally, studies would track each process from the very beginning (or even slightly before the beginning!) so that the stakeholders' choice of collaborative or noncollaborative approaches could be observed, modeled, and accounted for in later analyses. CBCs are dynamic, living creatures whose histories unfold over the course of many months and years, often cycling through several definable stages. Snapshots frozen in time tell only partial, unfinished stories.

Recommendations for CBCs

When scholars first started paying substantial attention to CBCs in the 1990s, the question of what makes collaboration work was fully up for grabs. Relatively little research had been published, and most of the available studies provided only anecdotal information about the keys to success. By the time the Community-Based Collaboratives Research Consortium hosted its sixth annual conference in November 2005, the field had converged around a relatively short list of perhaps two dozen primary factors (e.g., Tilt 2005), which are reflected in the preceding four chapters. Moreover, researchers had arrived at roughly the same conclusions by using a diversity of research designs, theoretical perspectives, and disciplinary orientations and by examining CBCs working on a variety of environmental issues across many different landscapes, scales, and political contexts. This confluence of findings suggests the field has made tremendous progress in a relatively short period. Today, we do know a lot about how to build effective CBCs. Careful readers of this book can collaborate with confidence, knowing that they can influence many of the factors that affect CBCs' success.

This chapter has attempted to synthesize this body of knowledge around a simple framework. If CBCs are ultimately about people learning to better understand themselves, each other, and the environments they all care about, then theory has a valuable role to play in helping stakeholders interpret each others' words and deeds. Theories can also help people better understand their own visceral reactions to the trials and tribulations of collaboration and to respond in a more deliberate and effective fashion.

Because the number of influential variables identified in the literature on CBCs is large, the theoretical framework presented in this chapter can also serve to organize and simplify this information so that it is easier to access and use. The framework consists of ten theoroids organized into three categories: (1) the essence of collaboration (how people learn, innovate, and negotiate in groups), (2) the legitimacy of collaboration (how people decide whether the process is fair), and (3) the economics of collaboration (how people decide if the process is worthwhile).

Each theoroid consists of a single postulate about human nature, coupled with one implication about how stakeholders should act or how CBCs should be structured for success. I hope that this simple "theory of action" will help stakeholders interpret new situations effectively and efficiently by relating them to what we know has worked well previously under similar circumstances. After elucidating each theoroid, the chapter focused on providing practical suggestions about what works on the ground, drawing conclusions mainly from empirical studies of CBCs working on environmental issues.

In using the theoroids, one should always realize that an individual stakeholder might not conform to the assumptions about human behavior that underlie each theoroid. Although a large body of research corroborates the validity of each assumption for most people most of the time, humanity is tremendously diverse. One should be vigilant for the occasional outlying stakeholder who breaks the mold. For example, what if some of the stakeholders have truly negative discount rates? How would that change the dynamics? What if one of the stakeholders judges the legitimacy of a CBC mainly in terms of the outcomes of the process, rather than procedural fairness? Stakeholders should be prepared to ask such questions as they arise.

Finally, good fortune may play an important role in the success or failure of particular CBCs. Because random variation is difficult for researchers to account for, we often overlook it. Stakeholders so inclined should consider taking affirmative steps to improve their luck. Then, after doing everything right, if a CBC should fail to meet expectations, stakeholders can chalk it up to a misalignment of stars, and be thankful for the chance to try again another day.

References

Abu-Nimer, Mohammed. 2005. "Islamic Principles and Value of Peacebuilding." *Collaborative Edge*, Fall.

Adler, Peter S., and Juliana E. Birkhoff. 2002. *Building Trust: When Knowledge from Here Meets Knowledge from Away*. Portland, OR: National Policy Consensus Center.

Argyris, Chris. 1993. *Knowledge for Action: A Guide to Overcoming Barriers to Organizational Change*. San Francisco, CA: Jossey Bass.

Argyris, Chris, and Donald A. Schon. 1974. *Theory in Practice: Increasing Professional Effectiveness*. San Francisco, CA: Jossey-Bass.

Ashford, Nicholas A., and Kathleen M. Rest. 1999. *Public Participation in Contaminated Communities*. Cambridge: Massachusetts Institute of Technology, Center for Technology, Policy, and Industrial Development.

Barrett, Robert C., Suzanne L. Frew, David G. Howell, Herman A. Karl, and Emily B. Rudin. 2003. *Rim Sim: A Role-Play Simulation*. Menlo Park, CA: U.S. Geological Survey.

Beierle, Thomas C., and Jerry Cayford. 2002. *Democracy in Practice: Public Participation in Environmental Decisions*. Washington, DC: Resources for the Future Press.

Birkhoff, Juliana E. 2002. "Evaluation and Research." In *Critical Issues Papers*, ed. S. Senecah. Washington, DC: Association for Conflict Resolution, Environmental Public Policy Section.

Blader, Steven L., and Tom R. Tyler. 2003. "What Constitutes Fairness in Work Settings? A Four-Component Model of Procedural Justice." *Human Resource Management Review* 13 (1): 107–26.

Booher, David E., and Judith E. Innes. 2005. "Comment." *Planning Theory & Practice* 6 (3): 431–35.

Born, Stephen M., and Kenneth D. Genskow. 2000. *The Watershed Approach: An Empirical Assessment of Innovation in Environmental Management*. Washington, DC: National Academy of Public Administration.

Bourne, Greg. 2005. "The Power of Peacemaking: Seven Biblical Principles for Dealing with Conflict in an Angry World." *Collaborative Edge*, Spring–Summer.

Brown, Harold I. 1977. *Perception, Theory, and Commitment: The New Philosophy of Science*. Chicago: University of Chicago Press.

Center for Collaborative Policy. 2006. "Conditions Needed to Sustain a Collaborative Process." Center for Collaborative Policy, Sacramento, CA. http://www.csus.edu/ccp/collaborative/stages.stm (accessed December 14, 2010).

Cheng, Antony S., Linda E. Kruger, and Steven E. Daniels. 2003. "Place as an Integrating Concept in Natural Resource Politics: Propositions for a Social Science Research Agenda." *Society and Natural Resources* 16 (2): 87–104.

Cheng, Antony S., and Katherine M. Mattor. 2006. "Why Didn't They Come? Stakeholder Perspectives on Collaborative National Forest Planning by Participation Level." *Environmental Management* 38 (4): 545–61.

Coglianese, Cary. 1997. "Assessing Consensus: The Promise and Performance of Negotiated Rulemaking." *Duke Law Journal* 46 (6): 1255–1349.

———. 2001. "Assessing the Advocacy of Negotiated Rulemaking: A Response to Philip Harter." *New York University Environmental Review* 9 (2): 386–447.

Dakins, Maxine E., Jeffery D. Long, and Michael Hart. 2005. "Collaborative Environmental Decision Making in Oregon Watershed Groups: Perceptions of Effectiveness." *Journal of the American Water Resources Association* 41 (1): 171–80.

Daniels, Steven E., and Gregg B. Walker. 1996. "Collaborative Learning: Improving Public Deliberation in Ecosystem-based Management." *Environmental Impact Assessment Review* 16 (2): 71–102.

de Tocqueville, Alexis. 1840. "How the Americans Combat Individualism by the Principle of Self-interest Rightly Understood." In *Democracy in America,* vol. 2. http://xroads.virginia.edu/~HYPER/DETOC/home.html (accessed December 14, 2010).

Dietz, Thomas, Elinor Ostrom, and Paul C. Stern. 2003. "The Struggle to Govern the Commons." *Science* 302:1907–12.

Dryzek, John S., and Simon J. Niemeyer. 2003. "Pluralism and Consensus in Political Deliberation." Paper presented at the American Political Science Association meeting, August 28–31.

Dukes, E. Franklin. 2004. "What We Know about Environmental Conflict Resolution: An Analysis Based on Research." *Conflict Resolution Quarterly* 22 (1–2): 191–220.

Dukes, E. Franklin, and Karen Firehock. 2001. *Collaboration: A Guide for Environmental Advocates.* Charlottesville: University of Virginia, Institute for Environmental Negotiation.

Ehrmann, John R., and Barbara L. Stinson. 1999. "Joint Fact-finding and the Use of Technical Experts." In *The Consensus Building Handbook: A Comprehensive Guide to Reaching Agreement,* ed. L. Susskind, S. McKearnan, and J. Thomas-Larmer. Thousand Oaks, CA: Sage.

Emerson, Kirk, Rosemary O'Leary, and Lisa B. Bingham. 2004. "Comment on Frank Dukes's 'What We Know about Environmental Conflict Resolution.'" *Conflict Resolution Quarterly* 22 (1–2): 221–231.

Festinger, Leon. 1957. *A Theory of Cognitive Dissonance.* Evanston, IL: Row Peterson.

Fisher, Roger, and William Ury. 1981. *Getting to Yes: Negotiating Agreement Without Giving In.* Markham, ON: Penguin Books.

Forester, John. 2005. "Policy Analysts Can Learn from Mediators." In *Adaptive Governance and Water Conflict: New Institutions for Collaborative Planning,* ed. B. Stiftel and J. Scholz. Washington, DC: Resources for the Future Press.

Frentz, Irene C., Donald E. Voth, Sam Burns, and Charles W. Sperry. 2000. "Forest Service–Community Relationship Building: Recommendations." *Society & Natural Resources* 13 (6): 549–66.

Green, Donald P., and Ian Shapiro. 1994. *Pathologies of Rational Choice Theory: A Critique of Applications in Political Science.* New Haven, CT: Yale University Press.

Greenberg, J. 1987. "Reaction to Procedural Injustices in Payment Distributions: Do the Means Justify the Ends?" *Journal of Applied Psychology* 72 (1): 55–61.

Gunderson, Lance H., and C. S. Holling, eds. 2002. *Panarchy: Understanding Transformations in Human and Natural Systems.* Washington, DC: Island Press.

Harrison, Glenn W., Morten I. Lau, and Melonie B. Williams. 2002. "Estimating Individual Discount Rates in Denmark: A Field Experiment." *American Economic Review* 92 (5): 1606–17.

Hibbing, John R., and Elizabeth Theiss-Morse. 2001. "Process Preferences and American Politics: What the People Want Government to Be." *American Political Science Review March 95* (March): 145–53.

———. 2007. "Voice, Validation, and Legitimacy." In *Cooperation: The Political Psychology of Effective Human Interaction,* ed. B. A. Sullivan, M. Snyder, and J. L. Sullivan. Malden, MA: Blackwell Publishing.

Huntington, Charles W., and Sari Sommarstrom. 2000. "An Evaluation of Selected Watershed Councils in the Pacific Northwest and Northern California." Trout Unlimited and Pacific Rivers Council. http://pacificrivers.org/science-research (accessed December 14, 2010).

Innes, Judith E., and David E. Booher. 1999a. "Consensus Building and Complex Adaptive Systems: A Framework for Evaluating Collaborative Planning." *Journal of the American Planning Association* 65 (4): 412–23.

———. 1999b. "Consensus Building as Role Playing and Bricolage: Toward a Theory of Collaborative Planning." *Journal of the American Planning Association* 65 (1): 9–26.

———. 2003. "Collaborative Policymaking: Governance through Dialogue." In *Deliberative Policy Analysis: Understanding Governance in Network Society,* ed. M. Hajer and H. Wagenaar. Cambridge: Cambridge University Press.

———. 2004. "Reframing Public Participation: Strategies for the 21st Century." *Planning Theory and Practice* 5 (4): 419–36.

———. 2010. *Planning with Complexity: An Introduction to Collaborative Rationality for Public Policy.* New York: Routledge.

Irvin, Renee A., and John Stansbury. 2004. "Citizen Participation in Decision Making: Is It Worth It?" *Public Administration Review* 64 (1): 55–65.

Jostad, Patricia M., Leo H. McAvoy, and Daniel McDonald. 1996. "Native American Land Ethics: Implications for Natural Resource Management." *Society and Natural Resources* 9:565–81.

Karl, Herman A., Lawrence E. Susskind, and Katherine H. Wallace. 2007. "A Dialogue, Not a Diatribe: Effective Integration of Science and Policy through Joint Fact Finding." *Environment* 49 (4): 20–34.

Katz, Nancy R. 2000. "Incentives and Performance Management in the Public Sector." Forth Executive Session, Kennedy School of Government, Harvard University, Cambridge, MA, June 20, 2000. http://www.hks.harvard.edu/visions/performance_management/katz_incentives.htm (accessed December 14, 2010).

Koontz, Tomas M., Toddi A. Steelman, JoAnn Carmin, Katrina Smith Korfmacher, Cassandra Moseley, and Craig W. Thomas. 2004. *Collaborative Environmental Management: What Role for Government?* Washington, DC: Resources for the Future Press.

Koontz, Tomas M., and Craig W. Thomas. 2006. "What Do We Know and Need to Know about the Environmental Outcomes of Collaborative Management?" *Public Administration Review* 66 (S1): 111–21.

Kuhn, Thomas S. 1962. *The Structure of Scientific Revolutions.* Chicago, IL: University of Chicago Press.

Kulongoski, Ted. 2005. State of the State Speech, State Capitol, Salem, Oregon, January 10, 2005. http://governor.oregon.gov/Gov/speech/speech_011005.shtml (accessed December 14, 2010).

Kusel, J., S. C. Doak, S. Carpenter, and V.E. Sturtevant. 1996. "The Role of the Public in Adaptive Ecosystem Management." In *Sierra Nevada Ecosystem Project: Final Report to Congress*, vol. 2, *Assessments and Scientific Basis for Management Options*. Davis: University of California, Centers for Water and Wildland Resources.

Lachapelle, Paul R., and Stephan F. McCool. 2005. "Exploring the Concept of Ownership in Natural Resource Planning." *Society and Natural Resources* 18 (3): 279–85.

Lane, M., and S. Hausam. 2003. "Native American Participation in Community-Based Collaborative Planning." Community-Based Collaboratives Research Consortium. http://www.cbcrc.org.

Langbein, Laura. 2005. "Negotiated and Conventional Rulemaking at EPA: A Comparative Case Analysis." Paper presented at National Research Council, Panel on Public Participation in Environmental Assessment and Decision Making, Workshop, Washington, DC, February 3–4.

Langbein, Laura I. 2002. "Responsive Bureaus, Equity, and Regulatory Negotiation: An Empirical View." *Journal of Policy Analysis and Management* 21 (3): 449–65.

Langbein, Laura, and Cornelius Kerwin. 2000. "Regulatory Negotiation versus Conventional Rule Making: Claims, Counterclaims, and Empirical Evidence." *Journal of Public Administration Research and Theory* 10 (3): 599–632.

Lawrence, Rick L., Steven E. Daniels, and George H. Stankey. 1997. "Procedural Justice and Public Involvement in Natural Resource Decision Making." *Society & Natural Resources* 10 (6): 577–89.

Leach, William D. 2006a. "Collaborative Public Management and Democracy: Evidence from Western Watershed Partnerships." *Public Administration Review* 66:100–110.

———. 2006b. "Public Involvement in USDA Forest Service Policymaking: A Literature Review." *Journal of Forestry* 104 (1): 43–49.

———. 2006c. "Theories about Consensus-based Conservation." *Conservation Biology* 20 (2): 573–75.

Leach, William D., and Neil W. Pelkey. 2001. "Making Watershed Partnerships Work: A Review of the Empirical Literature." *Journal of Water Resources Planning and Management* 127 (6): 378–85.

Leach, William D., and Paul A. Sabatier. 2005a. "Are Trust and Social Capital the Keys to Success? Watershed Partnerships in California and Washington." In *Swimming Upstream: Collaborative Approaches to Watershed Management*, ed. P. Sabatier, W. Focht, M. Lubell, Z. Trachtenberg, A. Vedlitz and M. Matlock. Cambridge, MA: MIT Press.

———. 2005b. "To Trust an Adversary: Integrating Rational and Psychological Models of Collaborative Policymaking." *American Political Science Review* 99 (4): 491–503.

Lee, Kai N. 1993. *Compass and Gyroscope*. Washington, DC: Island Press.

Lenard, Steven R., and Ian J. Finlayson. 2004. "The Role of the Scientist in Collaborative Environmental Policy Making." Cambridge, MA: MIT-USGS Science Impact Collaborative. http://web.mit.edu/dusp/epp/music/pdf/lenard_finlayson.pdf (accessed December 14, 2010).

Lord, Charles G., Lee Ross, and Mark R. Lepper. 1979. "Biased Assimilation and Attitude Polarization: The Effects of Prior Theories on Subsequently Considered Evidence." *Journal of Personality and Social Psychology* 37:2098–2109.

Lubell, Mark. 2004a. "Collaborative Environmental Institutions: All Talk and No Action?" *Journal of Policy Analysis and Management* 23 (3): 549–73.

———. 2004b. "Resolving Conflict and Building Cooperation in the National Estuary Program." *Environmental Management* 33 (5): 667–91.

Lubell, Mark, William D. Leach, and Paul A. Sabatier. 2009. "Collaborative Watershed Partnerships in the Epoch of Sustainability." In *Toward Sustainable Communities: Transitions and Transformations in Environmental Policy*, 2nd ed., ed. D. A. Mazmanian and M. E. Kraft. Cambridge, MA: MIT Press.

Macfarlane, Julie, and Bernie Mayer. 2005a. "What's the Use of Theory? How Trainer-Practitioners Understand and Use Theory." Paper presented at a conference, "Theory to Practice in Collaborative Problem Solving," Boulder, CO, February 4–5.

———. 2005b. "What Theory? How Collaborative Problem-solving Trainers Use Theory and Research in Training and Teaching." *Conflict Resolution Quarterly* 23 (2): 259–76.

Manring, Nancy J. 1998. "Collaborative Resource Management: Organizational Benefits and Individual Costs." *Administration & Society* 30 (July): 274–90.

Margerum, Richard D. 1999a. "Integrated Environmental Management: Lessons from the Trinity Inlet Management Program." *Land Use Policy* 16 (3): 179–90.

———. 1999b. "Integrated Environmental Management: The Foundations for Successful Practice." *Environmental Management* 24 (2): 151–66.

Maslow, Abraham H. 1943. "A Theory of Human Motivation." *Psychological Review* 50:370–96.

McCool, Stephen F., and Kathleen Guthrie. 2001. "Mapping the Dimensions of Successful Public Participation in Messy Natural Resources Management Situations." *Society & Natural Resources* 14 (4): 309–23.

McCreary, Scott T. 1999. "Resolving Science-Intensive public Policy Disputes: Lessons from the New York Bright Initiative." In *The Consensus Building Handbook: A Comprehensive Guide to Reaching Agreement*, ed. L. Susskind, S. McKearnon, and J. Thomas-Larmer. Thousand Oaks, CA: Sage.

McGinnis, Michael Vincent. 1998. *Bioregionalism*. London: Routledge.

McGinnis, Michael Vincent, John Woolley, and John Gamman. 1999. "Bioregional Conflict Resolution: Rebuilding Community in Watershed Planning and Organization." *Environmental Management* 24 (1): 1–12.

National Research Council. 1996. *Understanding Risk: Informing Decisions in a Democratic Society*. Washington, DC: National Academy Press.

Norton, Bryan G. 2002. *Searching for Sustainability: Interdisciplinary Essays in the Philosophy of Conservation Biology*. Cambridge: Cambridge University Press.

Olson, Mancur. 1971. *The Logic of Collective Action: Public Goods and the Theory of Groups*, 2nd ed. Cambridge, MA: Harvard University Press.

Ozawa, Connie. 1991. *Recasting Science: Consensual Procedures in Public Policy Making*. Boulder, CO: Westview Press.

Popper, Karl. 1959. *The Logic of Scientific Discovery*. New York: Harper and Row.

Potapchuck, William R., and Jarle Crocker. 1999. "Implementing Consensus-based Agreements." In *The Consensus Building Handbook: A Comprehensive Guide to Reaching Agreement*, ed. L. Susskind, S. McKearnon, and J. Thomas-Larmer. Thousand Oaks, CA: Sage.

Ravetz, J. R. 1999. "What Is Post-normal Science?" *Futures* 31 (7): 647–53.

Reza, Kathryn. 2003. "An Analysis of Native American Tribal Participation in Multi-Stakeholder Natural Resource Management Groups in Washington and California." Master's thesis, University of California, Davis.

Rieke, Betsy, and Douglas Kenney. 1997. *Resource Management at the Watershed level: An Assessment of the Changing Federal Role in the Emerging Era of Community-based Watershed Management*. Report to the Western Water Policy Review Advisory Commission, Denver, CO. Boulder: University of Colorado School of Law, Natural Resources Law Center.

Rose-Anderssen, C., P. M. Allen, C. Tsinopoulos, and I. McCarthy. 2005. "Innovation in Manufacturing as an Evolutionary Complex System." *Technovation* 25 (10): 1093–1105.

Sabatier, Paul A., Chris M. Weible, and Jared A. Ficker. 2005. "Eras of Water Management in the United States: Implications for Collaborative Watershed Approaches." In *Swimming Upstream: Collaborative Approaches to Watershed Management*, ed. P. Sabatier, W. Focht, M. Lubell, Z. Trachtenberg, A. Vedlitz, and M. Matlock. Cambridge, MA: MIT Press.

Schneider, Mark, John Scholz, Mark Lubell, Denisa Mindruta, and Matthew Edwardsen. 2003. "Building Consensual Institutions: Networks and the National Estuary Program." *American Journal of Political Science* 47 (1): 143–58.

Scholz, John, and Bruce Stiftel. 2005. "Introduction: The Challenges of Adaptive Governance." In *Adaptive Governance and Water Conflict: New Institutions for Collaborative Planning*, ed. J. Scholz and B. Stiftel. Washington, DC: Resources for the Future Press.

Schuett, Michael A., Steve W. Selin, and Debbie Carr. 2001. "Making It Work: Keys to Successful Collaboration in Natural Resource Management." *Environmental Management* 27 (4): 587–93.

Selin, Steven, and Debbie Chavez. 1994. "Characteristics of Successful Tourism Partnerships: A Multiple Case Study Design." *Journal of Park & Recreation Administration* 12 (2): 51–62.

Selin, Steve, and Nancy Myers. 1995. "Correlates of Partnership Effectiveness: The Coalition for Unified Recreation in Eastern Sierra." *Journal of Park & Recreation Administration* 13 (4): 37–46.

Senecah, Susan L. 2004. "The Trinity of Voice: The Role of Practical Theory in Planning and Evaluating the Effectiveness of Environmental Participatory Processes." In *Communication and Public Participation in Environmental Decision Making*, ed. S. P. Depoe, J. W. Delicath and M.-f. A. Elsenbeer. Albany: State University of New York Press.

Sherman, Marlon. 2004. "PRASI Anthology Discussion Concerning Native American Peacemaking." *Conciliation Quarterly* 23 (1): 3–4.

Shindler, Bruce, and Julie Neburka. 1997. "Public Participation in Forest Planning: 8 Attributes of Success." *Journal of Forestry* 95 (1): 17–19.

Simon, Herbert A. 1957. *Models of Man*. New York: Wiley.

Smith, P. D., M. H. McDonough, and M. T. Mang. 1999. "Ecosystem Management and Public Participation: Lessons from the Field." *Journal of Forestry* 97 (10): 32–38.

Stiftel, Bruce. 2001. "Can Governments Bargain Effectively? Lessons from a Waste

Transfer Station Location." Paper presented at the World Planning Schools Congress, Shanghai, July 9–15.

Stiftel, Bruce, and John Scholz. 2005. "The Future of Adaptive Governance: Learning about Learning." In *Adaptive Governance and Water Conflict: New Institutions for Collaborative Planning*, ed. J. Scholz and B. Stiftel. Washington, DC: Resources for the Future Press.

Susskind, Lawrence E., and Jeffrey L. Cruikshank. 2006. *Breaking Robert's Rules: The New Way to Run Your Meeting, Build Consensus, and Get Results.* New York: Oxford University Press.

Tedin, Kent L. 1994. "Self-interest, Symbolic Values, and the Financial Equalization of the Public Schools." *Journal of Politics* 56 (3): 628–49.

Thibaut, John, and Laurens Walker. 1975. *Procedural Justice: A Psychological Analysis.* Hillsdale, NJ: Lawrence Erlbaum.

Tilt, Whitney. 2005. "Lessons from Community-Based Collaboration in the West." Paper presented at the Fifth National CBCRC Conference, Plenary Session, Sedona, AZ, November 17.

Tuler, Seth, and Thomas Webler. 1999. "Voices from the Forest: What Participants Expect of a Public Participation Process." *Society and Natural Resources* 12 (5, July–August): 437–53.

Tyler, Tom R., and Steven Blader. 2000. *Cooperation in Groups: Procedural Justice, Social Identity, and Behavioral Engagement.* Philadelphia: Psychology Press.

Tyler, Tom R., and Steven L. Blader. 2003. "The Group Engagement Model: Procedural Justice, Social Identity, and Cooperative Behavior." *Personality & Social Psychology Review* 7 (4): 349–61.

Tyler, Tom R., and Yuen J. Huo. 2002. *Trust in the Law: Encouraging Public Cooperation with the Police and Courts.* New York: Russell Sage Foundation.

U.S. Forest Service. 2000. Collaborative Stewardship within the Forest Service: Findings and Recommendations from the National Collaborative Stewardship Team. http://www.partnershipresourcecenter.org/resources/publications/index.php.

Van Riper, L. 2003. "Can Agency-Led Initiatives Conform to Collaborative Principles? Evaluating and Reshaping an Interagency Program through Participatory Research." PhD diss., University of Montana.

Warner, John T., and Saul Pleeter. 2001. "The Personal Discount Rate: Evidence from Military Downsizing Programs." *American Economic Review* 91 (1): 33–53.

Weber, Edward P., and Anne M. Khademian. 2008. "Wicked Problems, Knowledge Challenges, and Collaborative Capacity Builders in Network Settings." *Public Administration Review* 68 (2): 334–49.

Webler, Thomas. 1995. "'Right' Discourse in Citizen Participation: An Evaluative Yardstick." In *Fairness and Competence in Citizen Participation: Evaluating Models for Environmental Discourse*, ed. O. Renn, T. Webler and P. Wiedermann. Dordrecht: Kluwer Academic.

Webler, Thomas, Seth Tuler, Ingrid Shockey, Paul Stern, and Robert Beattie. 2003. "Participation by Local Governmental Officials in Watershed Management Planning." *Society and Natural Resources* 16:105–21.

Weible, Christopher M. 2005. "Beliefs and Perceived Influence in a Natural Resource Conflict: An Advocacy Coalition Approach to Policy Networks." *Political Research Quarterly* 58 (3): 461–75.

Westley, F. 1995. "Governing Design: The Management of Social Systems and Ecosystems Management." In *Barriers and Bridges to the Renewal of Ecosystems and Institutions,* ed. L. H. Gunderson, C. S. Holling, and S. S. Light. New York: Columbia University Press.

Wikipedia. 2006. Mancur Olson. http://en.wikipedia.org/w/index.php?title=Mancur_Olson&oldid=73066996 (accessed December 14, 2010).

Wondolleck, Julia M., and Steven L. Yaffee. 1994. *Building Bridges across Agency Boundaries: In Search of Excellence in the United States Forest Service.* Research report to the USDA Forest Service Pacific Northwest Research Station, Ann Arbor: University of Michigan.

———. 1997. *Sustaining the Success of Collaborative Partnerships: Revisiting the Building Bridges Cases.* Ann Arbor: University of Michigan, School of Natural Resources and Environment, Ecosystem Management Initiative.

———. 2000. *Making Collaboration Work: Lessons from Innovation in Natural Resource Management.* Washington, DC: Island Press.

Woolley, John T., Michael Vincent McGinnis, and Julie Kellner. 2002. "The California Watershed Movement: Science and the Politics of Place." *Natural Resources Journal* 42 (1): 133–82.

Yaffee, Steven L. 1994. *The Wisdom of the Spotted Owl: Policy Lessons for a New Century.* Washington, DC: Island Press.

Yaffee, Steven L., Julia M. Wondolleck, and Steven Lippman. 1997. *Factors That Promote and Constrain Bridging: A Summary and Analysis of the Literature.* Ann Arbor: University of Michigan, School of Natural Resources and Environment, Ecosystem Management Initiative.

Zafonte, Matthew, and Paul Sabatier. 1998. "Shared Beliefs and Imposed Interdependencies as Determinants of Ally Networks in Overlapping Subsystems." *Journal of Theoretical Politics* 10:473–505.

7

The Promise of Community-Based Collaboration
Agenda for an Authentic Future

E. Franklin Dukes

This book marks a critical reflection point in a journey that began more than a decade ago with the questions posed by the Tucson gathering described in the preface: Is community-based collaboration transforming how people relate to the land and to each other? Do place-based collaborative efforts to integrate environmental resilience and economic gain promote social equity, broaden participation, and increase social capital? Do they improve local economic conditions? Do they really improve the environment?

In short, does community-based collaboration have value?

As with most questions of this sort, the answers the contributors to this book have offered are all some variation of "it depends." Yes, absolutely, community-based collaboration has value, and no, community-based collaboration certainly does not have value in all circumstances. The answers, as is shown in the earlier chapters, depend on many factors, including appropriateness of use and effectiveness of practice.

Enough evaluation and research exists to determine that community-based collaboratives (CBCs) can be of value. Charles Curtin in chapter 2 and María Fernández-Giménez and Heidi Ballard in chapter 3 demonstrate the effectiveness of CBCs in learning about the ecology of their region and the impacts of human activities through collaborative formal monitoring and adaptive management. Melanie Hughes McDermott, Margaret Ann Moote, and Cecilia Danks in chapter 4 document how CBCs can overcome obstacles to effective environmental decision making. Gregg Walker and Susan Senecah in chapter 5 show that CBCs are at the forefront of collaborative governance as government agencies ponder how to adapt to new roles. And William Leach, in reviewing the essential building blocks of successful CBCs in chapter 6, points to the many elements of that success.

I will go further: I argue that there is an absolute need for such work. If we are to have communities sustained ecologically, socially, and economically, it is essential that a capacity for productive, collaborative, place-based decision processes be developed. This chapter, building on the discussions in the previous chapters, argues this point forcefully.

But let us not confuse *what should be* with *what is*. We cannot predict what will happen on the basis of past actions or current needs. Nor is it possible to defend much of what has happened to date under the rubric of "collaboration." An argument for collaborative, place-based decision processes does not indicate satisfaction with community-based collaboration as it has been and is being practiced. A "naive and untempered enthusiasm" (Fung 2006) for collaboration is as inappropriate as its wholesale rejection.

Many examples exist of poorly conceived or poorly conducted CBC processes.[1] Participants in collaborative processes, who may devote months or years working to do right according to their own and their community's interests, may see that work negated through inadequate support, insufficient skills, misdirected authority, or even deliberate sabotage. These individuals will think long and hard before they consider participating in another collaborative effort. Unless substantial efforts are made to develop authentic and effective processes, this needed capacity may be lost amid the controversy of failed initiatives.

Another answer to the question of the value of community-based collaboration also is apparent. In one sense, it may not matter much how agencies or academics respond to the question, does community-based collaboration have value? For people throughout the United States and the rest of the world are doing this work even when support is lacking, and they show no indication of waiting while skeptics and outsiders ponder the meaning of that work. But the fact that many participants in this movement aren't waiting for outside approval doesn't change the need to address the question that will shape the future of community-based collaboration: Is community-based collaboration worth supporting? Is it worth developing the laws, regulations, agency structures, funding mechanisms, skills and capacities, evaluation procedures, and norms and processes, to grow and develop the right way? Can this work, much of it unregulated, ad hoc, and varying widely in character and effectiveness, ever be held to the standards of transparency, effectiveness, and efficiency needed to justify this level of support?

In this chapter I examine the future of CBCs based on the meaning of the knowledge we have gained through the extensive research, publication, conference discussions, and hands-on experiences sponsored by the Community-Based Collaboratives Research Consortium (CBCRC), as well as related work conducted by many people outside the consortium. The "authentic" future I suggest in the chapter's subtitle may imply insight into what community-based collaboration will become; in fact, I use the term in a normative sense. *If* community-based collaboration is to have a substantial role in public decision making, it must become a means of *authentic engagement*—"worthy of trust, reliance, or belief" (*American Heritage Dictionary of the English Language,* 4th ed., 2000).

The contributors to this book have probed the empirical research in great depth. However, at some point we move beyond empirical answers to address the types of questions that at best respond to informed judgment. As Jeffrey Sachs (2005, 2) declares in another setting, "The key is not to predict what will happen, but to help shape the future."

Why Community-Based Collaboration?

> Missoula is a thousand times smarter than I am ever going to be.
>
> —Dan Kemmis, personal conversation, June 30, 2006

The literature on collaboration of all sorts, including CBCs, supports many types of potential gains, whether environmental, social, or economic. However, participants in such processes may be motivated by interests entirely separate from potential gain (Dukes 2005). For them, the answers to "why collaboration?" can vary widely, and furthermore are likely to be specific to a particular place and context.

For an individual or a group, the answer may simply be the absence of another viable alternative, or pressure from a powerful elected official. This happens far more often than advocates for collaborative processes care to admit. For some citizens, collaboration may be seen as an opportunity to deal directly with an agency that may previously have been perceived as inaccessible. For others, such engagement may arise from a sense of responsibility, a willingness to understand and hence be able to mitigate the impacts of their actions on others. In any particular situation, such motivation varies with parties.

Motivation to participate also may vary with the passage of time: what brings parties together may not be what keeps them together. One long-term collaborative process that I facilitated began with most participants introducing themselves with "I'm here to see what's going on," and it took a year or more of meetings before any realization emerged that this effort could be helpful. This is not uncommon; indeed, it is customary for parties to enter a collaborative process unclear about their own goals (Forester 2005), much less knowing all that their participation might achieve.

Of course, many agencies and community members do understand the power of collaborative processes and convene or participate with the hope

Table 7.1 Possible initial motivations to participate in a CBC

Public agencies	Community participants
• Respond to local pressure to participate	• Respond to local pressure to participate
• Respond to persuasion from elected official	• Satisfy an authority (elected official, agency) who may have power to allocate resources or impact important decisions
• Follow policy or orders from a superior	
• Attempt to reduce conflict	• Delay or block an unwanted action
• Seek legitimacy and good will	• Persuade, tell story
• Observe and monitor others' activities	• Observe and monitor others' activities
• Secure support to achieve goals	• Secure support to achieve goals

Source: Adapted from Dukes 2005.

that success will lead to well-defined environmental, economic, and social outcomes. But an honest look at the range of motivations leads to a more complex picture of collaborative practice (table 7.1). And that complexity begs an explanation of what community-based collaboration can and should do—in short, its potential and its promise.

The Promise and Potential of Community-Based Collaboration: Fulfilling Vital Needs

The reasons listed above for why people participate in collaborative processes do not fully address the potential value and role of CBCs. As this book's contributors and many others have recounted, when conducted properly and in the right circumstances, community-based collaboration can fulfill significant needs and provide substantial value (see, e.g., O'Leary and Bingham 2003; Innes and Booher 2010).

The value has many facets; here I offer a broad look at why this collaborative capacity is necessary and deserves support. I offer four needs that can be met only through the processes of face-to-face deliberation and learning characteristic of the most effective CBCs:

1. *The practical need:* New processes of public engagement to achieve sustainable solutions.
2. *The moral need:* Moral development and an ethic of stewardship for people and place.
3. *The civic need:* Community capacity to solve problems and resolve conflicts.

4. *The adaptive need:* The learning and growth necessary to build resilient ecological and social systems.

It is important to separate these arguments supporting the development of community-based collaboration in general and the need to develop collaborative capacity for addressing natural resource issues from the decision to convene or participate in any particular effort. As has been shown repeatedly (see, e.g., Kenney 2000), and specifically in chapters 4 and 5 of this book, CBCs have value in some circumstances and not in others. With that caveat, I want to offer the reasons why CBCs not only are worthy of support in the first, general sense but are an essential part of a strategy for sustainable solutions to community-scale environmental and social problems. The argument boils down to four principles, one tied to each need, which I will explain in turn:

1. Programs and plans involving natural resource protection that are imposed on resource-based communities without authentic community participation in crafting those plans tend to fail miserably.
2. Programs and plans involving natural resources that fail to develop understanding and caring within affected human communities lend themselves to abuse.
3. Programs and plans involving natural resource protection that do not develop a communal capacity to solve problems and resolve conflicts tend to fail.
4. Programs and plans involving natural resource protection that do not provide for ways of learning and adapting to change tend to fail.

The Practical Need: Effective Processes of Public Engagement to Achieve Sustainable Solutions

As the bumper sticker proclaims, "If You're Not Completely Appalled You're Not Paying Attention!" Many of us are not paying attention. Arguments rage over the ultimate outcomes of accelerating climate change, destruction of species, fouled waters, or places with such toxic legacy they may never be habitable. We don't need to agree about what may happen generations from now to understand that many places—ecosystems—that do not have sufficient attention and protections are degrading miserably.[2] Crashed fisheries, lost species, contaminated water, toxic communities, the looming impacts of global warming—despite decades of laws, regulations, and work by countless individuals and institutions, with improvement in some important arenas, the uncontestable fact remains that we are failing in many ways and in many locations to ensure a safe, resilient, nurturing environment.

Why is this so? No greater consensus exists on the sources of our current dilemma than on its ultimate destiny. Globalization, capitalism, socialism, imperialism, corruption, competition, natural processes, ignorance, greed—these all are blamed by various people for all or part of these ills. These are subjects worthy of attention and debate. However, we don't need to identify all sources of environmental problems in order to understand the role that community-based collaboration can play in addressing these challenges. Here I assert a first principle that argues for the need for community-based collaboration to address community-scale environmental problems: *Programs and plans involving natural resource protection that are imposed on resource-based communities without authentic community participation in crafting those plans tend to fail miserably.*

Charles Curtin in chapter 2 notes how the centralized command of economic, ecological, or social systems has proved ineffective in responding to change. The failures of top-down planning domestically and internationally have been so well documented and are so intuitively apparent that they hardly bear repeating: well-meaning (and occasionally not so well-meaning) "experts" who identify a problem and a preferred solution misjudge local conditions, local capacity, or local willingness to go along with those solutions.[3] Network theory indicates that when power is dispersed, hierarchical authority becomes less effective than networks of people who have worked together collaboratively (Innes and Booher 2004.)

These failures argue for better public involvement, an argument that appears both relatively simple and easily accepted. But it is not. For public involvement rarely truly engages affected publics in decisions that impact their lives. Sherry Arnstein (1969) in her seminal critique of community involvement argued that public involvement too often demonstrates manipulation and placation. One could claim that much has changed since the publication of that article, and that would be partially true: many laws, regulations, and policies that promote an ideal of community involvement are in place now that were not then. But deep problems still remain. This critique from Innes and Booher (2004, 419) is worth quoting at length:

Legally required methods of public participation in government decision making in the US—public hearings, review and comment procedures in particular—do not work. They do not achieve genuine participation in planning or other decisions; they do not satisfy members of the public that they are being heard; they seldom can be said to improve the decisions that agencies and public officials make; and they do not incorporate a broad spectrum of the public. Worse yet, these methods often antagonize the members of the public who do try to work with them. The methods often pit citizens against each other, as they feel compelled to speak of the issues in polarizing terms to get their points across. This pattern makes it even more difficult for decision makers to sort through what they hear, much less to make a choice using public input. Most often these methods discourage busy and thoughtful individuals from wasting their time going through what appear to be nothing more than rituals designed to satisfy legal requirements. They also increase the ambivalence of planners and other public officials about hearing from the public at all. Nonetheless, these methods have an almost sacred quality to them, and they stay in place despite all that everyone knows is wrong with them.

Innes and Booher make a powerful argument that public participation needs reframing as *collaborative participation*. This new concept of participation does away with a model that assumes a simple government-citizen dichotomy, instead including a variety of parties engaged in a more complex network of relationships. Effective participation is collaborative in the most complete sense of the word: "communication, learning and action are joined together" in methods that are inclusive and self-organizing, challenge the status quo, build shared knowledge, and are adaptive (422).

Echoing Walker and Senecah in chapter 5, the new forms of public participation models are needed for sustainability because traditional practices that define government as decider and citizens as obstacles ignore both the need and the promise of interactive learning and deliberation as applied to natural resource issues. When important knowledge about a resource is held by different parties, when funds that could help a resource are controlled by multiple entities, when parties with interest and power are unconvinced by or even opposed to initiatives that other parties are certain are essential to their interests, when complex social, economic, or ecological systems face threats that require multifaceted responses, when problems transcend formal political jurisdictions—in short, when traditional forms of governance are overwhelmed by the realities of contemporary public issues, decision processes that can bring together diverse parties effectively are essential.

Thus we reach the conclusion that there is a need to go beyond stakeholder involvement to authentic collaborative processes that build knowledge, understanding, and shared commitment to effective and sustainable management of natural resources. Cormick et al. (1996, 3) put it strongly:

Unfortunately, the approaches that have been used to manage differences—the courts, the ballot box, and reliance on expertise and authority—are proving insufficient to address the challenge of creating a sustainable society. . . . Achieving sustainability is not primarily a technical or scientific challenge—although there is much to learn about how ecosystems work and respond to human activity. Nor is the challenge merely to manage our resources more effectively although there is much room for improvement in that, too. Rather, it is about dealing with people and their diverse cultures, interests, visions, priorities, and needs.

The Moral Need: Moral Development and an Ethic of Stewardship for People and Place

> If only it were all so simple! If only there were evil people somewhere committing evil deeds, and it were necessary only to separate them from the rest of us and destroy them. But the line dividing good and evil cuts through the heart of every human being. And who is willing to destroy a piece of his own heart?
>
> —Alexander Solzhenitsyn, *The Gulag Archipelago*

Environmental laws, regulations, and enforcement have brought progress in reducing direct harm previously done to natural systems, although violations continue to occur. But there is a limit to the role that laws and enforcement can play in protecting natural resources. There are not enough enforcement dollars available to keep our natural resources healthy: renegade recreationists invade protected areas, anxious watermen plunder replacement oyster beds, secretive collectors harvest threatened and endangered species, farmers allow cattle in streams, homeowners pour fertilizers and pesticides on their lawns, small-business owners dump chemicals behind their garages.

This is not an argument for less enforcement, it is an argument for the need for something more than enforcement: *an ethic of stewardship for people and place.* Sustainability is too important to leave to any single sector, including government. I assert a second fundamental principle that argues for community-based collaboration: *Programs and plans involving natural resources that fail to develop understanding and caring within affected human communities lend themselves to abuse.*[4] Without substantial awareness and commitment from all sectors, a sustainable future may not be possible.

The development of an ethic of stewardship requires moral conviction and commitment and, ultimately, an expansion of "me and mine" to "we and ours." This is as true for the protection of natural resources as it is for social well-being. People become stewards when they define their relationship to those resources and to community as one of responsibility and care.

To do so requires what I have defined elsewhere as a sense of relatedness (Dukes 1996).

Relatedness can be found in affiliation both to people and to place. Relatedness to place develops when one comes to value a place, whether through a practical understanding of its functionality or through deeper connections that may involve aesthetic and spiritual factors. Relatedness involving people can include friendship and love, but it does not depend only on warm feelings; rather, it includes qualities such as a sense of obligation to those who are dependent on us, loyalty to those who have given to us, respect for one's own and others' cultural practices, recognition of shared humanity, and empathy for others' needs, concerns, and interests.

This sense of relatedness can only be developed through sustained engagement with others that probes and ultimately understands those needs, concerns, and interests. Traditional democratic decision making, including public participation processes, systematically excludes many groups' needs and interests (Innes and Booher 2004). When done effectively, as Leach demonstrates in chapter 6, community-based collaboration allows people to discover a world beyond their already identified individual self-interest. Thus, common ground is not merely found by sharing existing preferences; it is created through the ebb and flow of discourse (Cole and Foster 2001, 112).

This profound process of moral development is not found, nor is it required, in all collaborative forums. But for those circumstances that have the most potential for significant impact on people and places, developing a sense of relatedness between and among people and with their land and environment may be the essential bridge that allows them to work together despite continuing differences and challenges.

The Civic Need: Community Capacity to Solve Problems and Resolve Conflicts

Chaskin (2001, in Innes 2002) declares that community capacity to address challenges requires four elements: (1) a shared sense of community, (2) a level of commitment among that community's members, (3) an ability to solve problems and to translate commitment into action, and (4) access to resources. The first two elements, community and commitment, reflect the caring and stewardship raised in the previous section. Community capacity, Chaskin argues, develops as members recognize their stake in the well-being of a place and so are willing to act to support that locale.

To attain the third element, the ability to solve problems and to translate commitment into action, the community needs to learn how to work collaboratively with others and to resolve conflict. And the ability of any community to solve problems is tied to the health of civil society. As Putnam (2000) has been documenting, when community ties deteriorate, community capacity declines; conversely, as community bonds strengthen, so too does capacity increase.

This leads to a third principle: *Programs and plans involving natural resource protection that do not develop a communal capacity to solve problems and resolve conflicts tend to fail.* One may have a community with many virtuous individuals and groups, but if they are isolated from one another or, worse, if they are constantly engaging in debilitating conflict, they are not able to accomplish social goals. Social capital—the types of connections among individuals that foster norms of reciprocity and generate trust—supercharges civic virtue.

Plummer and FitzGibbon (2006) confirm the role that social capital can play in enhancing collaboration in the management of natural resources. They offer empirical evidence demonstrating how social capital can lead to effective resource management. They argue that representatives of resource agencies need not only to understand the value of social capital but also to learn how to engage citizens in ways that develop social capital. As discussed in chapters 5 and 6, community-based collaboration that intentionally builds collaborative capacity can be one such vehicle.

The Adaptive Need: The Learning and Growth Necessary to Build Resilient Ecological and Social Systems

A fourth and final principle addresses the complexity of ecology and society: *Programs and plans involving natural resource protection that do not provide for ways of learning and adapting to change tend to fail.*[5] If we ignore those who hold different views, we risk encasement inside a shell where creativity, change, and growth disappear. At a structural level, a social system—a family, organization, or community—without sufficient interaction is no society at all but a static set of individuals. Healthy social systems need to adapt because we are in physical and social settings that continually change.

Charles Curtin in chapter 2 describes how groundfisheries and other commons can be destroyed if they do not have a learning capacity tied to power to effect change. Efforts to understand complex social and physical phenomena benefit from multiple perspectives and resources. Dialogue is an essential vehicle for translating knowledge into larger collective action (Innes and Booher 2010).

María Fernández-Giménez and Heidi Ballard in chapter 3 describe how CBCs are and should be developing knowledge and understanding and applying that learning through adaptive management. They note that stakeholders can contribute to assessment, management implementation, monitoring, and evaluation. The following comparison, adapted from Dukes (2006) and Lee (1999), illustrates how principles of adaptive management offer lessons for collaboration, but also demonstrates important differences.

Need
- The need for adaptive management is grounded in the recognition that people do not know enough to manage ecosystems with predictable results.
- The need for collaboration is grounded in the recognition that no single entity can know enough to manage a particular place with predictable results.

Focus
- Adaptive management focuses on managing people who interact with the ecosystem.
- Building authentic collaboration requires a focus on managing how people engage one another to foster mutual understanding, empathy, and problem-solving capacity.

Solutions
- Adaptive management explores questions to which there are few reliable answers by experimentation.
- Collaboration does not seek an answer that already exists; rather, it creates answers that can only be developed from the combined experience, resources, and ingenuity of diverse participants.

Type of learning
- In adaptive management, learning requires active participation from those most likely to be affected by actions. Those who depend on the resource may be those who know most about the condition of the ecosystem.
- Collaboration requires active participation from those most likely to be affected by planning. Those who will be most directly impacted by resource management may know most about the community, economic, and even ecological dynamics that must be considered.

Conflict
- Conflict in adaptive management is inevitable and essential, and should be conducted in ways that the disputing parties perceive as legitimate, or it will thwart learning.

- Conflict in collaboration is inevitable and essential, and should be conducted in ways that the disputing parties perceive as legitimate, or it will thwart learning.

Most appropriate application

- Adaptive management is likely to be costly and slow. This approach is reasonable for use in complex natural systems, including those most disturbed by human impacts.
- Collaboration takes time and resources. It is most appropriate in situations that are complex and involve significant resource and community impacts.

The Future Of Community-Based Collaboration

The future of community-based collaboration may very well include many futures. These will likely vary by geographic region, by scale, by subject focus, and by the types of parties involved. If collaboration is to grow, then institutionalization will continue with elements such as standardization of professional competencies for agency personnel, increased public funding, new regulatory definitions and mandates, and more university classes and degree programs. But the complex and chaotic nature of environmental issues also undoubtedly will mean a need for individual, ad hoc efforts whose design and purposes must be invented to address unforeseen circumstances.

This book focuses primarily on the North American experience, largely because of the need to address challenges peculiar to these circumstances. But CBCs are a growing global phenomenon, and the linkages between domestic and other efforts can and likely will strengthen both; indeed, those linkages are being made with exchange programs involving community members and agencies as well as the globalization of academic research and learning, as described by Curtin in chapter 2.

Bernardo Aguilar-González has thought carefully about the international arena:

Collaborative management represents one of the most ambitious and grounded ways to make operative notions such as strong sustainable democracy or ecological democracy (Prugh et al. 2000; Morrison 1995). As we are learning about it we realize that collaboration is the U.S. expression of other global trends that seek to enhance the role of civil society. Just as in the U.S., groups overseas seek to rescue the right and highlight the fitness of communities and grassroots organizations to decide the best ways to manage their bioregions without excluding themselves from nature. Just as in the Americas, expressions range from radical alternatives such as "Zapatista caracoles" in Mexico and endogenous development nuclei in Venezuela to more moderate ones like campesino associations trying to manage biological corridors in Costa Rica. This response to the centralizing and anonymous forces of corporate globalization shares a common language and hope with U.S. collaboratives. In the words of the prominent sociologist John Foran (2003), they share a magical political culture, a concrete utopianism. Learning from these alternatives abroad seems necessary for U.S. collaboratives not only to gain from their experience but also to develop a common language capable of uniting diverse views and allowing their not necessarily mutually compatible desires full expression globally. This process should also help develop international organizational forms capable of nurturing this expression and debate as well as enabling cooperative action when needed, both locally and across borders.[6]

Improving community-based collaboration will require entirely new institutional arrangements. Some, like Walker and Senecah in chapter 5, are calling these arrangements "collaborative governance";[7] a variety of other terms, such as "adaptive governance" (Scholz and Stiftel 2005), also exist.

Unlike traditional structures of governance, collaborative governance will involve the creation and recreation of many ad hoc, temporary systems of decision making. For example, a community group helping to develop a TMDL (water quality improvement) Implementation Plan was determined that its work would not conclude with a document collecting dust on shelves.[8] But the search for a responsible sponsor who could oversee implementation of the plan failed to secure sufficient commitment from any one organization with that capacity. Because responsibility for implementation was divided among public and private parties and several jurisdictions, the group decided that oversight would require a long-term (but not permanent), multi-jurisdictional and multiparty structure. Such a structure can encourage flexibility, adaptation, and resilience as it does not rely on a single entity for support, but it also risks diluting the leadership and accountability that might otherwise exist with a clear statutory authority.

Another easy forecast is that collaboration will continue to be controversial. Collaborative processes are human artifices and as such are too easily misused, mismanaged, and misinterpreted to expect that the field will ever get a free pass. Furthermore, CBC processes are typically responses to problems and change, often significant change, and change rarely is easy.

Finally, CBCs will continue to serve as laboratories, places where people gather to invent and practice the arts of democratic decision making (Kemmis 1990), of cross-community conflict resolution, of community development, and, of course, of conservation.

Tony Cheng, who credits Steve Daniels at Utah State University for orienting him to the entrepreneur model, suggests that the most likely future role for CBCs is as policy entrepreneurs,

catalyzing new forms of action and facilitating a different kind of dialogue about the interconnectedness of communities and the environment. CBCs will continue to:

- Bring in new voices and issues to the table that government agencies or industry do not address;
- Define and reframe community-environment relationships;
- Mobilize community members to engage in dialogue about future of community and environment as an integrated system;
- Increase availability and access to various resources for communities to draw upon—information, knowledge, technical, financial, personnel, and institutional resources;
- Build coalitions to change policies and programs;
- Build skills and opportunities for entrepreneurs and businesses;
- Retrain workers to meet broader ecological goals of environmental management—such as stormwater management through green roofs in urban areas, riparian restoration in the Southwest, invasive species management of Midwestern waterways.

In the future, CBCs in the U.S. need to bridge the urban-rural divide, so that "community" is thought of as an integrated system of neighboring urban and rural communities. CBCs will expand their issue sets from their initial land use concerns to broader community well-being and quality-of-life concerns. Many CBCs will become contract administrators for government programs and will directly provide public services to local communities in the form of water quality monitoring and testing, job retraining and outsourcing, energy savings tips and techniques, grant-writing support for other community nonprofits, youth and adult environmental educational opportunities, wildfire and other hazard mitigation services, and assistance to disenfranchised populations. CBCs will emerge as more full and equal partners with government agencies to provide for environmental and community goods and services.

Internationally, CBCs will need to get involved in water resource allocation, distribution, and quality to improve community well-being and quality of life. Once reliable sources of clean water are secured, CBCs in many countries will continue to address the linkage between loss of forest land, home fuel uses, family nutrition, and respiratory diseases from wood-burning stoves. CBCs will also be the leading edge of transforming the role of women in linking community economics and environmental management. CBCs will function as sub-state actors much more than in the U.S.[9]

Recommendations

What does this mean in the real world of community and place? What matters to community members, environmental advocates, recreationists, business owners, and other CBC participants seeking to maintain or restore healthy natural resources and sustain economically viable communities? What is most important for agencies seeking legitimacy for the difficult choices they make in managing resources for competing uses, or for elected officials seeking to balance essential environmental needs with economic and social concerns? What is most important for the many researchers and others seeking to understand and improve environmental decision making? How can these individuals and institutions make best use of the knowledge represented in this book through research and experience?

Earlier chapters addressed recommendations to these groups focused on issues that might occur in specific circumstances, such as monitoring, building relationships of trust, and seeking legitimacy. Here I offer a broader set of recommendations to community members, agencies, researchers, and funders for what needs to occur for the field of community-based collaboration to be nurtured and sustained in ways that fulfill its promise. These six recommendations are:

1. Develop, continually revise, and use guidance concerning best practices for determining how to use authentic collaboration as another tool that, when used correctly and in appropriate circumstances, can help achieve desired outcomes.
2. Define clearly the role and anticipated influence of any collaborative group relative to other decision processes.
3. Be proactive: parties and institutions other than public agencies can serve effectively as conveners and informed participants as appropriate.
4. Improve collaborative capacity (e.g., conflict skills, group leadership) among all participants.

5. Find ways to make new institutions of collaborative governance accountable and representative.
6. Participate in building knowledge about the appropriateness, efficacy, and conduct of collaboration.

I consider each of these in turn.

1. Develop best practices for determining how to use authentic collaboration to achieve desired outcomes.

Many "how-to" guides and manuals describe best practices in convening and conducting collaborative processes. Fewer books and guides help determine whether, when, and how collaborative processes can be effective (but see, e.g., Bernard and Young 1997; Wondolleck and Yaffee 2000; Dukes and Firehock 2001; Daniels and Walker 2002). However, research into collaboration is increasing, practices are being documented, and agencies are developing policies and procedures that support authentic collaborative processes. In this book, chapters 5 and 6 ("Collaborative Governance" and "Building a Theory of Collaboration") and chapter 4 ("Effective Collaboration") provide guidance about the appropriate circumstances for collaborative processes and best practices of such processes respectively. A number of organizations provide support for community and other participants in such processes.[10]

To argue for such best practices is not to suggest that these are immutable. As the use of CBCs grows and as practice, evaluation, and research mature, other lessons will be learned. Also, best practices are best used as guidance, not dogma; environmental and social issues can be formidably complex, and many situations arise that require judgment and may necessitate trade-offs.

Preparation for Successful Collaboration

Successful collaborative processes generally share the following conditions at the outset:

1. *Clear purpose and goals.* The effort must be driven by a well-defined purpose that is real, practical, and shared by the group (Innes 1999). Melanie Hughes McDermott, Margaret Ann Moote, and Cecilia Danks in chapter 4 point to the need for direct involvement of key decision makers in the process. Among decision makers' obligations is to provide clarity about purpose and goals early in the process, so that participants can make informed decisions about their participation.

Leadership and participants should recognize that group members may have additional goals as well, and that shifting conditions may necessitate adaptation in goals. But generally, convening a group whose purposes are not clear can lead to increasing frustration and wasted time and resources.

2. *Clear structure and process.* A CBC should have well-defined decision rules and process rules that are supported and periodically reviewed by the members. What are members' roles, rights, and responsibilities? How will the process be run? How will any decision or recommendation be determined, and how will it be used? What happens in the absence of agreement?

Again, these need not necessarily be laid out right at the beginning of the process. As with most elements of CBCs, co-design of structure and process can improve both the product and legitimacy of that product.

3. *Sufficient resources to conduct the process.* McDermott and colleagues again point to the importance of such resources. Some CBCs have started with little more than an agreement to sit down together and have ended up obtaining millions of dollars in resources. But as CBCs become institutionalized, and as expectations for defined outcomes grow, the need for resources to conduct an effective process becomes more predictable. This includes sufficient funding for various startup costs such as retaining skilled facilitators or conducting situation assessments or public outreach. On the individual participant level, success requires that agencies and organizations commit staffing and funding to support consistent staff attendance and participation.

4. *Inclusion and effective representation.* Successful CBCs include representatives of all relevant and significantly different interests (Innes 1999). At the same time, the right mix of participants is important to ensure compatible personalities and a diversity of skills and resources.

5. *Collaboration capacity among staff and participants.* Convening staff and other stakeholders are urged to seek out training for participants in communication, outreach, leadership, and collaborative problem-solving skills. Not all individuals have that capability, but few cannot improve.

Conduct of Successful Collaboration

Successful collaborative processes generally share the following characteristics of conduct:

1. *Early involvement and sufficient time.* Interested parties can be involved early and have sufficient time for effective consensus building. During high-stakes conditions, participants are more satisfied when involved in predecisional scoping activities rather then simply commenting on fully formed policy proposals. Successful public participation takes time. Refrain from judging collaborative processes prematurely.

2. *High-quality knowledge and monitoring and evaluation capacity.* Effective processes incorporate high-quality information (Innes 1999). As Leach notes in chapter 6, ambiguous evidence tends to cause people to interpret data as support for their prior conclusions, thus causing policy positions to polarize. Fernández-Giménez and Ballard in chapter 3 contrast that with the participation of diverse stakeholders who share responsibility for collaborative or multiparty monitoring; these conditions can help participants gain greater understanding of varying perspectives. Joint monitoring by stakeholders can even help resolve controversial issues.

Conveners should solicit both expert knowledge and local knowledge, which Fernández-Giménez and Ballard note can be invaluable. Provide information to help participants achieve common understanding, and design suitable protocols for monitoring and evaluating the outcomes of the process.

3. *Cultured conflict.* Effective collaboration follows principles of civil discourse while at the same time encouraging challenges to assumptions (Innes 1999). Civility does not mean the absence of conflict or disagreement; candor should be encouraged to ensure that all views are represented. It does mean that participants listen to one another, take each participant's perspective seriously, and attempt to address the concerns of each participant.

4. *Sustained dialogue.* Effective CBCs seek consensus only after discussions have fully explored the issues and interests and only after significant effort has been made to find creative responses to differences. Participants should be helped to distinguish between positions or demands and the actual needs and interests that underlie those positions—the "why."

Following that guidance, it is important to understand collaboration as one potentially powerful tool in an arsenal of such tools. As with mechanical tools, nobody should expect collaborative processes to be effective in circumstances not appropriate for their use.

2. Define clearly the role and anticipated influence of any collaborative group relative to other decision processes.

"Collaboration" can have many different meanings; some people use the term to describe any agency-convened process that involves even perfunctory consultation with individuals and institutions outside of that agency, or multi-agency initiatives that might have no private party role at all. Others describe collaboration as shared decision making[11] and expect no single group member, including agencies, to dominate. One of the most common and tragic outcomes of collaborative processes is the deep disappointment and disillusionment that follow months to years of hard work negated by aborted implementation. For the field to be successful, a norm must be developed such that collaborative efforts spell out the extent and nature of shared power and responsibility.

Elected leadership has a special role to play in this area, as elected officials are often in position to navigate the intricacies of policy and implementation (Policy Consensus Initiative 2006). Agencies also need to develop policies that provide clear guidance for agency-led processes, as well as those processes where the agency may be one of many participants. These policies need to allow for flexibility while at the same time including clear guidance about items such as boundaries of authority and authorization to share any such authority, criteria for participation, and use of data.

Participants will respect authentic efforts for inclusion that delineate what is and what is not part of the "decision space," that is, what may be open for discussion and what cannot be negotiated.

3. Be proactive: parties and institutions other than public agencies can serve effectively as conveners and informed participants as appropriate.

Although the overwhelming majority of CBCs, particularly those having an impact on large-scale areas and resources, are agency-led (Western Consensus Council 2003), many effective CBCs originated in the efforts of private individuals and organizations. There are potential disadvantages (weaker connections with established authorities, absence of formal oversight) to these efforts. However, some organizations have considerable capacity to help people work well together, and advantages such as flexibility and independence mean that each situation should be assessed on its own merits.

Many environmental advocacy organizations are sensitive to criticism that they only oppose and never propose. A successful collaborative can bring both substantive results and public acclaim.

One successful example of such an organization is the Elizabeth River Project, a community-based organization advocating for the health of the Elizabeth River and its watershed. In the mid-2000s, the Elizabeth River Project was determined to clean up its top-priority site, Money Point. Money Point consists of a dozen or more industrial parcels and a residential population of about 250 people living in older houses on streets approaching the industrial sites. A fire and later a spill at a creosote facility contributed contamination to the bottom of the Elizabeth River at some of the highest known concentrations of polycyclic aromatic hydrocarbons of any water body in the world.

The site was on no agency's list for cleanup. Rather than wait for an agency to step in, the Elizabeth River Project itself convened a collaborative group that included agencies, industrial landowners, and other key community interests to seek consensus for a plan to clean up the river bottom and prevent further contamination from land sources. The group was able to attract a university facilitator, who secured sufficient grant funds to support the process. This two-year effort concluded with a plan that secured substantial funding and voluntary cleanup efforts by the community and industry.[12] The plan won the 2007 Environmental Design Research Association Places/Planning Award.

Elected officials have always had the power to bring people together to work on problems. Now this power is being documented and formalized, as addressed by Gregg Walker and Susan Senecah in chapter 5, using the intriguing term "collaborative governance." Such officials can serve as conveners who help shape fair, effective, and authentic processes (Policy Consensus Initiative 2006).

An intriguing role is also emerging for universities (Policy Consensus Initiative 2005). Faculty and administrators at land grant universities, which have a traditional role of service, as well as at some public and private schools, have supported community-based collaboration at the individual level. Some schools now are explicitly assuming responsibility for convening public processes, with the University Network for Collaborative Governance the first network intended to assist in that development.

4. Improve collaborative capacity among all participants.

Foster, Fishman, and colleagues (2001) reviewed dozens of studies identifying essential skills and knowledge sets people need to collaborate effectively, among them the ability to work with others, leadership skills, conflict resolution skills, effective communication skills, and the ability to understand the norms and perspectives of other group members. Many of these skills can be developed with education and practice. Fernández-Giménez and Ballard in chapter 3 suggest that CBCs that plan to monitor should set up partnerships with scientists and natural resource professionals to build internal science capacity. Training is readily available throughout the country, and many web-based and published resources are available to help build appropriate skills and capacity for individuals and organizations.

Agencies with responsibility for convening such processes need to build collaborative capacity within their agency. Building capacity may include training to achieve desired skills for collaborative capacity (as defined by the agency), developing performance criteria that reward effective collaborative behavior, and mentoring. Leadership needs to offer clear guidance about when collaboration is and is not appropriate and what it actually means within the agency.

Agencies also can help build capacity outside the agency with those they engage. Rather than bemoan the obstinacy and enmity of the stakeholders, whose input many agency representatives come to dread, agencies can help them participate effectively. One way to do so is to invite stakeholders to participate with agency staff during such training rather than simply training one's own agency members.[13] A number of states have begun various forms of natural resources collaborative leadership programs that build such cross-sector capacity (Addor et al. 2005).

Facilitators vary widely by skill, experience, and commitment to authentic collaborative work. As Leach observes in chapter 6, theory tested by research is increasing in amount and utility. He notes that although some facilitators express reluctance to incorporate theory, all facilitators in fact incorporate theories in action anytime they act with an expectation of having an impact on group behavior. Reflexive practice should be the norm, not the exception, for what is a highly sophisticated and demanding practice of group facilitation. Professional associations such as the Environment/ Public Policy Section of the Association for Conflict Resolution foster best practices and continuing education.

5. Find ways to make new institutions of collaborative governance accountable and representative.

The world of community-based collaboration is growing because existing institutions of governance either don't work well or cannot serve the functions demanded by new problems. Yet community-based collaboration itself has already collected a litany of complaints and criticism that risks derailing the movement before it is well established. Agencies need to establish appropriate guidance at all levels that protect public resources while encouraging innovation and authentic collaboration.

A federal employee in Washington, D.C., who prefers to remain anonymous suggests that we are seeing more government policies, guidance, and directives encouraging the use of collaboration. This person writes,

This is a positive development for increasing awareness and providing support for those interested in pursuing collaborative approaches to resolving problems and making decisions. However, policy statements alone are not sufficient to actually change attitudes and behaviors. Making greater and better use of collaborative processes will take additional action both within and outside government agencies including:

1. Broad capacity building efforts to support collaborative approach.
2. Agency commitment and expectations of external partners that agencies keep their commitments to support collaboration—if you see policies not followed, opportunities missed, lack of collaborative behavior, then speak out, ask questions, and be a force for change.
3. Understanding within and outside government, that greater internal agency/government collaboration is crucial for sustaining external collaboration in local communities—e.g., communication and cooperation of components within agencies and between agencies at all levels of organization is essential for this approach to decision making and problem solving. Ensuring that everyone within the agency and across jurisdictions understands and is kept apprised so they can provide timely responses and keep commitments to local community efforts is a key to success. In addition, internal agency changes regarding budgets, procurement, policies and procedures, senior management roles, personnel, must shift to support community-based collaboration.

6. Participate in building knowledge about the appropriateness, efficacy, and conduct of collaboration.

At one point I considered titling this section, "What You Know about Collaboration, and Why It Is Wrong." This language is facetious, of course, at least for most of us. There are many people who work with CBCs who are quite capable, have had substantial and often surprising success in the face of formidable obstacles, and are smart and willing to learn—and do learn.

But there continues to be confusion and misrepresentation about the nature and practice of community-based collaboration. This is the case for several reasons. First, much of what individuals know is indeed based on what has worked (or not worked) in no more than a handful of experiences. Unless you are in a position to participate or observe dozens of those experiences, you are in no position to be making unexamined claims. But of course, people do just that.

Second, much of what is "known" is based on political and ideological preferences. That is, there can occur an ethos and even a culture of either compliance or opposition. Depending on your orientation, you can read Michael McCloskey's (1996) critique of collaboration and either accept it as unvarnished truth or define it as a grab for power, without understanding that McCloskey has a sophisticated and nuanced view that sees value in using collaborative approaches in appropriate circumstances. You may accept an agency's policy encouraging collaboration as an authentic effort to improve conservation and economic development or you may view it as a cover by a cynical leadership used to avoid making hard decisions required for authentic environmental progress. In other words, we often let our values and biases determine what we think is true.

Third, much of what is "known" is indeed based on research. But research should be understood to have limitations too.

All of this is a way of declaring a continuing need for knowledge building. This is based on the following premises:

1. The use of CBCs will increase as management of natural resources continues to evolve toward watershed and ecosystem scales involving multiple interests and jurisdictions.
2. Useful, research-based knowledge about collaborative efforts is eagerly sought by agencies, funders, community groups, and analysts of such processes.
3. However, research continues to be incomplete, isolated by discipline, and often dismissed as illegitimate by one or more stakeholders concerned with these issues.
4. Research and evaluation of CBCs will be effective only if conducted as a systematic effort.
5. That effort must develop a coordinated research agenda responsive to the needs of agencies, funders, community groups, and analysts of such processes; plan for the wide dissemination of its findings; and foster informed deliberation about the meaning of those findings.

How can this be done? Conferences, seminars, and research can be too insular, dominated by university researchers or public agencies. This need not be the case: community members also should seek and accept invitations to speak about their experiences and needs and partner with researchers in developing evaluations that bring authentic understanding. Many colleges and universities are eager to find connections to real-world community issues and, with guidance, would be able to support participants in learning what they need to learn. Researchers should seek learning partnerships with CBCs, with public agencies, and with larger private for-profit and nonprofit institutions. Researchers should also use and enhance participatory research methods (community-based research, action research) and find ways to have that type of research valued by research institutions.

Finally, researchers need to expand their community of learning and understanding beyond their research peers to those who want to gain knowledge but don't have access to the language, publications, conferences, and classes. A knowledge-building system that exploits stakeholders' time, knowledge, and identity without giving back will not sustain itself.

Conclusions

Many big questions remain to be answered. How do we make the exceptional—the well-run, just, effective, transformational effort—become the routine? How do we support equity, justice, and fairness in systems and histories that often are or were not fair or just? How do we legitimate essential conflict that helps identify real needs while promoting shared learning and decision making essential to resilient communities? And how do we ensure that we are meeting essential ecological needs?

Ultimately, CBCs can be a way of shaping the economic, social, and ecological changes that have been accelerated by human behaviors. Climates, landscapes, economies, and cultures change, sometimes rapidly, but individuals and communities may be unwilling or unable to accommodate those changes. Community-based collaboration can be a way to grab hold of change and guide it—perhaps, to use metaphors more familiar to those working with natural resource issues, like learning to ride a previously wild horse, or navigate a turbulent river, or bring a surfboard in on a long, powerful wave. We know that we don't fully control or even understand the momentum, but we can use it in ways that are productive and may even be enjoyable.

CBCs provide a vehicle not just for change, which can be forced, but for *transitions* (Bridges 1991) that have legitimacy and support to occur.

What will matter most, then, in the coming decades as people and institutions seek ways of improving collaborative processes?

Intention matters. Depending on purpose and goals, CBCs can be used to foster and support or to block change, to share power equitably or to consolidate unfair dominance, to promote authentic dialogue or to stifle dissent.

Policy matters. Whether and how agencies can convene and participate in collaborative processes, the leadership that agency staff may or may not offer, and how funding priorities are determined will all shape the future of CBCs.

Capacity for individual and institutional actors—local, state, and federal agencies, advocacy organizations, community members—matters. Without training, funding, performance criteria, and high-level support, collaborative efforts likely will be ineffective.

Knowledge matters. Community-based collaboration continues to engender skepticism among participants who have endured failed processes, as well as among many thoughtful critics (see, e.g., Kenney 2000). Community-based collaboration must be effective at improving environmental, social, and economic outcomes and not an ideologically driven choice by leadership that dislikes public expenditures or that seeks to exploit more than it seeks to protect natural resources. That requires a commitment to understand the reality of actual outcomes, good and bad, which are occurring throughout the country, and using that understanding to improve practice. Good research and evaluation build useful knowledge; bringing that knowledge into the world builds capable people.

Institutional support matters. Executive orders, financial backing, commitments of personnel, and performance-based management drive agency behavior.

Recall the question of whether CBCs are worthy of institutional support. Yes, it is worth developing systems of support for effective, authentic collaborative work, when the purposes, conditions, and resources are appropriate. Such systems can help ensure that CBCs are run effectively, that democratic and legal principles are followed, that public funds are spent in ways that are accountable. But such systems must be designed so that they don't risk subverting the very strengths of CBCs—their innovation, creativity, responsiveness, and flexibility. The tension between flexibility and the need for accountability is real and cannot be ignored by advocates for CBCs seeking institutionalization.

Change is a given. The question is whether or not people engaged in community-based collaboration can guide and shape that change or whether they must simply be observers. That will remain an open question—the future rarely follows a predictable course. The ideal of authentic collaboration likely will never be fully achieved (Innes and Booher 2004, 429). But that need not keep people who care from using their best judgment to prepare and advocate for what they need.

Notes

1. In 2006, Karen Firehock and I traveled around the country conducting training on authentic collaboration for environmental advocates, off-highway vehicle (OHV) advocates, and the U.S. Forest Service and other agency staff, as the Forest Service prepared to implement a 2005 rule on travel planning. One of the most energetic parts of the training occurred as participants described positive and negative experiences with collaborative processes. Many participants had positive experiences. However, without exception, each group of participants shared stories of distressing problems, including imbalanced recruitment of participants by agen-

.cies, insufficient science, failures to implement hard-fought agreements, and poor facilitation. For thoughtful criticism, see Kenney (2000).

2. See, for instance, Jackson et al. (2001) for an analysis of the collapse of fisheries and coastal ecosystems.

3. See Weissiger (2007) for a classic example of this. See Garande and Dagg (2005) for another example of failed planning due to inadequate involvement of the communities that must support the plans. Garande and Dagg also note that "Participation at the community level has been identified by the Organisation for Economic Development . . . as one of the most essential principles in rural development projects" (418).

4. An example from my own experience is an ongoing effort to restore oysters to Virginia's Eastern Shore. The reintroduction of nonparasitic oysters has been quite successful; however, local residents, who are not involved in the reintroduction, harvest the oysters despite laws and efforts at persuasion and enforcement.

5. See Kai Lee's celebrated 1993 treatise, *Compass and Gyroscope,* for an analysis of the key role of social learning in sustainability.

6. Bernardo Aguilar-González, email, December 16, 2005.

7. There already exists a University Network for Collaborative Governance, an informal network sponsored by the Policy Consensus Initiative.

8. From my experience as facilitator of this advisory group.

9. Tony Cheng, email, November 29, 2005.

10. As of 2008, these included the U.S. Institute for Environmental Conflict Resolution (www.ecr.gov), which provides guidance in cases in which federal interests are involved; the Policy Consensus Initiative (www.policyconsensus.org), which offers support for state and local officials; the Western Collaboration Assistance Network (WestCAN—http://westcan.sonoran.org); Red Lodge Clearing House (http://www.redlodgeclearinghouse.org); and the International Association for Public Participation (http://www.iap2.org).

11. From a November 18 keynote speech by Kirk Emerson at the CBCRC's 2005 conference, "Putting Knowledge to Work."

12. I served as lead facilitator for this effort.

13. The training sessions to prepare for collaborative planning for the U.S. Forest Service rule on OHV route designation were sponsored by the Natural Trails and Waters Coalition, made up of environmental advocacy organizations. The coalition invited OHV users and the Forest Service to participate, and the diversity of the participation received high scores on training evaluations submitted by trainees.

References

Addor, Mary Lou, Tanya Denckla Cobb, E. Franklin Dukes, Mike Ellerbrock, and L. Steven Smutko. 2005. "Linking Theory to Practice: A Theory of Change Model of the Natural Resources Leadership Institute." *Conflict Resolution Quarterly* 23 (2): 203–23.

Arnstein, Sherry. 1969. "A Ladder of Citizen Participation." *Journal of the American Institute of Planners* 35:221.

Bernard, Ted, and Jora Young. 1997. *The Ecology of Hope: Communities Collaborate for Sustainability.* Gabriola Island, BC: New Society Publishers.

Bridges, William. 1991. *Managing Transitions: Making the Most of Change*. New York: Addison-Wesley.

Chaskin, Robert. 2001. "Defining Community Capacity: A Definitional Framework and Case Studies from a Comprehensive Community Initiative." *Urban Affairs Review* 36 (3): 291–323.

Cole, Luke W., and Sheila R. Foster. 2001. *From the Ground Up: Environmental Racism and the Rise of the Environmental Justice Movement*, ed. Richare Delgado and Jean Stefancic. New York: New York University Press.

Cormick, Gerald, Norman Dale, Paul Emond, Glenn Sigurdson, and Barry Stuart. 1996. *Building Consensus for a Sustainable Future: Putting Principles into Practice*. Ottawa: National Round Table on the Environment and the Economy.

Daniels, Steven E., and Gregg B. Walker. 2001. *Working through Environmental Conflict: The Collaborative Learning Approach*. Westport, CT: Praeger.

Dukes, E. Franklin. 1996. *Resolving Public Conflict: Transforming Community and Governance*. Manchester, UK: Manchester University Press.

———. 2004. "From Enemies, to Higher Ground, to Allies: The Unlikely Partnership between the Tobacco Farm and Public Health Communities." In *Participatory Governance: Planning, Conflict Mediation and Public Decision-Making in Civil Society*, ed. W. Robert Lovan, Michael Murray, and Ron Shaffer. London: Ashgate Press.

———. 2005. "Why—and Why Not—Dialogue?" In *The Dialogue Forum Reflections*, ed. Glenn Sigurdson. Vancouver: Morris J. Wosk Centre for Dialogue, Simon Fraser University.

Dukes, E. Franklin, and Karen E. Firehock. 2001. *Collaboration: A Guide for Environmental Advocates*. Charlottesville, VA: Institute for Environmental Negotiation, The Wilderness Society, National Audubon Society.

Foran, John, ed. 2003. *The Future of Revolutions: Rethinking Radical Change in the Age of Globalization*. New York: Zed Books.

Forester, John. 2005. "Policy Analysts Can Learn from Mediators." In *Adaptive Governance and Water Conflict: New Institutions for Collaborative Planning*, ed. John T. Scholz and Bruce Stiftel, 150–63. Washington, DC: Resources for the Future Press.

Foster-Fishman, Pennie G., Shelby L. Berkowitz, David W. Lounsbury, Stephanie Jacobson, and Nicole A. Allen. 2001. "Building Collaborative Capacity in Community Coalitions: A Review and Integrative Framework." *Journal of Community Psychology* 29 (2): 241–61.

Fung, Archon. 2006. "Varieties of Participation in Complex Governance." *Public Administration Review*, Special Issue, December, 66–75.

Garande, Tarisai, and Suzan Dagg. 2005. "Public Participation and Effective Water Governance at the Local Level: A Case Study from a Small Under-developed Area in Chile." *Environment, Development and Sustainability* 7 (4): 417–31.

Innes, Judith E. 1999. "Evaluating Consensus Building." In *The Consensus Building Handbook: A Comprehensive Guide to Reaching Agreement*, ed. Lawrence Susskind, Sarah McKearnan, and Jennifer Thomas-Larmer. Thousand Oaks, CA: Sage.

———. 2002. *Evaluation Design for the Capacity Building Program of the California Center for Public Dispute Resolution*. Sacramento, CA: California Center for Public Dispute Resolution.

Innes, Judith E., and David E. Booher. 2004. "Reframing Public Participation: Strategies for the 21st Century." *Planning Theory & Practice* 5 (4): 419–36.

———. 2010. *Planning with Complexity: An Introduction to Collaborative Rationality for Public Policy.* Oxon, UK: Routledge.

Jackson, Jeremy B. C., Michael X. Kirby, Wolfgang H. Berger, Karen A. Bjorndal, Louis W. Botsford, Bruce J. Bourque, Roger H. Bradbury, Richard Cooke, Jon Erlandson, James A. Estes, Terence P. Hughes, Susan Kidwell, Carina B. Lange, Hunter S. Lenihan, John M. Pandolfi, Charles H. Peterson, Robert S. Steneck, Mia J. Tegner, and Robert R. Warner. 2001. "Historical Overfishing and the Recent Collapse of Coastal Ecosystems." *Science* 293 (5330): 629–37.

Kemmis, Dan. 1990. *Community and the Politics of Place.* Norman: University of Oklahoma Press.

Kenney, Douglas. 2000. "Arguing about Consensus: Examining the Case Against Western Watershed Initiatives and Other Collaborative Groups in Natural Resource Management." Boulder, CO: Natural Resources Law Center at the University of Colorado School of Law.

Lee, Kai N. 1993. *Compass and Gyroscope: Integrating Science and Politics for the Environment.* Washington, DC: Island Press.

McCloskey, Michael. 1996. "The Skeptic: Collaboration Has Its Limits." *High Country News* 28 (9): 7.

Morrison, Roy D. 1995. *Ecological Democracy.* Cambridge, MA: South End Press.

O'Leary, Rosemary, and Lisa Bingham, eds. 2003. *The Promise and Performance of Environmental Conflict Resolution.* Washington, DC: Resources for the Future.

Plummer, Ryan, and John FitzGibbon. 2006. "People Matter: The Importance of Social Capital in the Co-Management of Natural Resources." *Natural Resources Forum* 30:51–62.

Policy Consensus Initiative. 2005. *Finding Better Ways to Solve Problems: The Emerging Role of Universities as Neutral Forums for Collaborative Policy-Making.* June. Portland, OR: Policy Consensus Initiative.

———. 2006. *Legislators at a Crossroads: Making Choices to Work Differently.* April. Portland, OR: Policy Consensus Initiative.

Prugh, Thomas, Herman Daly, and Robert Costanza. 2000. *The Local Politics of Global Sustainability.* Washington, DC: Island Press.

Putnam, Robert. 2000. *Bowling Alone: The Collapse and Revival of American Community.* New York: Simon and Schuster.

Sachs, Jeffrey D. 2005. *The End of Poverty.* New York: Penguin Books.

Scholz, John T., and Bruce Stiftel, eds. 2005. *Adaptive Governance and Water Conflict: New Institutions for Collaborative Planning.* Washington, DC: Resources for the Future Press.

Weissiger, Marsha. 2007. "Gendered Injustice: Navajo Livestock Reduction in the New Deal Era." *Western Historical Quarterly* 38:437–55.

Western Consensus Council, and Consensus Building Institute. 2003. "Community-Based Collaboration on Federal Lands and Resources: An Evaluation of Participant Satisfaction." Paper presented at a conference, "Evaluating Methods and Outcomes of Community-Based Collaborative Processes," Salt Lake City, UT, September 14.

Wondolleck, Julia M., and Steven L. Yaffee. 2000. *Making Collaboration Work: Lessons from Innovation in Natural Resource Management.* Washington, DC: Island Press.

Contributors

Heidi L. Ballard is Assistant Professor of Environmental Science Education at the University of California, Davis. Her work focuses on participatory research approaches and citizen science efforts for ecological monitoring in conservation and natural resource management contexts. Her recent work examines the environmental learning outcomes of participatory action research for community members and scientists, and the relationship between youth wildfire education and socio-ecological resilience in fire-prone communities in the United States. Previously she worked with Latino migrant workers and a Native American tribe in Washington to research harvest impacts on nontimber forest products. She received her doctorate in environmental science, policy, and management from the University of California, Berkeley.

Juliana E. Birkhoff is a conflict resolution scholar and an experienced mediator, facilitator, and trainer. She is Vice President for Programs and Practice at RESOLVE. Birkhoff has an extensive background in multidisciplinary research on conflict and conflict analysis, in particular the use of collaborative decision-making processes in politically charged and technically complex issues. She has twenty years of experience as a mediator and facilitator with federal, state, and local level government, as well as with consumer, community, grassroots, and public interest groups. She has investigated how stakeholders and collaborative leaders integrate different ways of knowing into collaborative processes, and best practices for public participation. She studied with the Harvard Negotiation Project, Harvard University, and holds a doctorate in conflict analysis and resolution from George Mason University.

Charles Curtin is a biologist whose work links ecological and social systems. His research primarily examines how changes in climate and land use interact to alter landscape composition. Curtin has developed large-scale community-based science programs for the rancher-led Malpai Borderlands Group in the Mexico-U.S. borderlands. He has also developed collaborative projects between indigenous pastoral peoples in the U.S. Southwest and East Africa in conjunction with the African Conservation Centre and UNESCO, and community-based fisheries conservation programs in eastern Maine. He currently serves as core faculty in conservation biology at Antioch University, Keene, New Hampshire. He holds a master's degree in land resources and a doctorate in zoology, both from the University of Wisconsin–Madison.

Cecilia Danks is Associate Professor in the Rubenstein School of Environment and Natural Resources, the University of Vermont. Prior to joining the faculty at the University of Vermont she was director of socioeconomic research at the Watershed Research and Training Center, Hayfork, California, in the years 1997–2001. She has done extensive work in social science and statistical analyses of community forestry issues. Her research publications have focused largely on institutional issues in community-based forestry. Recent work includes community-based approaches to forest carbon markets and wood biomass energy. Formerly she served as a social science analyst for the Forest Ecosystem Management Assessment Team, which developed the Northwest Forest Plan. Dank received her doctorate in wildland resource science from the University of California, Berkeley, and is the author of numerous publications devoted to land and communities.

E. Franklin Dukes is Director of the Institute for Environmental Negotiation at the University of Virginia and the Environmental Conflict Resolution Initiative at George Mason University. He is both a researcher and a practitioner of collaborative environmental processes. He initiated the Community-Based Collaboratives Research Consortium and is past cochair of the Environment/Public Policy Section of the Association of Conflict Resolution. He teaches courses in public participation, consensus building, and mediation and has worked as a mediator and facilitator at the local, state, and national level on projects involving environment and land use, community development, education, and health. He is the author of *Resolving Public Conflict: Transforming Community and Governance* and co-author of *Reaching for Higher Ground in Conflict Resolution* and *Collaboration: A Guide for Environmental Advocates*. He holds a doctorate in conflict analysis and resolution from George Mason University.

María Fernández-Giménez is Associate Professor in the Department of Forest, Rangeland, and Watershed Stewardship, Colorado State University. Her research interests include the ecological dynamics of rangeland landscapes, management practices that maintain the productivity and natural variation of these ecosystems, and institutional arrangements that facilitate or enforce sustainable management practices. Recent projects have addressed community-based and collaborative natural resource management, adaptive management, traditional and local ecological knowledge, pastoralism and pastoral development, participatory research, and the effects of livestock grazing and other disturbances on the structure and function of rangeland ecosystems. She teaches integrated ecosystem management, community-based natural resource management, and rangeland monitoring and planning. She holds a doctorate in wildland resource science from the University of California, Berkeley.

Karen E. Firehock is a lecturer at the University of Virginia, School of Architecture, and director of the nonprofit environmental planning organization the Green Infrastructure Center Inc. She has been a planner and facilitator for community watershed plans and facilitates strategic plans for natural resource agencies and nonprofit organizations. She teaches graduate courses in watershed management, green infrastructure planning, and environmental ordinances, and is co-author of *Collaboration: A Guide for Environmental Advocates*. She holds a master's degree in urban and environmental planning and is a doctoral candidate in environmental studies at Antioch University New England.

Melanie Hughes McDermott is a researcher and consultant affiliated with the Department of Human Ecology at Rutgers University. Her research interests in community forestry, community-based collaboration, and indigenous land rights have taken her to the Philippines and southern Africa, as well as to different communities in North America. Her theoretical work is concerned with the causes and consequences of resource-use practices as shaped by environmental factors and the social relations of power, difference, and identity. She holds a master's degree in forestry from Oxford University and a doctorate in interdisciplinary social science/political ecology of environmental management and policy from the University of California, Berkeley.

William D. Leach is Assistant Professor in the Department of Public Policy and Administration at California State University, Sacramento. He teaches research methods, applied economics, and collaborative policy in the department's master's program. He also works closely with mediators at the university's Center for Collaborative Policy, where he serves as research director. The center facilitates conflict resolution and public involvement projects for local, state, and federal agencies in California. He received a doctorate in environmental policy from the University of California, Davis.

Margaret Ann Moote is a private consultant providing applied social science research and process design to natural resource management agencies and conservation groups. She conducts needs assessments, program evaluations, and policy analyses, and facilitates public participation and collaborative group processes. She has developed monitoring methods and performance evaluation protocols for federal, state, and local natural resource management programs and provided training and technical assistance in collaborative resource management and multiparty monitoring. Ann coordinated the Social Science and Community Outreach Program at the Ecological Restoration Institute at Northern Arizona University from 2001 to 2007 and the Community-based Conservation Program at the Udall Center for Studies in Public Policy at the University of Arizona from 1998 to 2001. She is the author of more than fifty publications.

Susan L. Senecah is Professor of Environmental Studies at the State University of New York College of Environmental Science and Forestry in Syracuse, New York, where she coordinates the graduate program in environmental communication and participatory processes and teaches courses in environmental public policy, dispute resolution, practical skills, and American environmental movement history. She served as editor of the two inaugural volumes of the *Environmental Communication Yearbook* and is on the U.S. Institute of Environmental Conflict Resolution roster of practitioners. In parallel with her academic activities, from 1993 to 2008 she served as environmental policy analyst and legislative aide to a New York State senator, providing district communities with capacity-building training. Since May 2008 she has been on leave from SUNY to serve the New York Department of State's Office of Coastal Resources, Local Government, and Community Sustainability. She holds a doctorate in communication studies from the University of Minnesota.

Gregg B. Walker is Professor of Communication, Adjunct Professor of Forest Ecology and Society, Adjunct Professor of Oceanic and Atmospheric Sciences, Adjunct Professor of Anthropology, and a member of the environmental science faculty at Oregon State University in Corvallis. On campus, Dr. Walker works with the Institute for Natural Resources and teaches courses in conflict management, bargaining and negotiation, natural resources decision making, and environmental conflict resolution. Off campus, he conducts training programs in collaborative conflict resolution, facilitates collaborative learning community workshops on natural resource and environmental policy issues, and researches community-level collaboration efforts. He is on the roster of the U.S. Institute for Environmental Conflict Resolution and on the editorial board of *Society and Natural Resources*. He has published numerous articles on communication and conflict resolution and is co-author (with Steve Daniels) of *Working through Environmental Conflict: The Collaborative Learning Approach*. He holds a doctoral degree in communication studies from the University of Kansas.

Index

collaboration (*continued*)
2; sustaining, 171; theories about,
146–47; when to pursue,177
collaborative adaptive ecosystem
management, 48
collaborative governance, 114–16, 201,
208; as adaptive governance, 115–16;
context of, 112–14; requirements
for, 115
Colorado State University (CSU), 50
community, sense of, 172
community-based collaboration: best
practices for, 204–6; capacity of,
12–13; challenges of, 10–11, 81, 85;
conflicts about, 6–7; contributions of,
7–10, 19, 70, 108, 141, 189; critiques
of, 81, 190; formation of, 12; future
of, 200–203; growth of, 4–6, 154, 200;
need for, 189, 192–200; —, adaptive,
192, 198–200; —, civic, 192, 197–98;
—, moral, 192, 196–97; —, practical,
192, 193–96; obstacles to, 82–91, 113;
questions about, 189, 212; recommendations about, 203–4, 213; and
related terminology, 1–2; and why it
matters, 2
community-based collaboration outcomes, 213; environmental, 11–12,
46, 81, 82–83; measuring, 11–13
Community-Based Collaboratives Research Consortium (CBCRC), 2, 58,
131, 190
complexity, 13
conflict, 199–200; cultured, 205
conservation, community-based, 28–30
convener, 207–8; universities as, 208
Cook, John, 33
Cooperative Conservation Partnership
Initiative (CCPI), 130
Coos Watershed Association (CWA),
58–59, 111
Coronado National Forest, 101
culture, 146; and differences, 165; Native
American, 165; role of, 170

decision space, 207
demonstration projects, 102–3
Diablo Trust, 12, 13, 53, 55–56, 58, 59,
60, 63, 72
Dombeck, Michael, 133

Downeast Initiative, 10, 27, 82, 94,
95, 103

East Africa, 24, 28
ecology, 23; community perspective on,
24; ecosystem perspective, 24; evolutionary perspective, 24; science of, 24
economics, 148; and incentives of
participation, 168–70; theoroid of,
167–68; and theoroid of costs and
benefits, 171
ecosystem management, 35; outcomes
of, 13
education, 97; of stakeholders, 155–56
Elizabeth River Project (Virginia), 97, 98,
100, 104, 207
Empire-Cienega Biological Planning
Team, 67
endangered species, 4
Endangered Species Act, 5, 85, 173
environmentalists, 91, 93, 102
Environmental Protection Agency, 129;
and pilot programs, 129–30
Environment/Public Policy Section of
the Association for Conflict Resolution, 209
Everglades, 137
Executive Order on Facilitation of Cooperative Conservation, 105
expertocracy, 7

facilitator, 159, 162, 209; impartiality
of, 147, 163; sharing process ownership, 167
fairness: and outcomes, 160, 161–62, 164;
and power, 162; theoroids of, 160, 162
Federal Advisory Committee Act
(FACA), 85
fire, 32, 35–37, 38, 53, 59, 68, 98, 125,
128–29
fisheries, 25–28; cod, 25, 26; decline of,
89; and groundfishing, 25
forgiveness, 165
foundations, 131
forests, 82, 92
funding, 97–98, 105

Gila National Forest, 93
governance, environmental, 1, 5, 13
Gray Ranch, McKinney Flats Project, 36

226   INDEX

National Environmental Policy Act, 85, 93, 94
National Estuary Program (NEP), 129
National Fire Plan, 99
National Forest Management Act of 1976, 9
National Marine Fisheries Service, 25, 26, 27, 94, 173
Natural Resources Conservation Service, 130
Natural Resources Working Group (NRWG) (Arizona), 91, 92, 94, 100–103
negotiation, interest-based, 158–59
networks, 91–92, 104, 194
New England Fisheries Council, 94
Nez Percé Tribe, 91
Northwest Atlantic Marine Alliance (NAMA), 27
Northwest Colorado Stewardship (NWCOS), 3, 10, 49, 50–51, 58, 59, 60, 62, 66, 111

off-highway vehicle (OHV), 49, 50–51, 58, 59, 60, 62
Ohio Environmental Protection Agency, 130
Oregon Water Enhancement Board, 130

Papillion Creek watershed (Omaha, Nebraska), 170
paradigm shift, 154
partnership, conflict about, 162
place, sense of, 172
policy subsystems, 155
political-economic factors, 84, 89
Ponderosa Pine Partnership, 102
power, 14, 32–33, 38, 103–4, 115, 124; devolution of, 6; differentials, 104–5, 162; researching, 139; of resistance, 84–85
postmodernism, 154
property rights, 4, 5
psychology: and bounded rationality, 20; and cognitive dissonance, 154
public engagement: authentic, 191; as collaborative participation, 195; to court support, 96; criticisms of, 194–95; research about, 177; reasons for, 9–10, 193–95

Public Lands Partnership, 46, 47, 82, 96, 98

Quincy Library Group, 7, 13

ranching, 30, 31–37, 69, 89
relatedness, 197
relationships, 175–76; improving, 8, 15, 69, 345; worsening, 69–70
representation, 3, 11, 83, 149–50, 205; and constituents, 151, 153; ensuring adequacy of, 150–52; evolving, 131–32, 137, 153; and inclusivity, 151–52; reassessing, 153
research: comparative, 177–78; as different than monitoring, 54; experimental, 32; methods of, 177; needs, 15; recommendations for, 72–74, 106–7, 138–40, 177–79; and testable hypotheses, 55–56
resilience, 12
Resource Conservation and Development (RC&D) program, 130
resources, 205; financial and human, 83–84, 170; stakeholder, 150
risk aversion, theoroid of, 175
Rockfish River Forum, 3
roles, 116–21, 128; as social constructions, 121; and role-playing, 159

Sand Wash Basin, 50, 58
satisficing, 157
scale, 85, 107
science: scale of, 36–37; and scientific method, 23, 40
self-determination, theoroid of, 166–67
self-interest, 168–70
Service First, 133
social capital, 69, 83, 84, 161, 178, 198; and effective resource management, 198
social dilemmas, 169–70
social status, theoroid of, 164–65, 166
standing: civic, 135–36; indicators of, 165–66
stewardship ethic, 196
strategies, 89–103
success, factors in, 22, 24, 83–84, 156, 171–72, 174–75
sustainability, 196